An
Ounce of
Prevention

Also by Lawrence E. Shapiro, Ph.D.

How to Raise a Child with a High EQ:
A Parent's Guide to Emotional Intelligence

An Ounce of Prevention

HOW PARENTS CAN STOP CHILDHOOD BEHAVORIAL AND EMOTIONAL PROBLEMS BEFORE THEY START

LAWRENCE E. SHAPIRO, PH.D.

HarperCollins*Publishers*

HarperCollins books may be purchased for educational, business, or sales promotional use. For information please write: Special Markets Department, HarperCollins Publishers Inc., 10 East 53rd Street, New York, NY 10022.

FIRST EDITION

Designed by Nancy Singer Olaguera

Printed on acid-free paper

Library of Congress Cataloging-in-Publication Data
Shapiro, Lawrence E.
    An ounce of prevention : how parents can stop childhood behavioral and emotional problems before they start / Lawrence E. Shapiro.—1st ed.
        p.   cm.
    ISBN 0-06-019301-8
    1. Emotional problems of children—Problems, exercises, etc. 2. Emotions in children—Problems, exercises, etc. 3. Child rearing. I. Title.

BF723.E598 S53 2000
649'.34—dc21   00-038324

00 01 02 03 04 ❖/RRD 10 9 8 7 6 5 4 3 2 1

To my daughters, Jessica and Tess

Contents

An
Ounce of
Prevention

1

Stop Emotional Problems Before They Start

All parents understand the importance of prevention when it comes to the physical health and safety of their children. Before the baby even arrives home from the hospital, parents begin plugging up electrical outlets and installing baby gates on the top and bottom of their stairs. They teach their toddlers to brush their teeth several times a day and to stay away from sharp objects. Parents conscientiously buckle their young children into approved car seats and make sure that bicycle helmets are securely fastened. They remind their children over and over not to speak to strangers. These are classic preventive measures, and parents everywhere adhere to them in order to keep their children physically safe.

But unfortunately, too many parents stop there. They think ahead when it comes to bodily harm, yet when it comes to emotional problems, most parents tend to start paying attention only when signs of maladjustment appear on the horizon. Depression, eating disorders, behavioral problems, school underachievement, shyness, and more come into focus only when the child displays disruptive symptoms.

Certainly these problems can be treated and/or managed once they appear, but it is always far more complex to undo a problem than it is to keep one from occurring at all. It would, in other words, be infinitely better if preventive measures for emotional problems were undertaken as early and automatically as are those for physical safety. There are no guarantees, of course, that doing so would completely eradicate emotional difficulties, but certainly preventive measures could keep such problems more manageable and less likely to interfere with a child's normal development.

The fact is that children are as vulnerable to emotional dangers as they are to physical ones. The statistics are staggering.

- Childhood and adolescent depression is rising at an alarming rate, nearly doubling over the last twenty years.

- Eating disorders affect almost 15 percent of teenage girls.

- Three thousand children a day start smoking, at an average age of 11.

- According to a recent Harvard study, nearly 45 percent of all college students are binge drinkers.

- Over 45 percent of children are affected by divorce, and studies show that 20 to 30 percent of these children will suffer long-term effects from the breakup of the family.

- American children use 90 percent of the world's Ritalin, more than five times the rest of the world combined.

- Every school day 17,152 students are suspended for misbehavior, and another 2,789 high school students drop out entirely. Over 5,000 children are arrested, 237 for violent crimes.

It's not that parents are unaware of potential emotional problems. All parents hope that their children will feel good about themselves, form close friendships, and enjoy a satisfying and challenging life as they grow up. Most parents experience concern at the slightest sign that their children are troubled. But it seems a far simpler matter to grip a child's hand firmly when crossing the street than it is, for instance, to figure out how to help him control his impulsiveness, make friends easily, or cope with divorce. Then, too, it is not only that parents don't know *how* to ensure their child's emotional health; many are unconvinced that their efforts would indeed have any effect at all.

DO PARENTS MATTER?

In 1998, Judith Harris touched on this chord of self-doubt in her book *The Nurture Assumption: Do Parents Really Make a Difference?*, which questioned whether parents really have any significant role in shaping the lives of their children when compared to the influence of their children's peers.

To be fair to Ms. Harrris, her stated intention in writing this book is not to degrade the role of parenthood but rather to put it into a realistic perspective. In questioning the omnipotence of parenthood, she seeks to relieve parents from shouldering 100 percent of the blame when, in spite of their devotion and sacrifices, their children fail to grow up to be happy, successful, and caring adults. As the description on her book jacket notes, "Parenting does not match its widely publicized job description. It is a job in which sincerity and hard work do not guarantee success."

To some degree I would have to agree with that. Children are not born as blank slates. They bring into the world their own unique temperaments, some of which are more open to modification than others. And yes, as they grow they will find themselves under the influence of many people, including peers, teachers, and other relatives—not to mention the media. But to conclude therefore that parents have a minimal impact on their children is an oversimplification of fifty years of developmental research and an affront to the tens of thousands of mental-health professionals and educators who dedicate their lives to helping parents raise happier, healthier, and more successful children. The paramount relationship in a child's life—the one in which there exists the most constancy and trust—is that with a parent. Only a parent is always there to reframe a life experience, guide a child through the dangerous rapids of life's challenges, and help to mold her into an emotionally healthy person.

Our knowledge about a child's inborn temperament is frequently traced back to the work of two physicians, Alexander

Thomas and Stella Chess, who conducted a study investigating the role of temperament in 140 children from birth to adolescence. It was concluded in this and subsequent follow-up studies that temperament is a highly stable part of development. A baby who hardly cries will become a toddler who does not complain when his clothes are pulled over his head, and still later he will likely be a ten-year-old who corrects his mistakes quietly. A baby who reacts irritably when being diapered will likely be a picky eater and have a hard time adjusting to change.

However, studies have also shown that even though temperament is a genetically loaded trait, it can sometimes be altered through intervention. Studies that compared parents who gently pushed their timid babies into being more adaptable with those parents who protected their shy babies from change revealed that the infants who were prodded to "venture out" grew out of their shy habits by age five.

In this book I intend to give you the skills you need to help your child grow into an emotionally healthy and satisfied person. I will help you understand the parameters of the key emotional trouble zones, assess the risk factors that affect your child for a particular problem, and offer practical and effective ways either to avoid a difficulty altogether or help to dissipate its disruptive effects.

Many of the suggestions I make will seem like common sense to you. Teach your child good eating habits to prevent obesity. Refrain from giving your child constant treats and rewards to help prevent her being spoiled and developing behavioral problems. If you're getting a divorce, spare your child from any vitriolic and mean-spirited arguments.

Other recommendations might seem counterintuitive to the way that you are now raising your children. Fearful babies should not be coddled if they are to outgrow their hypersensitivity. Toddlers should not be overly praised if you want them to become respectful and cooperative. School-age children should be involved in community service rather than spend hours in front of the TV or playing video games. Parents should become more involved in their teenagers' education even when their teens are pulling away.

The prevention of emotional problems is as much a part of a parent's job as is keeping that child physically safe. And while the path to this goal is not as straightforward as feeding a nutritious meal or providing a secure bike helmet, it can and should be achieved by any parent.

I am writing this book because, when it comes to your child's emotional health, *You do matter.* Children can be protected. Trends can be reversed. An ounce of prevention will offset a pound of trouble tomorrow and in the years ahead. And if you are reading this book because you can already see the signs of emotional pain, there is much you can do to prevent these problems from spiraling into even more serious ones and reverse the negative trend. Whether your child is an unsettled baby or a reclusive teen who has suddenly become obstinate and rebellious, *An Ounce of Prevention* can make a difference.

WHAT'S BEEN PREVENTING YOU?

It might be interesting (and guilt-reducing) to at this point to ponder why as parents we may have overlooked prevention when it comes to our children's emotional health. The most obvious reason is that parents do not have accurate information about emotional development. Parents know when their children should first sit up, or say their first word, or take their first step, but emotional milestones are much subtler. When should a child be able to talk about her feelings rather than act them out? When should a child learn to control his angry outbursts? When should a parent be concerned if a child has not made her first friend? If parents don't know the early signs of emotional problems, how can they know how to prevent them?

Another explanation is that we human parents, like parents in other animal species, are programmed to think about the immediate safety of our offspring and that pondering the future might distract us from seeing a danger that is closer at hand. When you're trying to stop your three-year-old from poking a fork into an electrical outlet or your eight-year-old from riding her skateboard without a helmet, it's hard to think about abstract emotional problems that might crop up in the future.

Finally we must take into account the inclination of today's parents to try to raise children who are never unhappy. When our children complain that they can't wait for dinner to be cooked, we take them out for fast food. When they're unhappy that their perfectly good sneakers aren't the sneakers all the other children are wearing, we buy them a new pair. Although parents see these acts as expressions of their love, they are also a reflection of an increasing tendency to indulge a child's every whim. Besides the fact that it spoils children and potentially causes behavioral problems, overindulgence is antithetical to many aspects of prevention. If your child whined that his seat belt was uncomfortable, would you let him take it off? If she said that she didn't want to take flu medicine because it tasted bad, would you cave in? Of course not. As we shall see, permissive parenting is a serious risk factor for children.

PREVENTION IN THE SCHOOLS

Over the last forty years there have been thousands of prevention projects started in schools. They range from suicide-prevention programs to programs intended to minimize the long-term effects of divorce to programs that keep children out of gangs.

The majority of school-based prevention programs teach one or more skills that form the basis of what we now call emotional intelligence, or EQ (as opposed to cognitive intelligence, or IQ). The term "emotional intelligence" was first used in 1990 by psychologists Peter Salovey of Harvard University and John Meyer of the University of New Hampshire. It was popularized by Daniel Goleman's 1995 bestseller *Emotional Intelligence*, whose thesis was that EQ may be even more important to success and happiness than IQ, the standard we commonly use to judge a child's potential. My own book *How to Raise a Child with a High EQ: A Parent's Guide to Emotional Intelligence* explores the subject in great detail.

Preventing mental health problems is neither a new idea or an unproved one. The Primary Mental Health Project, originally developed in Rochester, New York, and now in over seven hundred school districts in the United States and around the world, has been in continuous use for more than forty years. This program focuses on young children who show early signs of risk for adaptive or academic problems in school and has helped thousands of children avoid serious emotional and learning problems.

The I Can Problem Solve (ICPS) Program developed by Myrna Shure and David Spivak in Philadelphia has been in existence for over twenty years and is also used in hundreds of schools. Focused on teaching problem-solving skills, this program helps children reduce nagging and whining, emotional upset, and social withdrawal. As Dr. Shure writes in the introduction to her book of preschool activities (also titled *I Can Problem Solve*), "Regardless of temperament, children have become more aware of—even genuinely concerned about—the feelings of others. In brief, children who have learned the ICPS concepts are more successful in getting what they want when they can have it, and are better able to cope with frustration when they cannot."

What these and many other programs have in common is that they are time-limited (usually fifteen to thirty weeks), the children work with adults who are not trained psychologists (usually they are teachers or paraprofessionals), and the programs are clearly effective. Typically, children enrolled in these programs are followed for two to four years, and it has been found that the emotional and behavioral progress they've made continues through that period when compared to control groups of children who did not go through a prevention program.

Prevention programs, it should be noted, are not limited to younger children. The Penn Prevention Program under the leadership of Dr. Martin Seligman showed that eleven- and twelve-year-olds identified as being at risk for developing depression were only half as likely to fall victim to this illness after going through the program. This was the result of a twelve-week program that used comic strips, role-playing, games, discussions, and videos to teach children to think about the world optimistically and to develop social problem-solving skills. Another example, the Peacemaker Program tested in the Cleveland public schools, has shown that prevention activities can reduce the incidence of aggression-related disciplinary actions by as much as 41 percent and actual suspension for violent behaviors by 67 percent. All of this in just a seventeen-week program.

There are hundreds of other programs, offered primarily through the public schools, that have made an impact on children considered at risk for common emotional and behavioral problems. In fact, the public schools have become the de facto leaders in mental-health-problem prevention. From a purely sociological viewpoint, schools are certainly the best place to reach the largest number of children, particularly those who are most at risk for problems due to economic disadvantage. The Consortium on the School-Based Promotion of Social Competence writes in *Stress, Risk, and Resilience in Children and Adolescents:*

> Schools are widely acknowledged as the major setting in which activities should be undertaken to promote student competence and prevent the development of unhealthy behaviors. In contrast to other potential sites for intervention, schools provide access to all children on a regular and consistent basis for the majority of their formative years of personality development.

BUT PREVENTION IN SCHOOLS IS NOT ENOUGH

In spite of the many successes in school-based programs, you cannot count on schools to protect your children from developing emotional or behavioral problems. The most successful of these programs are being implemented in hundreds of schools, but there are over 110,000 schools in America, and the probability that the school that your child is attending has the right program for him or her at the right time is very small.

Although children's advocacy groups will continue to try to get every school to implement prevention programs at every grade level, this not likely to happen. Schools have been charged to educate our youth and prepare them for either higher education or a career, but as one elementary school principal put it, "We are not in the mental-health business." This is a blunt way of saying that schools are not funded for prevention programs the way that they are funded to teach academics. When programs do exist, even the most successful ones, they are subject to the changing priorities of school administrators and the ebb and flow of funds.

• • •

Parents, on the other hand, have none of the limitations of school-based programs when it comes to prevention. Parents have years, not weeks, to work with children. They have an investment in their children's future and a psychological connection that cannot be matched by even the most skilled professional. Parents don't have to wait for children to enter preschool or kindergarten; a family-based prevention program can (and should) begin at infancy.

The most important argument for making the home the first front for preventing emotional and behavioral problems is that only parents can reduce the risks associated with mild and serious disorders. Whatever a school-based prevention program can do to increase a child's emotional intelligence, it cannot change a child's diet, help her to be more comfortable with her body type, or encourage her to get more sleep or make exercise a regular habit. It cannot restrict the amount of time a child spends watching television or monitor the types of shows watched. Nor can it tuck him in at night with a story. Only parents have the power to make the day-to-day decisions that can shape a child's destiny. And only parents can know with some clarity all the risks their own child faces from both a genetic and an environmental point of view.

The only things parents don't have that the teachers in these school-based programs possess are the tools of prevention, which I hope these pages will provide.

IDENTIFYING WHEN YOUR CHILDREN ARE AT RISK

Advocates for the mental health of children have known for decades that some children are more at risk than others for serious problems. Many people use the term "at risk" as a euphemism for the "economically disadvantaged," but while very low family income is a significant risk factor, it is only one of the conditions that can affect a child's development and well-being. The following are some of the major risk factors that affect the short- and long-term mental health of children. I will be referring back to these factors throughout this book. As you review the factors below, you will see that some are more amenable to change than others, but every one can be reduced by parents who make prevention a daily concern.

RISK FACTORS

Emotional Intelligence

I am going to start with emotional intelligence because it contains so many elements that are critical to the management of life's challenges. In my previous book, *How to Raise a Child with a High EQ*, I explain how parents can use the same methods as the school-based prevention programs to teach such skills as anger control, realistic thinking, moral behavior, and friend-making skills.

A great deal of the excitement around the importance of emotional intelligence has to do with its basis in neuroscience. When we teach children specific emotional intelligence skills, we are actually affecting the way their brain and nervous system perform, affecting both their mental and physical health.

For example, whenever we are irritated or stressed, our sympathetic nervous system is stimulated. It then produces a group of biochemicals called catecholamines, which are the brain's way of calling the body to arms. The catecholamines include norepinephrine (related to adrenaline) and cortisol, which has been dubbed the "stress hormone." These biochemicals act as messengers to various organs of the body, causing the heart to beat faster, the blood pressure to rise, and the muscles to tense. This is the classic "fight or flight" syndrome, which can trigger aggressive behavior. A child's neurochemical makeup, in other words, may be part of a risk factor.

Yet despite this chemical reaction, you can still affect a child's level of emotional stress.

Take, for example, the simple techniques used to teach self-calming to children. Psychologists often prescribe these techniques for children who have problems controlling their tempers or who are overly aggressive, but in fact self-calming techniques will benefit all children (and adults, for that matter). The most commonly used techniques to teach children to relax and calm themselves include the following:

- Deep breathing: This technique is combined with all the techniques listed below.

- Listening to quiet classical music for at least fifteen to twenty minutes.

- Guided visualization: Many audiotapes are available that describe walking in a relaxing place like a quiet beach or the middle of a forest.

- Systematic muscle relaxation: The child reclines in a comfortable chair and consciously relaxes one muscle group after another, usually starting with the large muscle groups (chest, abdomen, shoulders, neck) and working out toward the smaller muscles (arms, legs, then hands, fingers, feet, and toes).

- Massage

Now let us look at what these simple techniques do to the mind and the body, by examining the case of Paul, who was referred to me when he was five years old as a severely disruptive influence in his kindergarten class.

> Paul had a very low tolerance for frustration. If he was having difficulty building a tower of blocks or zipping up his coat, or if he wanted a toy that another child was playing with, he would fly into a rage. His teachers had tried using a time-out corner, but he fought them tooth and nail. Paul was brought to therapy after he had been "suspended" from school, not to return until he got his behavior problem under control.
>
> What these teachers didn't understand was that Paul, like many other young aggressive children, didn't understand the meaning of self-control. When his teachers would admonish, "Now, I want you to calm down," Paul had no physical reference for these words. He had never learned to calm himself down. They might as well have said, "Now, I want you to go outside and drive the school bus."
>
> Paul's therapy consisted of teaching him self-calming. I taught him how to breathe deeply and relax his muscles while listening to quiet music. We did this for five-minute periods, then ten minutes, then fifteen. After each period Paul was praised and given a sticker. After three sessions he had clearly learned the meaning of "calm." He knew what it looked like because he saw himself on videotape. He knew what it felt like. He knew how people responded to him when he was successful. I then had

Paul's parents practice this technique at home, three times a day, explaining to them that self-calming must become a habit, and habits take practice.

After two weeks of home training, Paul was ready to try his new skill under pressure. He returned to school. I visited the school the day before, and with the teacher's permission we banned the time-out corner forever. Instead we created a relaxation corner. We laid down a blanket and several soft pillows. We added a tape recorder and headphones for playing soft classical music. When Paul arrived, I was there with the teachers to meet him. We had a class meeting, and I introduced the relaxation corner to the entire class. I taught all twenty children how to breathe deeply, relax their muscles, and calm themselves. I also told them how to recognize when they needed to go to the relaxation corner. If they felt unhappy, if they felt like hitting or yelling, they should go to the relaxation corner and calm down. If they still felt upset, they should tell the teacher.

It took a few weeks for the class to embrace these new techniques, but when I checked back several months later, the teacher described a remarkable change in Paul and in the tone of the class as a whole.

As you shall see throughout this book, there are many other emotional-intelligence skills that can be used to treat different disorders, and every new skill has the potential for long-term consequences by quite literally changing the way the mind works.

Temperament

As noted, psychologists believe that temperament is genetically determined and for the most part is very stable through a child's development.

But recent research also suggests that temperament can be changed through early intervention. Studies in shyness, a trait that has a high genetic loading, showed that it could be modified when parents were taught to coax their young children gently into being more adaptable. The problem is that parents who try to change their child's inborn temperament must often adopt a parenting style that is counterintuitive to their own nature. For example, one father came to see me with his moody and unhappy six-year-old, and when I asked him how he normally handled his son's uncooperative behavior, the father replied, "Why, I just tease him out of it. Like right now. See how he just sits there pouting? Now I'll say [turning to his son], 'What a little baby. Waa, waa, waa, waa. We're all just little babies 'cause we don't want to be here. Waa, waa, waa.'" But the child did not respond well to the teasing, and only looked more sour, ignoring his father's sarcastic attempt at humor. Things changed for the better when this father learned to set clear behavioral goals for his son and encouraged him with firm but compassionate statements, rather than taunting.

Parenting Style

Both children who are raised in an authoritarian home atmosphere and children raised in an overly permissive atmosphere are at risk for emotional and behavioral problems. If there are too many inflexible rules and too many unrealistic expectations wielded by inflexible parents, children may become angry, depressed, and riddled with self-doubt. Unable to control any aspects of their own lives, they have no chance to develop a sense of competence in the world. They also cannot easily reach out to others and treat them with consistent caring if they have not experienced this enough in their own lives. On the other hand, in households where there are too few rules and parents give in to every whim, children become frightened by their own power. They may become mini-terrors who seem to be constantly demanding "things" when what they really need and want are limits. The end result is an uncertainty about "the rules of society" and difficulty forming close relationships. A lack of discipline and too-low expectations has robbed them of the chance to understand why rules exist (including respecting others), and so they are often as demanding with their peers as they are with their parents. In both the authoritarian and the permissive homes there are often problems with the development of morality, including such important traits as honesty and empathy.

In contrast, an authoritative parenting style strikes a balance between an authoritarian and permissive atmosphere. Rules and limits are clear, but children are listened to, respected, and, when appropriate, given the power to participate in decisions. Dozens of studies have shown that children have fewer emotional problems when they are raised in a home where parents adopt an authoritative parenting style. These parents have high expectations for their children and provide the emotional support for them to obtain their goals.

Weight, Height, and Body Type

Our culture has a very clear idea of what people are supposed to look like. Study after study tells us that appearance makes a difference in popularity, in school success, and in overall life happiness. It is a sad commentary on our nature, but one we have to admit is true: physical appearance affects our sense of well-being.

Girls are typically much more self-critical of their appearance than boys. In research studies asking teenage boys and teenage girls to rate their own appearance, girls rate themselves as more unattractive than others see them, but boys actually see themselves as more attractive. Even though we have known for years that the way the media portray the "idealized" woman presents a risk factor for girls' development, the discrepancy between what we consider to be an ideal female body type and the way women actually look has never been greater. The average "supermodel" is five feet ten inches tall and weighs 107 pounds. The average American woman is five feet four inches tall and weighs 143 pounds.

Girls who are unhappy with themselves physically are more likely to have eating problems, as well as social and academic problems. Their insecurities whittle away at their ability to stay motivated and reach out comfortably to others.

Gender

If we look at the statistics on the children who are referred for psychotherapy, we find that boys generally have more serious emotional and behavioral problems before the age of twelve and girls have more emotional conflicts and adjustment problems as teenagers. We also know that gender plays an important factor in the types of emotional problems a child will have. Most children diagnosed with an attention deficit disorder or serious behavioral problem will be boys; most teens diagnosed with depression and eating disorders will be girls.

But the gender biases that can contribute to emotional problems can also be overcome. Boys, for example, tend to be slower in developing reading skills, but with patience and encouragement they will easily catch up. Girls lose ground in math and science as they reach adolescence, largely because of a cultural bias that seems to affect even the brightest students. However, when families and schools increase their efforts to keep ten- to fourteen-year-old girls interested in math and science, their grades and test scores do not decline.

Age

Generally speaking, a child is at risk for different problems at different ages, with the more serious issues tending to emerge in older children. Adolescence has always been considered the time when parents really need to begin worrying, but most trends show that the problems that we once associated with the fourteen- to eighteen-year-olds, such as eating disorders and depression, are now affecting children two to four years younger. Some studies suggest that the age of the parents may also be a factor in raising resilient children. One review of the literature found that resilient boys had younger mothers and resilient girls had older fathers, although we can only speculate on why this might be.

Age is a risk factor for another reason. Many parents don't realize that the building blocks of emotional health can begin to be put in place when children are infants and continue to be built up right through adolescence. There are windows of opportunity for prevention at every age, and this book will help you find the right things to do at the right time.

IQ

It makes sense that children with higher cognitive abilities (IQ) are less at risk for many problems than children with lower intelligence. Not only do brighter children typically do better in school, but they succeed with less effort. Children with lower intelligence or severe learning disabilities will have to work harder just to keep up with average children. They will most likely enter the school caste system at the bottom of their reading and math groups and, all things being equal, will remain there. Teachers, who are only human, are most apt to give attention and praise to the students who perform the best, and it is the rare teacher who can remember to give more to the children who need it most.

However, here is an example of where EQ, or emotional intelligence, can reduce the risk of failure for children with fewer natural abilities. Traits like self-motivation, an optimistic attitude, and friendliness can help children give the extra effort that they need or find other ways to compensate for cognitive problems or weaknesses.

Sleep

Many parents do not realize that a lack of sleep can be a serious risk factor for both mental and physical disorders. Studies suggest that between 20 and 25 percent of children do not get enough sleep. This can affect the balance of biochemicals that control a child's mood and behavior. Sleep deprivation is also a risk factor for parents. As with children, about one in four adults does not get the required amount of sleep. This has been linked to a variety of health problems, including premature aging. Certainly a parent deprived of sleep is not the best parent that he or she can be.

Diet and Exercise

I will explore the importance of diet and exercise in preventing eating disorders and obesity in Chapter 3, but parents should realize that this is also a risk factor for other emotional difficulties. In many ways it is a vicious cycle. A poor diet (high in sugar, salt, and fat and low in fiber) and lack of exercise can affect the mood and the attention span of your child, profoundly affecting both schoolwork and social development. But doing poorly in school and/or being unsuccessful socially can lead children to eat for self-comfort and to embrace a very sedentary life. Poor exercise and nutrition habits affect the immune system and may play a significant role in the physical health of your child for his entire life. In 1998, the American Heart Association estimated that 36.5 percent of children under age twenty had a borderline or higher cholesterol reading, putting them at risk for early coronary heart disease and strokes.

Even though parents are more aware than ever of the importance of diet and exercise, government statistics show most children and adolescents have a diet that is poor or needs improvement. And as children get older, the quality of their diet declines. In 1996, 76 percent of children aged two to five, 88 percent of children aged six to twelve, and 94 percent of children aged thirteen to eighteen had a diet that was poor or needed improvement.

Family Involvement and Sense of Belonging

A 1993 Harris and Associates survey commissioned by *Reader's Digest* found that high school seniors who frequently ate dinner with one or both parents (four or more times a week) had higher grades than students who attended a family dinner less often. Students in this survey who lived in two-parent homes scored higher than students who lived in one-parent homes. There are many ways to explain these findings, but it seems logical that family dinners represent a commitment to spending time together and are at least one way of measuring family cohesion. Other surveys support this conclusion, finding that students who are in more "traditional" homes, with stricter rules and curfews and high parental expectations, are also more likely to excel. Conversely, we know that children who are separated from their parents—whether due to war, natural disaster, divorce, or military duty—are more at risk for mental-health problems.

Parental Discord

It is not surprising that parental discord, no matter whether parents are married or divorced, is an important factor in determining whether children will have mental-health problems. Of course all parents argue sometimes, and there is nothing wrong with children witnessing this, providing they also see that the argument is resolved and it is explained to them that disagreement and occasional arguing are part of every loving relationship. However, parental arguing does become a risk factor to children when it is continuous (more than once a week), is mean-spirited (the argument ceases to be about a current issue, and past hurts or grievances become the main agenda), and there is no resolution to the argument or no apology. When arguments are characterized by shouting or rude behavior (slamming doors or throwing things) or when violence is even implied, children are at risk.

Community Involvement

Children who are considered to be resilient typically have a strong sense of belonging that comes from their family, their peer group, and their community. Studies show that children and teens who are socially isolated are at risk for a variety of problems, ranging from depression to antisocial behavior to drug and alcohol abuse.

Parents must lead the way in encouraging community involvement. To begin, they should seek involvement themselves, since we know that the best way for children to learn is from their parents' example. It doesn't matter whether you join the PTA, an adult sports league, hobby club, or a group with a religious affiliation. The important thing you want to show your children is that you value the opportunity to be with others and that this gives additional meaning to your life.

Children who have difficulty making friends usually do better in groups that share similar interests, as opposed to general-activity groups like the Boy Scouts or the Girl Scouts. It could be a computer club, a bowling team, or a model-train club. The only criteria are that the group meets together on a regular basis and that it provides experiences for children that are both challenging and fun. Groups geared toward specific interests will likely be composed of children or teens with similar personalities, making it easier for your child to fit in.

If parents find that neither they nor their children are drawn to any particular activity group, then community-service organizations might be the answer. There are many community-service groups that encourage family participation, like Habitat for Humanity (www.habitat.org) or FamilyCares (www.familycares.org). These organizations develop a sense of belonging and purpose in the family and in the community, while simultaneously lowering general risk factors for children of all ages.

Poor School Experience and Academic Failure

Many of our children view school as a negative experience and see their education as a burden rather than an exciting challenge. Certainly children who have learning disabilities or other special needs might be expected to have a poor attitude toward school, but some researchers suggest that as many as 20 to 30 percent of nonhandicapped children achieve significantly below their potential solely because of their lack of motivation and interest.

Involvement in a child's education is the most direct route to preventing a negative school experience, but this seems to be a difficult task for many parents to accomplish. As parents work longer hours and farther from home, they commonly find it harder and harder to be involved in their child's school. Parents also become less involved as their children grow older, even though children are more at risk for school problems with each passing year. In one survey of middle-school children (eleven to fourteen), 45 percent of the students said that their parents did not know all their teachers' names or even what they were studying.

If you can find the time to be more involved in your child's education, it will be time well spent. You will likely see your child's school performance increase, you will feel emotionally closer to your child and her experience of the world, and you will be reducing her level of risk for a variety of problems that affect children who feel alienated from their families.

ASSESSING YOUR CHILD'S RISK FACTORS AND RESILIENCE

As you read through the risk factors above, you probably made a mental checklist of which of them affect your child. If you are concerned because your child has several risk factors, there are two things you should know. First the bad news: The more risk factors your child is exposed to, the more concerned you should be. Some researchers believe that risk factors are not just additive but also multiplicative. One research study reported that having two risk factors doesn't double the chances of developing some form of psychopathology, but actually increases it by four times, and having four risk factors multiplies the likelihood of developing a problem by *ten.*

Now the good news: You must also take into account your child's natural resilience to stress. Many children are born with the traits that are a part of their emotional intelligence, making them naturally resistant to risk factors, the way children with a strong immune system are naturally resistant to disease. For example, in one ambitious study psychologists followed the progress of over two hundred high-risk children in Hawaii for a period of thirty-two years. The children in the study were picked because they had experienced four or more severe risk factors, including poverty, prenatal stress, family discord, divorce, parental alcoholism, and parental mental illness. Yet even with these multiple risk factors, a third of the children grew into competent young adults who enjoyed their work and had satisfying relationships.

Is your child naturally resilient? Is he or she born with a genetic makeup that can offset common risk factors? Use the table below to find out. The more statements you check, the better off your child will be. But even if you check off only a few traits, don't despair. All the traits listed can be taught to your child as part of your prevention plan.

Table 1: How Resilient Is Your Child?

Check off the traits that accurately describe your child. These are traits that seem to be consistently present in resilient children, teens, and adults.

___ Has a sense of humor.

___ Has insight into him/herself and others.

___ Has an active approach to problem-solving.

___ Is able to gain positive attention from others.

___ Has an optimistic view of the world, even in the midst of a problem.

___ Has a positive vision of him/herself and the world.

___ Is alert and energetic.

___ Seeks new experiences.

___ Is independent.

___ Sets high but attainable goals.

___ Makes friends easily.

___ Expresses affection openly.

___ Has good self-control.

___ Is adaptable.

As you can see, preventing mental-health problems in children and teens is a multilayered task. It involves reducing risk, increasing resilience or emotional intelligence, and achieving a balanced and practical parenting style that leaves your child the room she needs but also gives her the boundaries and support she craves. Your efforts will not guarantee that your child will be problem-free, but they will certainly move you forward on the road to preventing emotional difficulties.

HOW COMPUTERS CAN HELP

Throughout this book you will see how computers can help you accomplish your prevention goals.

First of all, computers can be used as a tool to increase your child's emotional intelligence and reduce the risks that can lead to serious emotional, behavioral, or social problems. Many parents are surprised when I prescribe activities on the computer as a way to help children with their development, but I can't escape the fact that computers and the Internet are changing the way we live, including the way we parent. Most of these changes are for the better.

> Mr. Snyder's wife had recently passed away. He took a few months off from work to be with his two children and get his life in order, but now he was back at work at his midsize accounting firm. He had enrolled his son in day care about ten miles from his office, but he was still able to keep a constant eye on him as he worked. The day care had a videocam that beamed constant images to its Internet site, allowing Mr. Snyder to view his son in a small box in the corner of his computer screen throughout the day.
>
> During his lunch break Mr. Snyder sent an e-mail to his eight-year-old daughter, Emily, which she would read when she got home from school. The e-mail message contained a joke, an animated cartoon of two bears hugging, and a list of chores that Emily had to do before dinner.
>
> When his children went to bed, Mr. Snyder, surfed the Internet for a little reassurance that he was doing everything right. He went to ParentSoup.com and joined a chat room on the best way to discipline a toddler, hosted by a child psychologist. Then he switched over to fathers.com, Web site of the National Center for Fathering, and read an article on "dating and the single dad." He thought that cyberspace might be a good place to meet someone and develop a friendship so that he could ease into a relationship with a minimum of disruption to his family.

The most important change that has taken place over the last five years is the amount of information now accessible to anyone with a computer and a modem. I used the Internet constantly to gather research as I wrote this book, visiting sites sponsored by government offices like the U.S. Census Bureau, associations like the American Academy of Child and Adolescent Psychiatry, and dozens of other organizations that are committed to the welfare of the nation's children. As a parent, you also have a world of information available to you with a few clicks of the mouse, on every aspect of parenting imaginable. If you have a question about a common or uncommon concern, you can likely find an answer just moments away. No generation of parents has ever had anything like this before.

A second benefit that the Internet brings to us is in the form of communication unlike any that our own parents could have imagined. The vignette about Mr. Snyder is fictionalized, but there is nothing particularly unusual about his story. An increasing number of schools have their own Web site to help parents stay involved in their children's education. Parents can join in chat rooms with the school principal, leave e-mail messages for a particular teacher, or keep track of a child's homework assignments. Videocams, like the one used at the day care attended by Mr. Snyder's toddler, are fast becoming commonplace. I know of one parent who was able to attend his daughter's school play by logging on to his computer, even though he was a thousand miles away on a business trip.

If lack of family and community togetherness is a risk factor for children, as already discussed, think of the ways that the Internet can bring people together. Children can e-mail their latest art masterpiece to their grandparents. A family Web site can bring together relatives from the far corners of the world. Children and parents can join virtual communities thousands of miles away, through interest clubs, self-help groups, and the hundreds of sites where people can go just to "hang out."

A third way that computers can help parents help their children is through the extraordinary software that has become available for both home and school use. For the child having difficulty in school, there are hundreds of programs that teach every subject imaginable, from beginning phonics to advanced algebra. These programs use colorful animated graphics, music, random surprises, and immediate feedback to motivate children to learn information that they might never even have attempted in a traditional classroom. Unfortunately, there are far fewer programs that help children with emotional and behavioral issues, but they are catching on. I've recommended *Pajama Sam and Who's Afraid of the Dark?* (Humongous Entertainment) for children with fears, and *The Berenstain Bears: Little Bears Make Big Helpers* (Sounds Source Interactive) for children who need to learn the importance of doing chores, and even a parenting CD-ROM, entitled *Active Parenting Today* (Active Parenting Press), that teaches basic parenting skills. You'll find other software titles geared toward prevention throughout the book, but because there are new titles coming out every month, you might do as I do and regularly check at www.childrenssoftware.com for current reviews and links to on-line catalogs.

HOW *AN OUNCE OF PREVENTION* WILL WORK FOR YOU

This book is organized so that in each chapter you can learn how to prevent a common emotional or behavioral problem. Most parents will want to read the book straight through in order to learn about the different risks for their child and construct a complete prevention plan. If you already feel that your child is at risk for one or more problems, you will want to first read the chapters about those problems thoroughly.

Chapters 2 through 7 (on behavioral problems, eating disorders, underachievement, fears and shyness, sexuality and gender problems, and attention deficit disorders) are organized so that parents can find out exactly what they can do to prevent problems at each stage of their child's development, infancy through adolescence. In Chapters 8 and 9 parents will learn the stages that predictably occur after a divorce or a trauma. These chapters are organized so that parents can quickly learn what they can do at each stage to ease the short-term suffering of their children and to mitigate the development of long-term problems.

As you read, I recommend that you fill in a copy of the Prevention Plan. Fill it in again on your child's next birthday, and every six months thereafter. Keep the plan in a place where you see it every day. Try and spend ten to fifteen minutes a day doing something that will help your child become more resilient or will reduce his risk. Make prevention a habit for your child, like having him brush his teeth or fasten his seat belt. Give your child an "ounce of prevention" every day. It will make a difference.

Table2: Prevention Plan

	Ways to Reduce Risks	Ways to Make My Child More Resilient
Daily		
Weekly		
Monthly		

2

Preventing Behavioral Problems

Jill and her two children were riding in the café car of an Amtrak train. A few businessmen were scattered about, working quietly.

"Stop that, sweetie," she softly admonished her son, who was busily attempting to push his loudly protesting little sister off the banquette.

Jill's words had no effect.

"Honey, if you do that again, I'm going to really be mad," she warned, but the soft tone of her voice belied her words.

Finally her son gave his sister a push, and she nearly fell into the lap of the man who was seated across from them.

Looking up at Jill, the man heaved a sigh and said, "Excuse me, but would you mind asking your children to be a little quieter? I'm trying to work."

Jill said nothing in reply, but her cold stare was response enough. Moments later she gathered up her children and moved to another car.

No parents like to think of their child as a "behavior problem," yet more than half the children referred for psychological treatment or counseling arrive with exactly that description written somewhere in their file. Usually the referral comes from a school and is written about a child whose lack of cooperation in the classroom has become as predictable as the morning bell. Occasionally the referral comes from a parent, usually a mother. I once treated a five-year-old brought to me by her harried mother, who explained, "She's running our entire life! We give her whatever she wants, because otherwise she will have a tantrum until she starts to convulse and throw up. My husband and I don't even tell her when to go to bed. *She* sends *us* to bed!"

Obviously this child did not get this kind of power over her parents overnight. Like every behavioral problem, it started with small demands that were met without question and minor infractions of household rules that were ignored. In virtually every child who is referred for a behavioral problem, there are a multitude of less serious behaviors that are the precursors to the ones that inspire the referral. If you are the least bit concerned about the behavior of your child, prevention should start today. There is no reason to allow children to be disrespectful, uncooperative, or ill-mannered, and confronting the minor behavioral problems will be your best hope of avoiding more serious ones.

WHEN PARENTS EXPECT TOO LITTLE

The unfortunate by-product of low expectations is the tacit acceptance of poor behavior, which heralds far more serious and destructive patterns. Yet while the population at large seems to agree that as a society we have become too lax in terms of the behavior we expect from our children, there seems to be little effort expended on correcting the situation. A 1996 survey found that 70 percent of adults thought incivility was one of the most significant problems facing our society. Another survey found that parents thought that children in general were much worse-behaved than a generation ago, but they did not know what to do about it. A teacher at a high school in an affluent New York suburb recently told me, "You wouldn't believe the language that these students use. Swear words are the norm, not the exception, and we are all so used to it that students never get punished. I've heard of schools where teachers are threatened and even beaten up by their students, so I guess we're pretty lucky. But it is still offensive."

Most parenting experts agree that an increase in behavioral problems is the result of fewer restrictions on children's behavior, fewer expectations for their talents, and fewer authority figures who get unquestioned respect. As William Damon, one of the nation's leading authorities on the moral development of children, puts it, "Too many children—the affluent and the poor alike—are drifting through their childhood years without finding the skills, virtues, or sense of purpose that they need to sustain a fruitful life." It is Damon's simple but sound reasoning that when less is expected of children, less is received.

WHEN MISBEHAVIOR BECOMES SERIOUS

Confronting even minor misbehavior and raising your expectations for your child's moral development is the basic recipe for bringing up compassionate and considerate children, but these ingredients become even more critical for children who are temperamentally prone to serious behavior problems.

Some children appear to be born more willful and demanding than others, and if they have parents who give in to these traits, they may earn themselves the unenviable diagnosis of Oppositional Defiant Disorder, or ODD. According to the diagnostic manual of the American Psychiatric Association, children with ODD are defined as having "a pattern of negativistic, hostile and defiant behavior lasting at least 6 months, which cause a significant impairment of academic or social functioning." Children with ODD can be extremely difficult to live with and equally difficult to teach, yet they may certainly have many good qualities as well. Research has shown that their misbehavior tends to occur in "chunks" of time, and at other times these children can be as loving and easy as any child. The goal of prevention is to increase the number and length of times these children are cooperative and compliant, and to help them learn more appropriate social and relationship skills.

The diagnosis of Conduct Disorder (CD) is much more serious. These children and teens exhibit behaviors that are truly unacceptable: skipping school, ignoring curfews, destroying property, and—

most disturbing—acting aggressively to animals and to other children, seemingly without remorse. Conduct Disorders can occur in children as young as five or six, but more commonly are diagnosed between ages nine and thirteen. Most mental-health professionals believe that Conduct Disorders have a biochemical origin and that when a child's behaviors have progressed to the point that they warrant this diagnosis, they will be extremely difficult to treat. Researchers who study the development of violent and destructive children believe that effective prevention programs should begin in infancy, emphasizing the creation of a strong emotional bond between the child and at least one adult. As toddlers and preschoolers these children need more intense efforts than the average child at stimulating their emotional development, with an emphasis on helping them control their anger and respect adult limits.

PROBLEM BEHAVIORS AND THE BRAIN

Although we can't pinpoint the neuropsychological makeup that determines which children become "difficult" children, scientists do believe that serious and persistent behavioral problems come in part from an impairment in the frontal lobe of the brain. This affects the ability to control impulses, plan ahead, problem-solve, and, most important, to learn from negative outcomes.

From a biochemical point of view, serotonin appears to play an important part in determining "good" or "bad" behavior. When the level of the mood-determining neuropeptide serotonin was measured in one study of children with Conduct Disorders, it was found to be significantly lower than in a control group of children. Dopamine and norepinephrine are two other neuropeptides that appear to be involved in behavioral problems. When children with ODD or CD are given Ritalin, which adjusts the level of dopamine and norepinephrine in the brain, they typically exhibit more cooperative and less aggressive behavior toward their peers and their teachers. But while medication may be necessary for extreme problems, there are other ways parents can affect the biochemistry that determines a child's behavior.

As discussed in Chapter 1, your child's basic lifestyle habits—eating, sleeping, and exercise—can be important contributors to the risk of developing behavioral problems. Not getting the right kinds of food, enough sleep, and sufficient exercise will affect the biochemicals that determine emotions and behaviors. Unfortunately, even many professionals overlook the importance of a healthy lifestyle in determining our moods and our responsiveness to others.

Parents don't realize it, but effective discipline and activities that stimulate a child's moral development may also literally affect the child's developing brain. When you set and enforce clear limits and when you encourage children to act repeatedly with empathy and kindness, you are stimulating the parts of the brain that govern a child's self-control and, ultimately, positive behaviors.

RISK FACTORS FOR DEVELOPING BEHAVIORAL PROBLEMS

In Chapter 1 we looked at general risk factors for emotional problems. But sometimes when it comes to behavior problems, there are other, more specific risks of which parents need to be aware. A difficult temperament, inconsistent discipline, and a permissive parenting style will all increase the likelihood that a child will develop some form of behavioral problem. Since risk factors are cumulative, each of these areas must be considered carefully and kept in mind throughout your child's developing years.

A Difficult Temperament

Children who are born with a calm temperament are easy babies to relate to. They tend to be quieter, more self-contained, and highly responsive to the social cues of others. As they grow older, they are constantly reinforced positively for their easygoing personality and social awareness. They are characteristically hardier, more adaptable, and predisposed to be both self-disciplined and self-sufficient.

Difficult babies, on the other hand, cry often, do not like

change, and are slow to settle down. If you have such a baby, you know that they are harder for parents to feed, harder to dress, and they frequently take more time to develop a predictable sleep pattern. As a result, your tension levels may rise, so that the baby and later the young child senses the strain. In what becomes a vicious cycle, behavior worsens, and you feel less confident about your parenting abilities and less connected to your child. When nothing is done to reduce this risk factor, the cycle may be repeated over and over again as a child grows.

LACK OF CONSISTENT DISCIPLINE

There are hundreds of books proclaiming the "best" way to discipline children, but all this advice boils down to about a dozen or so techniques that work because they are based on proven behavioral principles. I will review these in Chapter 7 and rank them according to their developmental appropriateness, though I strongly believe that each family must come up with its own strategies for managing children's behavior. The litmus test for whether you are using the right strategy is simple: "Does it work?" Once I had a parent consult me because her eight-year-old wouldn't listen to her. "I have him in the time-out corner twenty times a day," she explained, "but how much time can I spend disciplining him?" I responded that discipline should take very little time if the technique is effective. Discipline takes a lot of time only when it doesn't work. If you find yourself disciplining your child over and over again, then your strategy, or at least the way you are applying it, does not work. You should consider getting some professional advice, for until you find a strategy that works, you are putting your child at greater risk for future problems.

Too Few Demands on Our Children

As mentioned, a common risk factor for behavioral problems is low parental expectations, which usually translate into overly permissive parenting. Permissive parents tune out "bad" behaviors. They may think, "Oh, this is just a stage. She'll grow out of it." They give in to their children's demands because it is the path of least resistance and because they like to see their children happy when they get what they want. Parents forget, however, that giving in to demands deprives their children of opportunities to improve their behavior. They forget that their primary job is to set behavioral standards for their children to achieve and to teach them how to reach them.

As you think about preventing behavioral problems in your child, it is important to create a clear vision for both of you of the kind of positive qualities you want your child to work toward. There are millions of children and teens who do admirable and altruistic deeds, who feel connected to their parents, who treat others with respect, and who make their choices from a core set of values and ethics. Your child can be like these children when you set your standards high.

Below is a list of qualities you might like to consider as goals for your child's behavior. Use this list as a reminder of what you are working toward whenever you find yourself caught in a never-ending disciplinary cycle or feeling defeated by problems that seem insurmountable.

You want a child who is:

- flexible

- able to tolerate frustration

- able to calm him/herself

- able to talk about positive and negative feelings

- able to offer and receive constructive criticism

- able to make other people feel good

- able to express affection and caring

- empathic

- honest

- cooperative and helpful

- considerate of others

- polite

- able to compromise

- able to resolve interpersonal problems

- in control

- capable of understanding that his or her behaviors affect others

Remember these qualities as you read through the chapter. They are achievable no matter how your child is currently behaving.

INFANTS

KEY TO PREVENTION: KEEPING CONNECTED TO YOUR BABY

Easy babies are a joy. They sleep well, take a bottle or breast eagerly, and make eye contact. They do not cry often, and when they do, it is for a reason. Easy babies are responsive to their parents and to others, so that adults are constantly getting reinforced for their attention. This reciprocal pleasure builds a baby's sense of competence, trust, and sense of self-worth and goes a long way toward preventing emotional difficulties.

But difficult babies can try anyone's patience and cause parents to question both their own abilities and the strength of the bond that they are forming with their child.

The process of natural selection has seen to it that human parents, like every other animal species that nurtures its young, have a "grace" period, during which expectations are minimal. But that grace period takes a toll. There is no question that high-need babies require parents who are more responsive, patient, and willing to do whatever it takes to adapt and emotionally connect with a demanding infant.

Establishing a pattern of "love with limits" will help parents maintain a sense of confidence about their parenting ability and begin habits that will sow the seeds for self-control and coopera-tion. A difficult baby need not grow into a difficult child.

AN OUNCE OF PREVENTION

As babies become less egocentric, they will come to see that getting what they want is conditional to certain kinds of behaviors. A baby who whines or screams does not get a cookie; a baby who sits qui-etly in his high chair does. At least this is the way it should be. When parents find themselves giving treats or rewards to try to soothe a baby older than twelve months, they should be aware that they are also reinforcing difficult behaviors. Leniency during cer-tain times of the day, when a baby is hungry or tired, is fine, but if a baby is over a year old and irritable whenever he doesn't get his way, then this is the time to begin looking at the limits you will need to set for your child.

By ten to twelve months a baby begins to understand the word "no," or if not the word itself, then the tone that accompanies it. Most babies will also shake their head no when they hear the word spoken by their parents, showing that they are beginning to inter-nalize self-control.

Whether your baby is low- or high-need, the following preven-tion techniques will keep difficult patterns from emerging in your relationship, creating a sympathetic bond between you and your child and minimizing his chances of developing behavioral prob-lems as he grows.

Introduce Change Slowly

Difficult babies are less adaptable, perhaps because of slower neurological development. Make their schedules as predictable as possible, introducing changes (feeding, sleeping arrangements, new people) one at a time. Difficult babies are not only more sensitive to change, they are also less able to calm themselves when they are upset, but these are things that all children learn with time and patience.

Learn Your Baby's Cries and Gestures

A baby cries to communicate discomfort, but there are many things that can be causing this discomfort. Experts believe that babies have as many as twelve different cries, which can indicate that they are wet, hungry, frustrated, too cold, just bored, or in real pain. Try to identify different cries by their tone, volume, and accompanying breathing pattern, and also observe your child's skin color and level of physical tension. As your baby gets older, you will realize when you can ignore cries for attention and when there is a real need that must be met. The more consistently you react correctly to your baby's cries, the more trust will exist between you and the more secure and satisfied your baby will feel.

"Wear" Your Baby

In most primitive cultures parents carry their babies around in a sling. This seems to be both comforting and stimulating for fussy babies. Find a commercially available sling that allows you to carry the baby in different positions, depending on her mood and yours. She may need more soothing and physical closeness to achieve a comfortable level of intimacy and security. Holding your baby close reinforces a connectedness that she will enjoy and that will translate into the sense of security all children need.

Infant Massage

Infant massage is promoted for both its physical and psychological benefits to your baby. Even though some fussy babies do not like to be touched, most will respond well to some form of massage. There are several good books on this subject, such as *Baby Massage* by physical therapist Peter Walker. Massaging your baby will help calm her and also will promote a closeness between you. Massage brings enjoyment to you and your baby and creates quiet moments that will grow longer as she grows older. Most important, massage will make you feel like a competent teacher, instructing your fussy baby on how it feels to be at peace.

Play with Your Baby

Playing with your baby stimulates his overall development, contributing to the bond that you are establishing with him. There are many ways to play with your baby—peekaboo, finger play, making faces in a mirror—and he will be sure to make his preferences known. Set aside several times a day to play with your baby when he is in a good mood. Joining him in pleasurable moments will assure him of your presence, love, and ability to care for and be with him. It will set the stage for years of cooperative play and enjoyment. But choose your moments carefully. Playing with him when he is in a bad mood probably won't distract him and may actually overstimulate him, leading to increased irritability.

Avoid Parent Burnout

The worst result of having a cranky and irritable baby is not being able to enjoy your child. Feeling connected and responsive to your baby is the single most important job you have as a parent. This is why it is important for you to realize that you don't have to be Supermom or Superdad, or spend every waking minute with your baby. Find other caretakers who can help you out. Spend time with supportive people, particularly other parents who have had "difficult" babies themselves and who can give you advice and consolation. But it is critical that you do whatever is necessary so that in the time you do have with your baby you are communicating patience, love, and your undivided interest. Without these messages a difficult baby will only become crankier and unhappier. Babies are quite capable of picking up a parent's tension and alienation. So be sure that what gets through is your patience and affection.

Computers Can Help

Raising a temperamentally difficult baby can wear you out, but your personal computer is a link to the thousands of mothers and fathers who are struggling with the same issues that you are. Through the act of sharing your own disappointments and frustrations, as well as your pleasures and successes, you will likely find a renewed sense of purpose as well as practical ways to help your baby and yourself. Some of the more popular sites on the Internet for information and support about babies include Parentsoup.com, Family.com, and Babyonline.com, but search until you find one that suits you best.

TODDLERS AND PRESCHOOLERS

KEY TO PREVENTION: INSIST ON GOOD BEHAVIOR

Two to five years is the critical stage when children learn to behave according to adult social standards. By the end of this period, when children are ready for formal schooling, they should be respectful, helpful, able to follow two- or three-step directions (without complaint), and they should understand the intrinsic and social value of "being good." They are also developing an internal sense of right and wrong. Serious behavioral problems can begin to develop if this rudimentary beginning is not in place.

Children naturally try to emulate our best qualities. Even before a toddler can string two sentences together, she will want to help her parents set the table, or dust the bureau, or sweep the floor, and will derive great joy from their approval. If a toddler passes her father sleeping on the couch, she may cover him with a blanket. If she sees another child cry, she will try to comfort him.

But young children are also very egocentric, and they will just as naturally look after their own interests before the interests of others. Take for example, Ginny, age four, who in an experiment on moral development was given eight small dolls that she was told she could share with a friend.

Adult: You have eight dolls here. Would you like to give some to a friend of yours?

Ginny: No, my friend Tara has a lot of dolls at her house, so I don't want to give her any.

Adult: But what about another friend who does not have any dolls and might like one of these?

Ginny: Oh! My friend Vicky likes dolls, but she isn't here, so she doesn't want these dolls.

Adult: But what if she were here? Would you share your dolls with her?

Ginny: Yes, if she were here, I would give her two little dolls, because she is my friend.

Adult: But then Vicky would have two dolls and you would have six dolls. Is that fair?

Ginny: Yes, because I like dolls better than Vicky.

Ginny's reasoning shows the first moral awakening of a four-year-old, but it's also clear that her ideas of fairness are far from complete. Ginny understands the importance of sharing and being concerned about others, but these values dim somewhat when confronted with the need for self-sacrifice. Children are born with the capacity for empathy, but this develops slowly, over time. The fact that we can chart the predictable moral growth of children as they age certainly suggests that it is a genetically programmed trait. But the fact that there is also a wide variance in children as they age tells us that moral behavior can be easily modified by experience.

Studies show that adult authority figures, namely parents and preschool teachers, provide moral direction to children by their very presence. For example, when researchers standing in a playroom observe children, they note many more examples of sharing, helping, and kindness than when the same researchers observe the same children left on their own from behind a two-way mirror. Children have a natural drive toward socially appropriate behavior, but it takes adult guidance to make this behavior dominant.

RISK FACTOR

Shame and Guilt

Although many parenting experts don't like to admit it, shame and guilt play an integral role in forming a child's personality. Shame is a form of extreme embarrassment that occurs when children are caught breaking important social rules. It is certainly not something that we want our children to feel often, but we do want them to feel shame when they have done something to be ashamed about. If a child hits another child, deliberately hurts someone's feelings, or takes something that belongs to someone else, these are shameful acts. Shame occurs when children (or adults) behave in a way that is considered contemptible by others. It is a horrible feeling, but one that discourages us from doing the same thing again.

The emotion of guilt similarly serves a developmental purpose. While shame comes from the disapproval of others, guilt occurs when we have failed to meet our own expectations. Guilt is the closest thing to what we call our conscience. Guilt occurs when we set goals for ourselves but then lack the motivation or willpower to achieve them.

Many children never need to be punished. Their natural drive to emulate adult behavior and seek adult approval, combine with the self-imposed punishments of shame and guilt to make such children consistently cooperative and eager to please. Other children, for reasons we don't really understand, seem to be less sensitive to their own internal voices as well as to social disapproval, and require more active discipline from their parents. Here's what parents can do when their toddlers and preschoolers misbehave.

AN OUNCE OF PREVENTION

Don't Deprive Your Child of Guilt or Shame

Many parents make the mistake of depriving their children of experiencing the normal emotions of guilt and shame. They can't tolerate seeing their children in any kind of distress and want them to feel good even when there is no reason to feel good. I remember observing one mother in a store who yelled briefly at her son when she saw that he'd dismantled a display of dozens of packages of cookies. She then apologized herself to the disapproving clerk and proceeded to fix the display. I then heard her say to her five-year-old, "Okay, sweetheart, now let's get you something to eat."

Develop a Zero Tolerance for Misbehavior

I know that toddlers are expected to have periods of testing and misbehavior (i.e., the terrible twos and fearsome fours), but the fact that we can anticipate misbehavior does not mean that we should accept it. To the contrary, this is a time that parents must be the firmest in their resolve to socialize their children. Parents need to be clear in the boundaries that they set in order for children to feel safe and learn respect for others. Toddlers feel more secure (though temporarily infuriated) when it is clear that parents are in charge. If they sense themselves able to have their way, they can become frightened by their own power—which only increases misbehavior.

There are five basic steps to teaching children to behave, as we can see in the example of Anna, a four-year-old who was caught throwing her blocks at the family cat.

1. **Set clear rules:** In a firm voice, her mother tells Anna, "Pets must be treated kindly. It is wrong to throw things at the cat."

2. **Recognize, label, and describe misbehavior:** Her mother says, "Throwing things at the cat will scare and hurt her. It is bad to throw things at the cat. She is our Fluffy, and we need to treat her gently. Stop that right now." But Anna doesn't stop.

3. **Give a warning: "Anna, this is your second warning.** If you don't stop, you will go into the time-out corner for four minutes." Anna is now running after the cat to throw more blocks at her. Anna is giggling excitedly. She is not trying to hurt the cat, but trying to tease her mother.

4. **Immediately provide a consequence:** Her mother sweeps Anna

up in her arms and says firmly, "Now you have to take a time-out as a punishment. Your time will begin once you are sitting quietly."

5. **Emotionally disengage from the struggle:** Anna begins to scream with outrage, struggling in the time-out chair. Her mother holds her in the chair from behind, remaining calm. "Anna, your time-out will not begin until you are calm, and then I will let go. You have to be punished when you throw things at the cat. That is the rule." Her mother holds Anna in the chair until she is calm, then sets a timer for four minutes. When the time-out is over, she tells Anna that she can go back and play.

Keeping your own cool is critical. Discipline techniques are most effective if you are dispassionate and keep a clear head about what is happening. Parental feelings of guilt, anger, or hurt are common and understandable, but they get in the way of giving your children the consistent message and behavior that they need from you.

The Overcorrection Technique

There are many forms of discipline, and I usually suggest that parents use the mildest form first (e.g., a firm reprimand). If that does not work, I suggest going to the next step (usually a time-out). If a child continues to misbehave, more comprehensive techniques, like using points to win or lose privileges, are usually effective. But typically, by the time children are referred to me for behavioral problems, their parents have tried innumerable techniques without success. When this happens, I recommend the two-part overcorrection technique, which is almost always guaranteed to be quick and effective (though, as we shall see, not particularly easy or pleasant).

The overcorrection technique was devised more than twenty-five years ago by two behavioral psychologists, Nathan Azrin and Richard Foxx, working with developmentally disabled children and adults who did not respond to more traditional techniques. Since that time it has been used successfully with a wide range of intransigent behaviors, from thumb-sucking and nail-biting to aggressive and destructive outbursts.

It can be used with older toddlers through school-aged children.

Stage One: Positive Practice

The first stage of this technique is designed to teach the child the correct behavior and to rehearse it over and over again. When a child misbehaves, there is always a positive behavior that is the opposite of the "negative" one, and is the behavior you want your child to practice. In traditional discipline techniques, children are punished for misbehaving, but they are not taught the behavior that is expected of them. They learn what they shouldn't do, but not what they should do.

In the positive-practice stage, the parent makes it clear exactly what behavior was expected of the child in the first place and then has the child repeat the positive behavior (the opposite of what occurred) five to ten times or for five to ten minutes (the length of time depends on the child's age and the type of negative behavior). Here are some examples:

- A four-year-old boy drove his parents crazy by slamming the bathroom door when he was the least bit upset. He was asked to practice going downstairs, opening the bathroom door quietly, then shutting it quietly, then going back upstairs, ten times.

- A five-year-old wouldn't clean up his toys when asked, and made a sarcastic remark to his parents. He had to put away his toys, then take them out again, then put them away again, five times. Each time he had to report to his parents that he was done in a calm and respectful manner.

- A three-year-old refused to put on her coat to go out to the school bus on time, so that her mother had to bring her to preschool and be late for work. She had to practice putting on, taking off, and putting on her coat again 5 times.

As you might have gathered from these examples, this technique is usually used with very stubborn children, and as I'm sure you can imagine, it becomes a test of wills. But parents are much bigger than their kids, and with resolve (and the good of the child in mind) they should easily be able to win such a test. Often this technique requires physically standing or sitting behind children and gently guiding them to do what they don't want to do. If children openly fight their parents, they must take a time-out for five minutes, until they are willing to cooperate.

As I have said, this behavioral technique is not fun. It is a form of discipline. But it is one that conveys to even the stubbornest child the correct balance of power and the determination of the parent to restore it. Unlike other forms of discipline, this technique gives children practice in the positive behavior that they should have demonstrated in the first place.

Stage Two: Making Things Right

The second stage of this technique is technically called "restitution." A younger child may be told, "Now it's time for us to work together," and an older one, "Let's set things right." This part of the technique recognizes that the child's misbehavior has taken a lot of parent time and caused unnecessary grief, and that amends must be made so that the behavior can be forgiven. Stage two of the overcorrection technique restores the balance between the parent and the child as you can see from the examples mentioned above.

- The three-year-old door-slammer took a sponge and wiped fingerprints off the doors and walls.

- The boy who wouldn't clean up his toys spent fifteen minutes helping his father clean up the garage.

- The girl who wouldn't put on her coat helped her mother make sandwiches for her school lunch the evening before, so that her mother wouldn't be as rushed in the morning.

As you can see, the second stage of the overcorrection technique brings a positive end to the original problem and brings parents and their children together in a mutually supportive way. Younger children will readily see the pleasures in helping their parents instead of opposing them.

If this technique seems a little cumbersome and time-consuming, then you are understanding it correctly. But it rarely has to be repeated more than once or twice, because when done correctly, it works.

Computers Can Help

It is difficult to find computer software that teaches children the importance of helping and caring behaviors, but I have found a few programs for preschoolers that I recommend to parents. For example, *The Lie* (Davidson Publishers) tells the story about a girl who lies to her mother about not having any homework. As the story progresses, a little green monster appears and gets bigger with every new lie. Throughout the story the child using the program must perform a variety of helping tasks, like cleaning up the girl's room.

SCHOOL-AGE CHILDREN

KEY TO PREVENTION: TEACHING VALUES AND THE BEHAVIORS THAT REFLECT THEM

By the age of six or seven, children begin to think consciously about their values and choices, and by twelve they should have a well-developed system of beliefs that they use to distinguish right from wrong.

Although the groundwork for good behavior is laid in the previous developmental stage, the ages between six and twelve are the time when children become able to behave as "good" people. It is at this stage, the age of reason, that the thinking part of the brain, the neocortex, gives children the capacity to analyze a conflict and see that there may be several solutions to the same problem.

Of course, good moral values are relative to the culture in which a child lives. In a 1987 study by Richard Schweder and his colleagues, comparing American children and Brahmin Hindu children from India, each was asked to rank the worst offenses that a person could commit. The number-one offense the Indian children could imagine was an eldest son, the day after his father's death, getting a haircut and eating chicken. Number two would be committed by a woman who prepared and then ate rice with her husband and his eldest brother as opposed to letting them dine alone. Among the top deeds that the American children considered wrong were hitting a child and eating with your hands.

Even though we like to blame television, video games, or toy manufacturers for ignoring their responsibility in shaping children's values, truthfully they are only a backdrop against which parents make choices about the behaviors they want their children to emulate and the ones they want them to avoid. Consider, for example, the Simmons family, sitting around the TV watching Monday-night wrestling. Mr. Simmons and his son Mark, age ten, are following the action intently. Mrs. Simmons is reading the newspaper, trying to ignore the staged mayhem.

Goldberg, a goliath ex–football player and reigning champion, has just lifted Macho Man high over his head and, with animal ferocity, is asking the crowd what he should do.

"Body-slam him," Mark responds.

"Slam him," Mr. Simmons chimes in.

Mrs. Simmons pauses for a moment and incredulously peers over her paper at the TV.

A third wrestler has now appeared from somewhere at ringside and is hauling a metal chair into the ring with him, demanding that Goldberg release his friend.

"Don't do it," Mark implores. "Body slam them and then stomp both their heads."

"Or throw the Undertaker out of the ring, and then wrap him around his own chair," Mr. Simmons says more calmly than his son, thinking his strategy a little more refined.

The camera pans to the horde of young men in the audience (and a token woman or two), making rude gestures and calling for their own particular brand of violent mischief.

According to the Nielsen ratings, professional wrestling has become one of the most popular forms of "entertainment" on television.

The people that produce violent or sexually suggestive TV shows, or who make the toys and video games that children beg

their parents to buy, say that they are just offering a form of entertainment and that it is the responsibility of parents to turn off the
TV or just say no. Although this may be a rationalization, it is still
good advice (if parents would only take it). But it doesn't go nearly
far enough. Certainly it is the parents' job to set limits and define
the values of what their children should and should not do, but
they must also be the moral authority whom children look to and
learn from. Considering the influences in today's culture, this job
cannot be a benign or passive one. Here are some of the things our
children learn from watching television and playing video games an
average of twenty-four hours a week:

- Rude behavior is seen as socially appropriate.

- Aggressive and sexually provocative behavior is rewarded.

- Adults are often the objects of rude behavior and derision.

- There are rarely any reasonable or permanent consequences to
  dishonest or unethical behavior.

Many shows (particularly talk shows) teach disrespect, high-
lighting the audience members who mock the guests, get in the last
word, and use insolent body language.

School-age children live in a world in which much is expected
of them. They are up against a vast number of influences, and we
expect them to distinguish the good influences from the bad. We
encourage them to be more empathic than they have ever been
before and increasingly to be able to put themselves in someone
else's shoes. They need to have enough control to contain their
negative impulses.

But while some kids are able to glide into these new under-
standings, many do not. They need to be encouraged to think about
the feelings of others. They need to be helped to imagine what others might think or how they might react. They need to be given the
tools necessary to control an impulse.

All of this is possible when parents take steps to prevent the
influence of the media from providing inappropriate role models and
to create a home full of opportunities to teach children appropriate

values. All children will ultimately learn appropriate behavior from seeing the consequences of their own actions, but parents shouldn't wait for a child to come home complaining because he punched someone and was punched back, or until she relates a story in which she treated a friend unkindly only to be rebuffed herself. There are many opportunities during each day to help a child to understand principles of fairness, compromise, and empathic thinking.

AN OUNCE OF PREVENTION

Raise Your Expectations and Give Explanations

School-age children should be well mannered and respectful. There is no reason for them to behave otherwise to you or anyone else. Make it clear early on that anything short of polite behavior is just not acceptable. It's helpful to give children some tips before the moment arrives. "When you meet Mr. Smith today, it's important to say hello clearly and to smile." You might also want to place this advice in the context of how it can make another person feel as opposed to presenting it as some arbitrary rule. "When you say hello, look someone in the eye and smile. It helps people feel important. It also helps them see what a good person you are."

School-age children are often told what to do, but not always why they should do it. In offering an explanation of why you expect certain behaviors, you are teaching them to respect others because you are respecting them.

Share Your Moral Reactions and Let Your Child Share His

Children have many influences that shape their values, but none are as powerful as the family. Don't hesitate to talk to your children about what you read in the newspaper or see on TV, or about what happens in your everyday experiences. Here is an example of how you can teach your children values in a meaningful way.

Susan and her seven-year-old son, Pete, were watching an afternoon special about a child who was always teased for being small.

Pete was clearly upset for the child. "They should stop," he said. "He can't help it."

Susan nodded. "I agree. What would you do if you saw that happening to someone?"

Pete shrugged. "Well, I wouldn't say that stuff."

"I know," Susan said. "But do you think you could help in some way?"

Pete thought about that. "If he was my friend?"

"Even if he wasn't," said Susan.

That seemed to give Pete pause. He turned and looked at his mother quizzically. "I don't know. If I didn't know him, you mean?"

Susan nodded. It was understandable that Pete hesitated. They were approaching a topic of social awareness that Pete was too young to come to on his own. "It's important to try to help people who are being hurt. If it's not safe to do it yourself, then it's good to get help. Watching out for people is a good thing," said Susan.

Your child will learn this kind of lesson best when it is in the context of a real problem he is having. Take such opportunities to help your child explore his moral reasoning as well as to model yours.

Teach Children an Emotional Awareness of Themselves and Others

Children must be sensitized to understand their own feelings as well as the feelings of others. It is important to remember that emotional awareness includes nonverbal as well as verbal communication. Children are not often taught how to read gestures, postures, facial expressions, and so on, but this is an invaluable skill that can easily be acquired.

While you are watching your child play with a friend, countless opportunities may arise to encourage him to reflect on the feelings of others. This can be done right out in the open, or by pulling a child aside.

Jim was watching his eight-year-old son Tom take turns batting with his friend George. Each was to bat three times, then be the pitcher. Tom had just pitched the third ball when a car honked, and George, startled, looked over his shoulder and missed the ball.

"That's it!" Tom cried out. "My turn."

"No fair!" yelled George. "I wasn't watching."

"Too bad," replied Tom, confident in the rightness of his views. He started walking toward George to get the bat.

"Hold on!" Jim called out, quickly approaching the two of them.

He looked at George. "That was a really sudden loud noise, wasn't it?"

"Yes," George said, clearly upset. "I got scared."

Jim turned to his son. "How do you think you would have felt standing there if a horn went off behind you really loudly?"

Tom hesitated. He shrugged.

Jim just stood there looking at him. "Well?"

Tom shrugged again. He looked at George. "I guess I'd have looked or something."

"Okay, then," said Jim. "And what would have happened? You'd have let the ball go by, too?"

Tom nodded. "I guess so . . . but I want to bat!"

"I know," replied Jim. "But what do you think is fair? Didn't you guys decide to have three turns each?"

Tom sighed. "Yeah. He should go. But just one more time!"

"Right," George said quickly. "One."

By helping his son assess the situation more fairly and put himself in his friend's shoes, Jim took advantage of what seemed like an insignificant moment. But in fact it was a perfect opportunity to mold Tom's moral development. Learning in the simplest of situations to put aside one's own needs to understand what might be going on for another will be a springboard to more complex situations, when negotiating and compromise are more critical.

Teach Cooperation

Because we live in such a competitive society, it is important to actively teach children the habit of cooperation. School-age children enjoy the feeling of camaraderie and welcome the opportunity to have more cooperative experiences when they are not tempted away by their desires to "be the best" or to be the winner. Involving children regularly in cooperative activities, where there are no winners or losers, is the simplest way to combat the more common competitive message they usually hear: "Status and self-worth depend on you winning and others losing." One example of such a cooperative activity is Create a Story. Have the kids sit in a circle. Make up the first line of a fairy tale. Then have each child create another part of the story until they've all decided that it is done.

A child might begin, "One day a beautiful princess walking by a stream found a rock so shiny she could see her face in it. . . ."

And the next child continues, "But in the rock her face looked kind of funny, and so she threw it and by accident hit a tiny goldfish. . . ."

And so on. When the tale is done, the children will feel successful and unified and will likely seek more activities where there are no losers because everybody wins.

Teach Altruism

According to developmental research, children are naturally helpful to friends and family members from the time that they are toddlers. By twelve or thirteen they also begin to express concern for people they don't even know: the homeless, the poor, the sick. Most children are also eager to express their concern in deeds, demonstrating altruism, the highest form of moral development.

But if these values are not nurtured, they can disappear. In a materialistic culture like ours, it is easy to become self-centered and ignore the problems of others. Parents can counter this cultural trend by making charitable acts and deeds a regular part of the family's life. Working in a soup kitchen, or wrapping presents for the homeless, or helping an elderly neighbor with her groceries can teach your children a great deal about the pleasure of caring for others. If your child has a history of behavioral problems, this is the quickest way to create a new behavioral pattern that all can admire.

Teach Social Problem-Solving

Children can learn to solve social problems as early as four or five years of age when they are instructed in specific techniques such as negotiation, compromise, and seeing another person's point of view. Learning how to resolve conflicts is important in every aspect of life. When your child is grown, it will be a key to success in relationships as well as at work.

When your children are five or six and you witness a struggle over who gets to play with which action figure, suggest that they take turns. If both girls want to be the princess in a skit, suggest that they make up two skits so that each gets a turn. As they get older, help them to think of solutions on their own. "What are the different ways you can each get a chance to play?"

Encouraging your children to think of possible resolutions before an argument starts will teach them an invaluable social skill and save you from the job of being the mediator of all their problems.

Take Back the TV

Few will argue that children watch too much TV. We have heard it hundreds of times. But as noted above, it is not just the time that children spend watching TV, it is how their parents respond to what they are seeing. Children need to be educated consumers of television. Go through the TV listings and help children decide what they want to watch and why. View some shows with them. Share your values. Don't just condemn what you don't like, but help your children develop their own critical awareness. Don't hesitate to forbid shows that you feel are inappropriate, but do tell your children why, and use this opportunity to share your values: "I know you like that police show, but the truth is, people are always getting hurt. I don't view that as entertainment. I think it's serious stuff that can actually happen and is not something you should watch for amusement. It isn't fun to have a gun aimed at you."

True, your child might just go over to a neighbor's house to watch a forbidden show, but you will have stated your values and priorities clearly, and that is what children will remember.

COMPUTERS CAN HELP—OR HURT

The Internet offers endless opportunities for children to learn and express their values. They can learn about other cultures by developing e-mail pals or express their concerns by working on volunteer projects (you can get ideas at www.kidscare.org or www.volunteers.com). Of course, they can also learn how to make an incendiary bomb or download pornography. As in other aspects of moral development, the encouragement and guidance of parents make the difference. Certainly you need to stay vigilant about what your children are doing online, and view the computer as a small window to a very large world. Move your computer into a room where you can observe your children and use it with them. The Internet can provide both good and bad experiences for children, and you can help them make the right choices.

TEENAGERS

KEY TO PREVENTION: STEP FORWARD INTO THE ROLE OF GUIDING YOUR TEEN, NOT BACKWARD

Parents can spend the first twelve years of their children's lives reducing the risks that cause serious problems, only to find that their teenagers begin creating new risks for themselves. This is a trying stage for both teens and their parents. On the brink of adulthood, teens are anxious to grasp their independence, but they do so with ambivalence (though they would never admit it) and can be frightened by the temptations placed before them. Breaking rules can seem both exciting and terrifying.

> *For a six-week period not a week went by at a Chicago suburban high school when a student wasn't suspended for smoking marijuana. With each "bust" the police would arrive at the*

school, handcuff the offenders, and make a big deal about the arrest, hoping that it would act as a deterrent. But it never did. The same thing happened again and again. These were smart kids, from well-off families, who at the very least should have had more sense than to take drugs on school property. But apparently the "high" that the teens got from tempting fate was just as important as the high they got from the drug.

The traditional explanation for why teenagers are attracted to high-risk behaviors is that it is part of their normal development. Recent research in neuropsychology, in fact, shows that high-risk behavior in teens may actually be a biochemical/physiological characteristic of this age. Although by age sixteen a teenager's brain development reaches adult levels, teenagers are likelier to use the higher centers of their brains for creativity than for judgment. In other words, they employ their "adult powers" to originate ideas, not to assess them.

Successful prevention programs that deal with high-risk behaviors in teenagers are aimed at helping them think about the consequences of their actions. Programs may fail, however, when they do not acknowledge that teenagers have the final choice over their behavior.

AN OUNCE OF PREVENTION

The good news about today's teens comes from surveys that tell us that adolescents now feel closer to their parents than they have in several generations. The majority of teens report that they would confide an important problem to their parents before they would talk to a friend.

But this good news is contingent on the assumption that parents *know how* to talk to their teens. If teenagers feel that they will only get a lecture or criticism when they talk to their parents, they soon learn to be quiet and avoid important topics. According to Charles Schaefer and Theresa Foy DiGeronimo, authors of *How to Talk to Teenagers About Really Important Things*, teenagers will seek the advice of their parents when they feel that their parents know what they are talking about, and when parents present their information with respectful authority.

Let's take as an example the conversations that every teen and parent should have about drinking and driving. Almost one-quarter of the people who died in speed-related crashes in 1997 were between the ages of fifteen and twenty. Car crashes are the leading cause of death for teens.

Understand a Teen's Point of View, Even If You Don't Agree with It

Teens are subject to intense peer pressure. They might, for example, choose to get into a car with an intoxicated driver rather than being seen as a spoiler. Their fear of being embarrassed or ostracized is a significant factor in impairing teens' judgment. It may seem odd to adults, but teens don't fear death as much as they do disfigurement. Helping them see that pain and bodily harm are the most likely consequences of a car accident might actually be a more effective deterrent than pointing out fatality statistics. "You could have severe burns from an accident, or live the rest of your life in a wheelchair" is a sobering argument for any teen.

Know the Facts

Proclamations without explanations won't work. Your teen may know nothing concrete about drunk driving, and may in fact think that he's being conservative if he waits twenty minutes after having a drink before climbing behind the wheel. Teens need to know the facts. They need to know, for instance, that cold showers don't sober up people who are drunk, or that just two drinks can make a person too intoxicated to drive.

They need to know the medical risks of different drugs and the statistics of unsafe sex. They need the facts delivered in an even, clearheaded way. Avoid scare tactics. Comments like "You'll fry your brain if you . . ." is the kind of approach that makes teens tune out. They'll consider it high drama on your part.

State Clear Rules

The rules about a dangerous activity like drinking and driving must be stated clearly, with no room for exceptions. A teen should never get into a car with someone behind the wheel who has had even a single drink. There is no guarantee that your teen will listen, but if you've expressed understanding and offered the facts, you will have stacked the odds in your favor.

Anticipate Problems

As part of your discussion with your teenager, anticipate problems that might occur and the best ways to address them. Don't conduct an interrogation, but bring up hypothetical situations like "What would you do if your date takes drugs at a party?" or "What happens if a driver denies that he is drinking but you smell alcohol on his breath?"

Your teen might say nervously, "Oh, that won't happen." But push a little. Get her thinking. If she gives you an innocuous or pat response like "I'll tell him to stop," try to get her to think further. If she refuses, brainstorm for her.

"Well, one thing you can't do is let him take you home from the party. Go home with someone else, or call me."

"I'd ask him to pull over at the first phone booth and calmly say, 'I can't drive with you. It's not safe. I don't think you should either. Let's call someone to come and get us.'"

Planning how to react, even running it by your teen like a movie, is referred to as a "cognitive rehearsal." This simple exercise programs the higher centers of the brain to react rationally when the actual event is at hand. It encourages the ability to assess a situation and plan an action.

Make a Formal Agreement

It may seem juvenile, but making a written contract about expected rules can have a significant influence on behavior. For example, in a study of cheating among college students, subjects were asked to sign a contract at the beginning of the semester promising that they would not cheat. As a result, self-reported incidents of cheating were reduced by more than 25 percent. A contract is a simple statement of what is expected in a particular circumstance. A contract on drinking and driving might state:

Teen: I agree to call you when I get into a situation where someone is drinking and driving.

Parent: I agree to come and get you at any hour. If I am not available, I will pay for a taxi.

Helping your teenagers become the responsible adults you want them to be is a difficult job in such complicated times, but you may be comforted to remember that it is a job with a definite beginning and an end. After all, your child is a teenager only for 2,555 days.

Computers Can Help

There are a growing number of software programs that can help teach children about specific risks such as drugs, alcohol, cigarette smoking, and sexuality. See the list of programs and their publishers in the Appendix. These multimedia programs show real teens talking about real problems, and are designed to help users see the consequences of their choices.

• • •

You can prevent behavioral problems. You can prevent merely annoying behaviors like whining and rudeness and major problems that could change the course of a child's development. The first key is staying attached to your child, no matter how difficult the behaviors might be. The bond that you create with your child begins in infancy, but it must be nourished throughout a lifetime.

The second key is finding a way to discipline your child that works. Do not ignore minor misbehaviors, for they are much easier to address. Set your standards for good behavior high. There are many discipline techniques to choose from when your child tests your rules. If you can't find one that is effective, seek professional guidance rather than letting your child continue to misbehave.

The third key is to take an active role in teaching your child values. Have high expectations for her to acquire all the virtues that you admire in the best people you know. Guide her toward the experiences that will reinforce these values.

Finally, as your children grow into adolescence, step forward into your role as an important influence in their lives rather than fading into the background. Many parents have the misconception that teenagers want to be left alone, when in fact they seek their parents out if they know they will find an understanding and thoughtful audience for their concerns.

3

Preventing Eating Problems and Disorders

Samantha looked down at her plate with painfully mixed feelings. It was filled with fried chicken, mashed potatoes, and gravy, and it looked good.

Unfortunately, it seemed to be the only thing in her life that did.

Twelve-year-old Samantha had been heavy throughout her childhood. Now that she was a preadolescent, her weight was really starting to bother her. Every day she heard children at school calling her "Fatty" and "Blimpy." She hated the way she looked.

She wished she didn't have to go to school at all.

Samantha picked up her fork and dug in.

Eating is often a very complex experience. It *should* just be a matter of feeling hungry, throwing together a balanced meal, and sitting down to eat, but most of the time it's not that simple. Eating can be either a positive or negative emotional experience. As in Samantha's case, it's often both at the same time. Eating can be the center of a social event or an isolating, lonely experience. It can be a way to comfort oneself or another person, or it can be an expression of deep emotional turmoil. A balanced diet can be a source of energy and a way to ward off disease. An unhealthy diet can lead to both short- and long-term health problems.

As adults, many of us struggle with emotional conflicts around eating, and, unfortunately, we pass this predisposition along to our children. Despite the fact that we live in a health-conscious world and are well aware that eating low-fat, low-salt, high-fiber diets and exercising religiously is important for physical and emotional health, parents frequently neglect to concentrate on their children's eating patterns. Many parents fail to adequately supervise the eating patterns of their children until a monumental problem appears on the horizon.

It's hard to believe that something so basic as teaching children to eat nutritious meals can be so difficult for parents. But the statistics are irrefutable:

- An estimated 6 percent of preschoolers, 14 percent of school-age children, and 12 percent of teenagers are overweight.

- The incidence of type-2 diabetes, a common complication of obesity, typically seen in adults over forty, has increased tenfold in children and adolescents over the last decade.

- Potentially life-threatening eating disorders (anorexia and bulimia) affect an estimated 10 to 15 percent of the population. An estimated 86 percent of these problems will start before the age of twenty.

The physical tolls of obesity and eating disorders are well known (premature cardiovascular problems, elevated blood pressure and cholesterol levels, decrease of growth hormones, and more), and the psychological damage can be equally devastating.

Eating problems are associated with a wide variety of serious emotional and behavioral disorders, including depression, social inhibition, and underachievement. These, like the physical effects of eating problems, can last a lifetime.

Although it is hard for most of us to accept, everyone is born with a preset body type and a propensity for weight gain that will largely determine our size and shape. If a child isn't happy with the genetic hand he's been dealt, he needs to reach a philosophical acceptance and set a healthy and realistic goal for improvement. Once a child registers any dissatisfaction with his body or appearance, it becomes critical to work on issues of emotional health such as self-acceptance, a sense of competence, social skills, and the strength to take control of whatever is in his power. Building the emotional health necessary to withstand disappointments is a process that can start at infancy.

The good news is that eating problems and disorders are preventable. The increase in the number of children and teens having problems around food is relatively recent and, as we shall see, involves risk factors that parents can limit. Also, the science of nutrition has made many advances in the last decade, and the information now available to parents may help them raise children who are better protected from more physical diseases than any generation before. Now it is time to pay attention to how better nutrition and eating habits can help children avoid emotional disorders.

Obesity and eating disorders are caused by a combination of factors: social, psychological, developmental, and genetic, with the last of these being by far the most important. Genetic makeup applies to biological issues as well as temperament.

But while there are certain genetic or biological components of an eating problem that are more difficult to manage than others, in general the risks can be contained. I will begin with the risks that are the least malleable and then move forward to the nutritional and emotional risk factors that are more amenable to change.

RISK FACTORS FOR POOR NUTRITION, EATING DISORDERS, AND OBESITY

Body Type

The two most important inherited factors that determine the relationship between food intake and how much we weigh are our metabolism, controlled by the thyroid gland, and our "set point," a genetically programmed level of body fat. These factors, along with the genes that predetermine our height, bone structure, and natural muscle density, will set the parameters for what we look like as children, as teens, and as we age.

Brain Function

There are many theories about how the brain works to control hunger and satiety, and even more theories about how it can fail to work and allow us to overeat, undereat, or fail to eat what our bodies really need. All these theories, however, agree on the basic fact that the brain acts as a "control tower" for managing food intake, receiving signals from the various body systems, such as the need for immediate energy. The hypothalamus is the section of the brain thought to be most responsible for the regulation of food intake. One section of the hypothalamus sends the "feed me" message to the higher centers of the brain, and another delivers the message, "Okay, I'm full." The brain conveys its directions to eat or not to eat by sending out chemical messengers in the form of neuropeptides and hormones. One biochemical, cholecystokinin (CCK), seems to be a particularly important messenger that tells the hypothalamus to "Shut down the food supply. I'm full now." According to recent theories, some of us have bodies that fail to produce sufficient CCK to control our appetite, and a lack of this neuropeptide may be a factor in why obese children never seem to get enough to eat and why bulimic teenagers go on eating binges. Some researchers also believe that the bingeing and purging associated with many eating disorders are triggered by lowered levels of the neurotransmitters serotonin and norepinephrine. This discovery was made when physicians saw that antidepressant drugs like Prozac, which raise serotonin levels in the brain, also seemed to diminish the bingeing and purging symptoms of bulimics.

Cultural Pressures

It's a beautiful and thin world out there. Or so say the media.

Our children are constantly picking up the messages that thin is great, and fat is bad. How they will react to the images that bombard them depends on the particular relationship they have with food, their feelings about themselves, and their coping mechanisms. Overeating to comfort themselves, or starving to be the "ideal" weight are two ways children and teens express dissatisfaction with themselves, and they can be symptoms of a deep insecurity.

Americans are obsessed with the merits of low body weight and slimness. However, even with a healthy diet and a regular exercise program, most of us will never be able to achieve and maintain the idealized body images that we constantly see on TV and in the movies. Yet it seems to be hard for many American adults to accept this reality, and we are passing along this attitude of denial to our children. It is extraordinary and tragic that in a culture obsessed with an unrealistic image of beauty, our very genetic makeup has become a risk factor for most of us.

Family Food Attitude

Parents not only pass on their genetic code that predisposes a child to be fat or thin, they also pass on their attitudes about food. These attitudes can either teach healthy food habits or contribute to eating problems and disorders. Many psychologists feel that the best and the worst of a family's dynamics can be seen at the dinner table. Is food consistently used to appease and avoid a fight? Is it used to punish or reward? Are meals the occasion of predictable arguments? Do parents overeat when they are upset?

Children are affected by their parents' behaviors and their words as well. For example, teenage girls diagnosed with anorexia tend to have mothers who are overly concerned about their daughters' weight or fathers and brothers who are overly critical.

Family Conflict

Studies have shown that unresolved family conflicts are also major contributing factors to the development of eating disorders and obesity. Children faced with emotional difficulties may reach for food, even without such modeling by parents, to comfort themselves, satisfy frustrations, ease tension, and even to express anger. Children can begin to eat to symbolically fill up the emptiness they feel inside. The more extreme the tension in the house, the less control a child or teen might feel, and the more eating becomes the only arena where she feels completely in charge of her life. Also, families in conflict will tend to pay less attention to the importance of nutrition and good eating habits.

Temperament

Research indicates that certain eating disorders are associated with specific personality traits. Teenagers with eating disorders tend to be perfectionistic and obedient, and keep their feelings to themselves. Anorexics are commonly sensitive to the wishes of others as a primary means of coping with interpersonal conflicts. Controlling their weight simultaneously gives them a sense of controlling their bodies and gaining approval from others. Binge eaters, on the other hand, tend to have more impulsive temperaments that lead to risk-taking. This is why they are more likely to abuse alcohol and drugs. Obese children tend to be introverted and shy. They rarely see food as part of a social experience, but rather as a substitute for social pleasures.

Age

Finally, time itself must be considered a risk factor for eating problems. A delay in addressing the issue of nutrition in your children will have both physical and psychological consequences. While the window of opportunity for adopting a healthy diet and lifestyle never really closes, the earlier a healthy lifestyle begins, the greater the chances that it will be continued. The most serious risk factors for eating problems increase with age. For example, an obese infant has about a one-in-ten chance of becoming an obese adult, while an obese preschooler has a one-in-four chance. The likelihood of an obese seven-year-old becoming an obese adult is 40 percent.

According to the National Research Council, more than 80 percent of obese adolescents will remain obese throughout their lives.

The earlier you help your child establish a healthy attitude toward food, the less likely it is that eating habits will become a symptom of emotional problems. When parents accept their role in shaping their children's habits of eating and exercise, they are preparing them for a lifetime of mental and physical well-being.

INFANTS

KEY TO PREVENTION: LOVING, CONNECTED FEEDING

Certainly the most critical task of parenting a very young baby is to provide the infant with good nourishment, but feeding also provides many emotionally charged choices for parents that can affect their bond with their infant.

The first important choices parents will make is whether to feed a newborn by the breast or the bottle. There are many benefits to breast-feeding (a hundred of which are listed on the Web site www.promom.org), but the most important involve bolstering the baby's immune system with the mother's antibodies and providing some degree of antiallergy protection. Still, countless millions of happy, healthy infants started out life entirely on the bottle, and if breast-feeding is something you simply cannot do for any length of time, feeling guilty will not make things better. As we shall see, parents have many other opportunities to ensure that their children get the lifelong advantages of good nutrition.

The second choice that parents face will be when to introduce solid foods to a baby, and this, too, can have emotional repercussions. In general, pediatricians advise parents to wait until at least five or six months old to make sure that the infant's digestive system is mature. They advise introducing foods slowly, one at a time, waiting until the age when they are unlikely to cause allergic reactions. But even cautious parents may encounter food allergies in their infants. About 8 percent of children will experience food allergies in the first three years of life, which will cause extreme initial distress and sometimes make parents overconcerned about their child's eating. However, almost all of these children will outgrow their allergic reactions, with only about 1 percent remaining allergic throughout their childhood. The one noteworthy exception is children who are allergic to peanuts, certain shellfish, and some seeds. These substances can cause systemic anaphylaxis, an extreme allergic reaction in which the throat closes up, blood pressure drops, and the child may quickly lose consciousness. These allergies present a lifelong risk to children, and they must be taught as early as possible to be vigilant about knowing what is in their food.

By the time that a child is twelve to fourteen months old, parents will have introduced many different foods, and many will have been rejected. This is a period during which many parents begin to struggle with their children over what they are eating and the way they are eating it. Many babies dislike sitting in a high chair for more than five or ten minutes, and they'd just as soon throw their food off their plate as eat it. Couples who were used to eating leisurely evening meals before the arrival of their first child are often very surprised at this change in their lifestyle. Patience is the only remedy to this problem.

The important thing to remember with each of these milestones is that feeding is a developmentally timed behavior for infants, not so different from learning to walk or talk. Feeding is natural for most children, but difficult for some. Each change comes slowly at first, and then all at once the child has success. Parents should avoid struggling with their children about food, taking heart that they all will eventually learn to eat well and healthy. Instead, see feeding times as opportunities to be emotionally supportive to your growing child, guiding her to enjoying this simplest and most important of life's pleasures.

TODDLERS AND PRESCHOOLERS

KEY TO PREVENTION: KEEPING FOOD FROM BECOMING AN EMOTIONAL STRUGGLE

Between the ages of two and five the key to establishing healthy eating habits is developing an "authoritative" relationship with your child regarding food. This means taking a firm approach to nutrition and not allowing food to be used consistently as a reward or as a crutch for a difficult moment or emotion.

The most common complaint of parents of young children is that they are "picky" or "finicky" eaters. One child will eat only peanut butter for breakfast, lunch, and dinner. Another child will eat only crackers dipped in strawberry yogurt. Many parents worry about their children's lack of appetite and interest in food, causing daily struggles and unnecessary emotional strife.

Dr. William Wilkoff notes in his book *Coping with the Picky Eater* that most eating problems in young children arise from misinformation or unrealistic expectations. He lists some of the most common concerns of parents and explains why parents do not need to worry. Here are a few:

"My toddler doesn't eat well and he doesn't seem to be growing."

> Children's growth slows down after one year. In the first year a baby's weight triples, and parents may get used to this rapid growth. By the time a child is two, she is growing at only one-tenth the rate as in her first year. Your pediatrician will alert you to any serious growth problems.

"My child does not like to eat."

> The preschool child needs only half the calories per pound of body weight that she did as an infant. This is why the two- to five-year-old may appear to be eating less as she grows older.

"My child has strange eating habits."

> Almost all children are finicky eaters. Toddlers may like one type of food for weeks or months and then inexplicably stop liking it. This can be unsettling to parents, but it is perfectly normal.

"My toddler only likes to eat sweets."

> Babies are born with a preference for sweet things and a dislike of things that are sour. Their preferences will gradually change, but this may take a long time in some children.

"My child won't try anything new."

> Children are naturally wary of new foods. This may be nature's way of protecting humans from eating things they shouldn't.

"My child hardly eats any dinner."

> Young children usually eat only one and a half to two full meals a day, and their appetite decreases as the day wears on. Working parents who look forward to enjoying an evening meal with their toddlers are likely to be disappointed. It is common for children to eat a good breakfast, be less interested in lunch, and have only a little appetite for dinner.

While most pediatricians and counselors advise parents not to worry too much about young children who are fussy eaters, this does not usually mean that your child's eating preferences should be given full reign. Some experts, however, seem to argue this point. Jane Hirschmann and Lela Zaphiropoulos, in their book *Preventing Childhood Eating Problems*, urge parents to "remember that children have a remarkable inborn mechanism that lets them know how much food and which types of food they need for normal growth and development. The aim is not to make the child eat, but to let her natural appetite come to the surface so that she wants to eat." They suggest that parents prepare a variety of foods and let children choose what they want, even if they don't seem to be eating a balanced diet. The authors cite Dr. Benjamin Spock, who believed that given the chance to choose their own foods, within a two-week period young children will naturally choose the foods their bodies need.

This "listen to your body" approach sounds fine on the surface; however, it does not fit with the way we know the brain works. As noted, some children are undoubtedly born with brain chemistry that does not tell them what they need or don't need. In addition, today's children are not raised in a "natural" environment, such as on an isolated farm. Rather, they experience a daily onslaught of clever messages from the media to eat foods high in calories, fat, and sodium. Finally, the naïve advice to let children tell you what they want, rather than the other way around, ignores the fact that today's children have a much more sedentary lifestyle than even children of a few decades ago, and there is no question that this affects appetite and metabolism, creating a very unnatural habit of eating and calorie usage. A permissive, child-centered, approach to eating isn't likely to develop good eating habits in children or ward off later problems and conflicts around food. The following suggestions will help you gradually develop good eating habits in your children, while avoiding the high drama around meals that can lead to later problems.

AN OUNCE OF PREVENTION

Monitor Snacks Carefully

If you want mealtimes to go well, you need a hungry child. Limit drinks and snacks between mealtimes. Water is okay anytime, but let your child have juice or milk only at midmorning or midafternoon snack. When your child is hungry, he is less likely to balk at the food that is set before him. Limiting eating to specific times of the day will also teach your child that it is okay to be hungry. The stomach is not supposed to be filled all the time, a fact that many overweight children (and adults) seem to disregard.

Guide Your Child to Healthy Eating

Eating should never be a battleground, but that does not mean you should lower your expectations for having your children eat nutritious meals. Authoritative parents know what their children should be eating, consider what the children like, and find a way to make the two meet:

- If your child won't eat all green vegetables, establish which ones he can tolerate and serve him those (even if it's only two or three) on a regular basis. He will understand that his preferences are being attended to.

- Small portions can be fine as long as they are "eaten up." Or serve your child a full portion and require that she eat half. This will give her the message that you are willing to compromise.

- Always inform your child about why you want him to eat well. Don't be afraid to repeat the same message again and again. Explain that "healthy nutrition helps you grow and gives you the energy to be active and feel good." Your child may get tired of hearing this, but the message will be remembered.

Establishing your authority at mealtimes while you respect your children's preferences could become a blueprint for resolving other areas of potential conflict. So in addition to promoting healthy attitudes toward food and their own bodies you are reinforcing an effective approach for managing disagreements.

Invite Your Child to Help Prepare a Meal

Most children love to help cook, and having them do so gives you an important opportunity to teach about nutrition in a creative and fun manner. It also helps teach about responsibility, making children feel that they're contributing to the well-being of the family. Many parents invite their young children into the kitchen only when it's time to make cookies or other sweets, but there's no reason you can't involve them in creating nutritious snacks or even whole meals.

Leave Problems in the Living Room

Don't bring problems to the dinner table. Family meals should be a time to enjoy each other and the pleasures of eating. If arguments constantly erupt, or if you use mealtimes to remind a child of some problem that she has caused, your child will naturally begin to associate eating with anxiety and discomfort.

Don't Use Food to Reward or Punish

There are many kinds of rewards and punishments that can be used in teaching children appropriate behavior, but using food as a behavioral-management tool is a sure way to pile one conflict on top of another. Make a list of appropriate rewards for good behavior, which could include renting a video, engaging in some special activity, or having extra time on the computer. If your child asks for a special dessert or other sweet treat, explain that you have rules for when it is okay to eat sugary things and those are different from the rules for good behavior. In the same vein, when a child needs to be disciplined, use a technique that is appropriate to the problem, preferably one that will help your child learn from the misbehavior (see Chapter 2). When parents use food to try to control their young children, they give them a very inappropriate message, which may backfire when their children grow older.

REQUIRE GOOD TABLE MANNERS

Meals should be pleasant social experiences, so children need to learn acceptable social rules and behaviors. You can explain to your children that every time people are together, there are rules. There are rules when you play a game. There are rules when you ride in a car. And there are rules, called manners, when people eat together. It often helps to write down a list of these rules for young children to remember. This will save you from mealtime arguments over what is and is not appropriate behavior, because you can just refer to the specific, agreed-upon rules.

Limit meals to twenty minutes for young children. If your child is done by this time, she should be allowed to leave the table and play quietly, but not to return.

Encourage Regular Physical Exercise

Toddlers and preschoolers have plenty of energy, and typically they wear us out expending it. But this age is not too early to get children into a regular exercise program, particularly one in which they can develop an interest in basic sports skills. Besides giving your children many chances during the day for active play, make sure that you also take time to teach them to throw and catch, to kick a ball, to run an obstacle course, or to swim. Cultivating an interest in specific sports is the most direct way to get children to develop a lifelong habit of vigorous exercise, and it all begins with the basic skills.

SCHOOL-AGE CHILDREN

KEY TO PREVENTION: RECOGNIZING THE EARLY SIGNS OF EATING PROBLEMS AND ADDRESSING THEIR CAUSES

School-age children need to develop a realistic understanding of how food, eating habits, and exercise affect their bodies and their self-image. From a developmental perspective, this is the best time to prevent the irrational thinking and denial that underlie all eating disorders.

Megan's mother did not think too much about it when her ten-year-old announced that she was going to go on a diet with her. Like many women in their forties, Mrs. Herman had gone on one diet after another, trying to fight nature's insistence on thickening her waist and expanding her hips. Megan had always been a robust girl—one might even say a little round—so her mother thought that some dieting might not be so bad. Maybe it would give her daughter more of the angular, "coltish" look that most of her friends had. Mrs. Herman was also afraid that Megan had more of her father's body-type genes than hers, and her father seemed to be getting fatter by the day. He was now at least forty to fifty pounds too heavy.

Mrs. Herman and Megan went on an all-protein diet. Chicken, eggs, meat, and cheese were all allowable, plus one portion of a green vegetable each day. No carbohydrates or sugar were permitted. Mrs. Herman considered this to be a lot healthier than Megan's present diet, which consisted of lots of pizza, macaroni and cheese, canned spaghetti, and large quantities of cookies and other snack foods. Mrs. Herman lasted about six days on her diet, which was average for her. A dinner party given by her husband's law firm was her undoing. Two glasses of wine before dinner had loosened all her resolve. But Megan stayed on her diet and lost three pounds the first week. Too much, her mother thought, for a ten-year-old body. But Megan persisted. Another two pounds the second week, and three pounds the third. By now Megan and her mother were having daily battles over her food.

Eating disorders are an insidious problem that frequently begin during the elementary-school years. Studies indicate that children are dieting at an ever younger age, and since the number of children dieting is directly proportional to the number of children with eating disorders, this is certainly an alarming trend. Not all eating problems in children are considered to be eating disorders, and it is important to note that although the symptoms of problems and disorders may be the same, the causes and recommended treatments can be quite different. I have set forth below the major eating problems that occur in childhood.

RISK FACTORS

Food Refusal

Some school-age children who do not have a history of being picky eaters refuse to eat certain foods or to eat certain foods at certain times. Unlike a true eating disorder, this food refusal doesn't relate to a concern about weight or body shape; rather it is typically a part of a behavioral problem that reflects conflicts within the family. Children who are angry at authoritarian parents and want a place to express themselves may choose the dinner table to take control or make a statement. They may also refuse food because emotional tension at the table decreases their appetite.

Appetite Loss as a Symptom of Depression or Trauma

It wasn't so long ago that psychologists believed that depression was exclusively a disorder of teenagers and adults, and could not really be diagnosed before the age of twelve. Now we know that this is not true. According to epidemiological researchers, depression is more and more common in children. Depression can occur as a reaction to a specific event, such as a death or a divorce, or it may seem to appear out of nowhere, presumably caused by a biochemical imbalance. Whatever the cause, a sudden change in appetite and eating habits is a common symptom. Other symptoms of depression are sleeplessness, moodiness, faltering friendships, lack of interests, and self-enforced isolation.

Anorexia in Prepuberty

About 10 percent of the people who are diagnosed with anorexia are children under the age of twelve. The consequences of anorexia are severe and often irreversible. Anorexia is diagnosed when a child's behavior can be characterized by two or more of the following symptoms:

determined food avoidance

preoccupation with body weight

preoccupation with energy intake

distorted body image

fear of fatness

self-induced vomiting

extensive exercising

laxative purging

Anorexia is considered an intransigent psychological disorder and often requires a period of hospitalization. Letting anorexia go untreated can result in a predisposition to cardiac disease and diabetes, a failure to establish normal weight, and height and cortical atrophy when weight loss is extreme. Some cases may even result in death.

Bulimia

Bulimia is characterized by recurrent episodes of binge eating, during which time the child cannot stop eating even when she is full. Eating-disorder specialists believe that bulimia is an expression of a need to self-comfort and fill an emotional void, but it may also reflect a biochemical imbalance. To compensate for the overeating, the child often prevents weight gain by self-induced vomiting; misuse of laxatives, diuretics, enemas, or other medications; fasting; or excessive exercise. Effects can include metabolic disorders, dental erosion—particularly of the front teeth, with corresponding decay—fatigue, weakness, and even seizures. Full-blown bulimia does not usually occur until adolescence, probably because the eating habits of younger children are more supervised. "Experimenting" with aspects of bulimia, such as self-induced vomiting, has been known to occur in younger children, particularly girls who mature early or who have older siblings.

Obesity in Children

Being overweight is not considered a psychological disorder, yet the disease of obesity affects millions of children, and the numbers are growing. According to Gayle Povis Alleman in her book *Save Your Child from the Fat Epidemic,* there has never been such a high percentage of children and teens who are overweight. It is double the number of twenty years ago. Statistics tell us that there is a window of opportunity between ten and twelve, when obesity can be restrained from becoming a lifelong problem.

This is an age during which maintaining an appropriate body weight can be quite difficult. Part of this may be due to a sharp drop in the physical activity of children as they age. In elementary school the majority of children are naturally active and participate in at least one organized sport on a regular basis. But by the time that they are teens, nearly 80 percent of children who once participated in organized sports no longer do so. Prior to puberty there is a 30- to 50-percent chance of an obese child becoming an obese adult. By midadolescence the probability becomes 70 to 80 percent.

This is also an age when children are cognitively ready to understand the importance of eating the right foods and getting regular exercise for their health, yet parents still have considerable control over what they eat and when. By age thirteen or fourteen, this will surely change, as a teenager's natural drive toward independence will significantly lessen a parent's influence.

AN OUNCE OF PREVENTION

When school-age children begin to show symptoms of eating disorders, it is always a good idea to consult an experienced mental-health professional. However, most problems in childhood are "subclinical," meaning that they can be picked up by an objective observer but are not yet serious enough to interfere with other areas of functioning. The challenge for parents, of course, is to be sensitive to minor problems and intervene before they take hold.

The following recommendations will help establish a healthy attitude toward food and create an atmosphere in which emotional problems to do with eating, weight, and appearance are directly confronted and appropriately treated.

Provide Nutrition Education

Most parents are content to leave the task of talking about nutrition to the school nurse or the health educator, but this is clearly insufficient. I'm not diminishing the role of today's health educator, who brings children important new information about weight control, fad diets, and the evils of junk food, as well as the traditional information about nutrition and the food pyramid. But information alone is rarely enough to prevent emotional problems. Only parents can take this information and make it part of a child's day-to-day experience.

Recently I took an informal survey of twenty-five parents of school-age children, asking them to list the five most important things that they do regularly to influence the development of their children. Only two parents listed preparing food as part of their foremost responsibilities and none of the parents listed teaching their children about nutrition as part of their role. Most parents feel that their children will not listen to their "lectures" about food, but this is not the case. Children are very influenced by what their parents say and do, as long as parents act in ways that are realistic and respectful of their children's views and concerns. Remember that listening is as important to communication as talking.

Help Children Accept Their Appearance

Parents should take the time to combat the ever-present influence of the media on how children feel about their appearance. You might want to read aloud articles in which models admit to their figure flaws or talk about their awkwardness when they were young. You can explain the tricks photographers do with lighting, shadow, and angle to produce a certain image. Also try to help your children understand that advertisers are trying to "sell" them beauty.

It's important to share your own perspective on what makes someone attractive, as well as your own experiences. Don't be afraid to express your self-doubts and conflicts. Children will always respond to open and frank discussions, even when there are no easy answers.

Correct Irrational Self-Criticism

While we all have self-doubts and times when we are less confident, this is very different from being persistently self-critical. Psychologists have found that most people with emotional problems, including most children, have specific kinds of distorted thinking. One common type of irrational thinking is called absolute thinking. A child might say, "I will never be popular because I am fat," or "Everyone is a better athlete than I am, so why even bother trying out for a team." Words like "always," "never," and "everyone" should clue you to the fact that your child is not thinking realistically. You should take immediate steps to correct this dysfunctional thought pattern.

When you hear your child making this type of comment about herself, write it down and ask her to give you just one reason the statement is *not* true. One reason will lead to another, and that reason will lead to yet another. This is the way that parents can help their children become less self-critical. Simply arguing with them does not help.

Be a Good Role Model

It is obvious that parents should model a healthy lifestyle to their children, but for most of us this is easier said than done. A large percentage of Americans don't eat nutritiously, don't get enough exercise, and constantly express dissatisfaction about the way they look. Begin by being aware of what you say around your children. Don't be self-critical or overly critical of the appearance of others. If you do not currently have a healthy lifestyle, begin to change in small steps. Make good health a family project, and you'll be preventing future problems for all of you.

Encourage Sports and Exercise

The simplest way to encourage a lifelong habit of physical exercise is to develop a love for a particular sport in childhood. Unfortunately, even though many children participate in organized sports like soccer or Little League, the way we approach children's sports in America may do more harm than good. For example, a poll done by USA Today found:

- 41 percent of children said that they have awakened in the night worrying about an upcoming game.

- 51 percent observed that they frequently see other children acting like "poor sports."

- 71 percent said they wouldn't care if no score were kept in the games.

- 90 percent said they would rather play on a losing team if they could really play rather than sit on the bench.

According to Rick Wolff, author of Sports Parenting, parents must guide their children through the developmental stages of enjoying athletics, just as they guide them through other areas of development. He notes that since preschoolers are naturally active and energetic, and since there is a sudden drop in organized athletics in the early teens, the ages from five to twelve seem to be the window of opportunity for developing a lifelong passion for sports. Mr. Wolff suggests that parents expose children to many sports during this period, emphasizing fun and skill acquisition rather than winning. He notes, "Keep in mind that it's your kid's sense of self-esteem, not some objective standard of play, that determines whether he wants to go on playing. If he feels that he's a good player—not necessarily a great player, or a star or the best on the team—and he enjoys the competition, why should he ever give up playing?"

Recognize the Early Warning Signs of Eating Disorders

As mentioned, about 10 percent of severe eating disorders are diagnosed in childhood, but undoubtedly many other serious problems go undetected. If your child exhibits any of the signs listed below, you should immediately seek advice from a qualified psychologist or pediatrician:

- unexplained change in weight, food consumption, or amount of exercise (unrelated to a sport)

- preoccupation with uncompromising desire to control food, weight, or exercise

- harsh and demeaning attitude toward herself and particularly her body shape and weight

- feelings of shame and guilt about her eating behavior and her body

- strong beliefs that his experiences in life are dramatically affected by his body weight

- irrational fear of getting fat combined with a desire for rigid control of exercise or food intake to prevent gaining weight

- signs of any type of purging, including vomiting and the use of diuretics and laxatives

- more than 20 percent above his recommended body weight, and does not respond to age-appropriate diet restrictions

Computers Can (and Cannot) Help

There are a number of nutrition education sites on the Internet for you to "bookmark," as well as numerous sites to give you information on eating problems in children and many support groups. Search on the phrase "children's nutrition" in your favorite Internet search engine.

When it comes to exercise and physical activity, however, computers can't help, and in fact may impede your child's development. Of course computer activities that involve learning should be distinguished from activities that are purely for entertainment. Studies are beginning to show that children are watching less television and spending more time in front of the computer. Although this is in one way a step in the right direction, it is obviously still a sedentary activity. Make sure that your children get at least an hour of moderate to vigorous physical activity every day, and put realistic limits on TV watching and computer time.

TEENAGERS

KEY TO PREVENTION: ONGOING PARENTAL INVOLVEMENT AND EMOTIONAL SUPPORT

Eating disorders like anorexia and bulimia can have very serious physical as well as psychological consequences, but many other less dramatic eating problems may affect your teenager for years to come. Some teens end up spending their lives trying one ineffective diet after another, never happy about the way they look. Others don't pay any attention to their diets or the need for exercise, not realizing that they are acquiring habits that will have long-term health consequences. Your role in prevention can range from calling immediate attention to serious problems and getting professional help to guiding your teen toward developing a positive self-image reflected in a positive lifestyle.

One of the serious problems for today's teens is the cultural myth that they can achieve an "ideal" body. With the right video or gym equipment or diet, they can get "buns of steel" or "abs of iron" and look just like a model or a movie star. We can blame the marketers of diet foods and exercise equipment, or the entertainment industry, or ourselves, but the fact remains that teenagers are the single group most susceptible to the myth that we all can be thin and beautiful, and they are the least prepared to cope with the hard truth that this just isn't so.

Compounding this problem, attracting the opposite sex is one of the strongest determinants for a teen to feel socially accepted and valuable. For many teens there is no greater priority.

> Darlene was considered one of the brightest students in her suburban high school of over three thousand students. Although her father had died when she was just eight years old and she had an older sister with Down's syndrome, she was considered a well-adjusted, vivacious young woman by her teachers. She was not thought of as a "beauty," but she had a pleasant face and was average weight for her height and frame.
>
> In her junior year in high school, she met Ted, who was handsome, popular, athletic, and also very bright. Ted was a freshman at a local college. They began to see each other every weekend and talk on the phone daily.
>
> Darlene confided to her friends that she did not feel that she was "good enough" for Ted. She was sure that he would find someone who was prettier and skinnier. So she began a strict regimen to get "the body that men die for." She went on a nine-hundred-calorie diet, ran three to five miles each morning, and lifted weights for an hour in the evening. She lost fifteen pounds in three weeks and was exhausted and irritable. She and Ted began to have their first fights.

*Within another week they broke up, and although Darlene felt dev-
astated by the loss, she vowed to keep working on her body until
Ted drooled with envy when he saw her with her next boyfriend.*

Eating disorders can become a very serious problem for tens of
thousands of teenage girls, and it is widely recognized that they are
related to a marked decrease in self-esteem in midadolescence.
Almost half of all teenagers know someone with an eating disorder.

Although it is not nearly as common in boys, they do still com-
pose an estimated 10 percent of the teens diagnosed with an eating
disorder, and some experts feel that this number is an underestimate. Eating disorders in boys are most common for those participating in highly competitive sports. One study found that over 40
percent of boys enrolled in high-school wrestling regularly used
vomiting or laxatives to reduce their body weight. Young men, like
young women, want to look good and be attractive, and an increasing number find compulsive exercise along with bingeing and purging a part of their daily routine.

While both anorexic and bulimic teens tend to be depressed
and have a family history of depression, bulimic adolescents are typically more socially and sexually active. Bulimia patients are also
more outgoing, angry, and impulsive. Shoplifting, suicide attempts,
histories of sexual abuse, and involvement in self-destructive sexual
relationships are associated with bulimia. Paradoxically, bulimia
patients tend to be high achievers.

Although it is not classified as a psychological disorder, overweight teens can also have serious emotional problems in addition to
the obvious physical ones. Being overweight is the one psychological problem that people seem to have no sympathy for. Overweight
teens may be openly ridiculed, with little or no social repercussions
for their tormentors. Understandably, many overweight teenagers
avoid any social interaction, adding social isolation and depression
to their growing list of emotional problems. As with other eating
problems, parents are the most logical people to make a difference in
helping an overweight teen. If parents don't try to address this problem, who will?

AN OUNCE OF PREVENTION

Many parents feel as if they are being forced out of the picture when their teenagers begin to experience emotional problems, and this is particularly true with a teenager who has an eating problem or disorder.

Of course parents can't make their teens eat or not eat. Nor can they make teenagers turn off the television and go jogging if they don't want to. But looking the other way is not the answer, no matter how tempting this might be. By definition, a teenager with an eating problem or disorder is not looking after her own best interests, so parents must become more involved than ever. The mental and physical toll of an eating disorder can be severe, and in some cases irreversible, so even though it may go against your own developmental instincts and fear of conflict, this is not the time to disengage from your child. The following are some suggestions that should help.

Give Your Teen Emotional Support, Even When She Doesn't Seem to Want It

Adolescent girls in general tend to get less emotional support from their families, who often feel out of sync with the "young woman" in their midst. Fathers may have difficulty in dealing with the underlying body and sexual issues. This withdrawal of family support comes at a time when girls are most self-critical and socially anxious, with a very high incidence of depression. While parents should be careful not to be invasive, it is an important time to stay available and offer acceptance. Riddled with fears about maturing too quickly, or too slowly, or not well enough, girls need to feel that there is a place where they are appreciated just for being themselves.

Even if your teenagers don't want to talk to you, there are many ways to show your support and concern. What they really need is your time and your commitment to their health and happiness.

Keep Life as Predictable as Possible

Your teen may act unpredictably, but she certainly doesn't want you to do the same. If your teenager has either mild or serious problems related to eating and weight, the most important thing you can do is to provide a supportive and predictable family environment. Studies consistently show that teenagers do best in families where members eat dinner together, where there are clear family rules that are consistently enforced, and where religious services or other family-oriented activities are practiced.

Continue to Advise Your Teen About Good Eating Habits

One of the biggest problems with severe dieting is that it works. A teenager who is intent on losing weight and who drastically cuts her caloric intake while increasing physical activity can lose two to five pounds a week. If she is at an average body weight to begin with, she will begin to look significantly different in just three or four weeks. You can't control what your teen does or does not eat, but you can serve nutritious meals, act as a good role model, and educate your teen about the hazards of fad diets.

Trust That Your Words Are of Keen Interest to Your Teen

A shrug of indifference. A sigh of impatience. An irritated grimace. All of these are classic teen behaviors in response to parental advice. Many parents don't find it particularly easy to have conversations with their teenagers, especially when they are abrupt, sarcastic, or just plain unpleasant. Yet surveys of teens make it clear that they do value their parents' interest and input.

When talking to your teenager about eating or weight concerns, you must begin by being open and honest about what you know and what you don't know. You certainly know about the importance of a healthy lifestyle and the consequences of abusing food. You don't know exactly how your teenager feels about herself, her eating problem, or her daily life, and you should not assume that you do. When you decide to have a conversation about eating, be clear about what you are going to say and the most important points that you want to get across. Do you think that your daughter should see a counselor because she is losing too much weight? Then state this clearly. Do you think that your son has put on extra pounds and spends too much time by himself? Then say this directly. Teenagers are naturally defensive when you start talking about their weight or appearance (just as most adults would be), so be brief. Respect your teens' views, and talk with them, not at them.

Unhappy teens will be more likely to answer questions or volunteer information if they trust that they will find an open mind when they start talking. Teens who think that their parents "live in a dream world" will stay silent or answer with words that they think a parent wants to hear.

Get Family Counseling

If you believe that your teenager has an eating disorder or if she is clinically obese (more than 20 percent above her recommended body weight), you should certainly consider going for family counseling. It is almost impossible for a counselor to deal with the psychological issues related to eating unless the teenager's family is involved.

Family counseling will look at the eating habits of the family, the foods available in the house, and the degree to which weight gain or loss is a symptom of family struggles. In milder cases only a few family meetings will be necessary, providing that each family member agrees that changes must be made by everyone, not just the diagnosed teen. Moderate and severe cases frequently require longer-term interventions, since, when unchecked, eating disorders can lead to irreversible physical problems and even death. Antidepressants such as Prozac have been shown to be helpful in treating some adolescent eating disorders, but medication only deals with the immediate symptoms, not the underlying problems. In-depth family counseling for eating disorders can take many forms, but there is rarely a quick cure. Make sure that you have family and community support for yourself, as well as for your child.

Computers Can Help

As I have mentioned throughout this book, teenagers are prime candidates for the self-help opportunities on the Internet. There are dozens of sites with information and chat rooms for people with eating disorders. For example, Something-fishy.org has several chat rooms on mental-health issues, including one on eating disorders. Concernedcounseling.com provides around-the-clock support for people with eating disorders and their families, sponsored by a residential treatment center for eating disorders. Since Web sites change all the time, however, you may wish to do your own Internet search by entering key words like "eating disorders + chat" in one of the popular search engines, such as Yahoo, Lycos, or Excite. Chat rooms can offer valuable support for teens, but you should be aware of their inherent dangers, including bad advice.

• • •

Development of healthy eating habits begins in infancy, when parents are forming an intimate bond with their children. Feeding a newborn is one of the most enjoyable activities for parents, but by the time a child is a year and a half, mealtimes can be filled with struggle. As with any other aspect of a child's development, parents must guide their children toward healthy habits and appropriate behaviors.

As toddlers, children begin to develop very idiosyncratic ideas about food, driving many parents crazy. Some professionals advise giving in to their whims, assuming that they will eventually eat what their bodies need. But this permissive parenting style is not a habit that you want to get into. Parents must find ways to resolve food conflicts with their children, which will also set a pattern for other areas where negotiation and compromise are required.

The years from six to twelve are a time when parents need to take a very active part in guiding their children to a healthy lifestyle. They need to continue informing their children about good nutrition and making sure that they develop the habit of daily vigorous exercise. This is also a time when parents must be aware of early signs of eating disorders, particularly with high-risk children.

Teenagers will likely resist their parents' attempts to bring up issues of weight, appearance, eating, and exercise, but this is certainly not the time for parents to give up. Serious eating disorders can cause irreparable physical problems, but even mild eating problems can affect a child's self-esteem and social development. Staying involved as a guide for your teen is the key to preventing something as basic as eating from becoming a lifelong struggle.

4

Preventing Underachievement

According to standardized intelligence tests, children are getting smarter and smarter. Most children recognize school success as a highly valued achievement in today's world. Our culture celebrates high achievers, and we are one of the most productive nations in history. Yet many educators agree that underachievement is among the most serious problems facing our schools today, affecting nearly one out of four children.

As early as the second or third grade, your child may show signs of not performing up to his or her potential. There is no clear personality profile or temperament that we can associate with this problem. Family conflicts and emotional problems might contribute to underachievement, but even here there are no definitive patterns.

Underachievement can take several different forms. Some children do poorly in all subject areas—a problem known as pervasive underachievement. They may have specific learning disabilities or emotional problems that interfere with their learning, or they may just dislike school. Some children simply see school as a low priority in their lives and are there only because they have no choice.

Another form of underachievement can occur when a child has

difficulty with one specific subject area. This type of child essentially succumbs to his frustrations in math, or language, or science, and does not feel the need to work harder in these areas. Educators refer to this as "topical underachievement."

Unfortunately, because underachievement can come in many shapes and sizes, the early signs of school difficulty may be overlooked or mislabeled. The child is thought to be bored instead of unmotivated, or perhaps a learning disability is diagnosed where none exists. Some educational researchers believe that so many children are uninterested in school because of what they term "insufficient rewards." This theory explains that human behavior is motivated by the desire for certain rewards, particularly social rewards like praise or recognition. High-achieving students are constantly rewarded for their efforts by teachers, parents, and peers, but moderate- or low-achieving students do not have these same reinforcements. If these students get social rewards from being the best video-game player, or having the largest baseball-card collection, then it is no wonder that they are unmotivated to do schoolwork.

There are many other theories about why so many children don't perform up to their potential; in fact, there are probably as many theories as there are children who underachieve. On the other hand, there is much more agreement on how to prevent or reverse underachievement, and as we shall see, this can be done at any stage of a child's development. But first let's look at the risk factor for underachievement.

RISK FACTORS FOR UNDERACHIEVING IN SCHOOL

Socioeconomic Level

It's hard to argue that the most common and serious risk factor for underachievement has to do with the socioeconomic level of the family. Children who are born into poverty (22 percent of American children live at or below the poverty line, according to 1997 statistics) will likely be deprived of the best nutrition, high-quality health care, educational toys and books, and parents who have the time to spend on early stimulation. Research strongly suggests that a deprived early environment will impede both the emotional and cognitive development of children, but even with appropriate early stimulation, children who are born into families with low incomes will likely suffer from fewer parental expectations, lower-quality schools, and a greater exposure to family and community risk factors. Many child advocates are particularly concerned that these children will fall even further behind in the upcoming decade, since they won't have the same access to computers and the Internet as will children from higher-income families. Although most schools and libraries have computer centers with a collection of software programs and Internet access, it's not the same as having immediate access to a computer in the home.

A Disruptive Family Event

A specific disruptive event in a child's life—such as a move to a new school, a divorce, or a serious illness in the family—can trigger an episode of underachievement. Children who are categorized as "situational underachievers" previously performed well in school and enjoyed learning, and their sudden poor grades and lack of interest in work are out of character. Situational underachievement occurs as a symptom of an underlying problem, and when that problem is addressed through some form of intervention, the child will typically bounce back, after a period of three to six months. When the underlying problem is not addressed, however, these students may not easily find renewed success in school. In extreme cases the underlying causes can lead to a form of learned helplessness, in which children feel that they have no control over their lives and that it is not in their power to master the tasks before them. Underachievement then becomes a chronic problem.

Overindulgence and Permissive Parenting

In earlier times, before television and video games and the dozens of household appliances we take for granted, children were expected to work hard around the house and contribute to the well-being of the family. Today most children are required to do only perfunctory chores, and even these are met with complaints. Parenting articles on getting children to do chores advise us to "make chores fun." But that does not teach today's children what their grandparents knew when they were little: sometimes it is necessary to do difficult work without any short-term rewards.

A permissive parenting style is characterized by having low expectations and bestowing an excess of material possessions. When children have difficulty in a particular subject, permissive parents find many reasons that the problem is not their child's fault. They may reason that the textbook is too hard. They may blame the teacher for being overly critical. They may think that the child has an inherited problem with this particular subject.

One unfortunate trend in some school districts has been to overdiagnose learning disabilities or other handicapping conditions, giving children who are topical underachievers an excuse for their problems in some subjects, rather than just demanding more from them.

A child whose parents only look to find blame for poor performance will never learn to look to her own actions to find answers. The message is that her problems are beyond her control.

Temperament

An impulsive temperament is a significant risk factor for many children. Some of these children are labeled as having behavioral problems and others are diagnosed as ADHD, but nearly all impulsive children tend to be delayed in their language development as well as in their problem-solving skills. Because of their slower development, they often start school below their real potential and, all things being equal, continue to perform that way throughout their school career.

Children with an impulsive temperament have trouble thinking before they act. On the other hand, children who are born with a reflective temperament typically have a variety of coping strategies to resist temptation, including the ability to persist with a task, literally talk themselves through the necessary steps, foresee the future consequences of their actions, and comprehend that there are multiple solutions to a given problem. As we shall see, although some children do not seem to innately possess these cognitive skills, they can be taught to control their impulsivity so that the path to learning is easier.

Gender

As discussed in Chapter 1, a child's gender must also be considered a risk factor for certain kinds of underachievement. Boys are more at risk for problems in early reading, and girls are more likely to have problems in math, especially when they enter middle school. According to psychologist Sylvia Rimm in her study of a thousand successful women, as reported in her book *See Jane Win,* many of the most motivated and ambitious women that she interviewed were turned off to math in their middle-school years. She advises parents, "Whether you liked or feared math, encourage your daughters to enjoy the subject. Your daughters will have more choices if they conquer math. . . . If you have a choice, find a school that encourages girls to take math and science."

Sibling Dynamics

Some experts believe that certain sibling combinations may also be a risk factor for underachievement. Children who are fewer than two years apart may be very competitive with each other, particularly if they are the same gender. If one sibling has more natural aptitude than another, the second sibling may feel that it is useless to try to compete. He may use his seeming indifference to school to get attention from his parents. The so-called class clown is often the younger sibling of such a family constellation, getting attention by testing authority rather than risking failure in the eyes of his parents and the world.

Siblings of gifted children can also be at risk for underachievement. Their needs may be overlooked in the adulation of the more talented child. Some parents recognize this problem and mistakenly overcompensate for it—the less gifted child may find himself the recipient of false compliments, leaving him to believe neither in himself nor in his parents. The siblings of gifted children often harbor great strengths of their own, but fail to find them or trust in them, given the excitement generated by the gifted child.

Children with a sibling who has a handicap may also be at risk for low achievement. Sometimes these children use poor school performance as a means to compete with the sibling for their parents' attention, and in some cases there is a guilt factor, with the nonhandicapped sibling feeling somehow responsible for her sibling's problems. The guilt this child might feel both for her potential success at school and for being the one who is not handicapped can lead to various emotional problems, with underachievement a common symptom.

In most of these cases the underachieving students will usually respond to increased, straightforward encouragement and acknowledgment by their parents of the special situation they are in.

A Sense of Entitlement in Gifted Children

Finally there is the paradox of the gifted child, who is born with innate intelligence or special talents but who all too frequently does not fulfill his or her potential. A considerable amount of the psychological research on underachievement has focused on these children. Many psychologists have concluded that underachievement in gifted children frequently stems from too much attention paid by one or both parents, leading to a sense of entitlement. When these children inevitably encounter teachers or instructors who do not give them the same level of attention or the special considerations they feel they deserve, they may become uninterested in school as an act of defiance.

Virtually all of the problems mentioned in this book—divorce, trauma, behavioral problems, and shyness—can be a factor in underachievement. However, preventive measures can be taken at every age to keep underachievement from being an additional obstacle to a child's healthy development.

INFANTS

KEY TO PREVENTION: HELP INFANTS ACHIEVE A SENSE OF MASTERY

On April 17, 1997, the White House sponsored a three-day conference on early childhood development entitled "What New Research on the Brain Tells Us About Our Youngest Children." In her opening speech, Hillary Rodham Clinton emphasized the advances in neuroscience that have given us a new understanding of the developing brain of a child and of the important role that parents play. She explained that neuroscience has now confirmed what parents have long intuitively known, that "the song a father sings to his child in the morning or a story that a mother reads to her child before bed help lay the foundation for a child's life."

A side effect of this attention to new brain research has been an explosion of interest in how infant-stimulation techniques could enhance a child's development. In the last two years there have been at least half a dozen books and hundreds of articles in parenting magazines on what parents can do to raise smarter babies, presumably loading the dice for their child's future success. As a result, parents play Mozart to increase spatial and logical thinking, or lullabies sung in other languages to make their babies more receptive to later learning. They show them videotapes and flash cards with the hope of stimulating more neural connections to form in their infant brain. Yet there is no scientific evidence to support the claims that any special techniques or products can make a well-cared-for baby any smarter than nature intended.

However, the way that parents relate to their children *may* make a difference to their later learning. Developmental psychologists believe that helping children acquire a sense of mastery, the mental connection between action and outcome, will help them develop early traits of inquisitiveness, persistence, and optimism, which are the hallmarks of successful achievers.

Researchers have found that infants as early as two months of age begin to exhibit purposeful action. In an experiment by John Watson of the University of California at Berkeley, three groups of eight-week-old infants were given a special pillow for ten minutes a day. In the mastery group, every time the baby pressed his head against the pillow, a mobile spun around. In the control group, the mobile spun around just as much, but it was not connected to anything that the babies did. In a second control group, babies had a mobile that did not spin at all. As you might expect, the children in the mastery group significantly increased their activity, learning to press their heads against the pillow to make the mobile respond. But what makes this experiment more than just conditioned learning is that the two-month-old babies enjoyed this activity, smiling and cooing when they made the mobile spin around, while the other two groups showed little or no enjoyment of the mobile.

AN OUNCE OF PREVENTION

All infants have an innate drive to explore and interact with their environment. Parents simply need to follow their instincts in playing with and enjoying their babies. Still, a few basic suggestions will help you stimulate an infant's natural desire to learn.

Make Mastery a Part of Everyday Life

Each day presents hundreds of opportunities for your baby to learn about her world and how she can affect it. Just because your infant can't yet slip on a shirt, pick up a fork, or tie her own shoes, that doesn't mean she can't enjoy her own level of mastery. Each time she cries and you come to sort out what's "wrong," she will feel more in control of the world. When you notice that she likes a particular toy and you get down on the floor with her to play with it and talk about it, she will know that you're responding to her joy of discovery. As your baby grows, you will soon find that she'll want to do things on her own, even though many activities will be beyond her abilities. Still, you can find many things that she will be able to do. Let her toss a toy or two into the toy basket. Let her help you undress her when it is time for a bath. When your baby accomplishes these tasks, clap your hands and let her know of your approval with a loud "Good girl!" You have just taught her the joy of achievement.

Give Your Baby Choices

Maximize the amount of choices that you give your child as soon as he can distinguish between yes and no (nine to ten months). For example, at snack time take out two kinds of crackers and ask your baby which one he prefers by holding each up in turn and asking, "Do you want this cracker or this one?" while you nod your head yes. If your baby nods his head yes or points in response, then he gets the cracker. Of course, babies can become very willful if they think that they have unlimited influence on their environment. This is certainly not a trait you want to reinforce. In the above example, two crackers are sufficient for a choice. Do not become like a parent I once counseled who kept over a dozen types of crackers and cereals in the cabinet to make sure that her ten-month-old's slightest whim was satisfied.

Create an Environment That Says, "Yes! Explore!"

Give your baby plenty of time and space to explore. If you can, create a space in a section of a room where she can check things out without having you hover over her. Active babies and toddlers do not like to be confined to a playpen, yet some limits are necessary for your sanity and her safety. If you need some ideas for creating an environment with the right balance of limits and freedom to explore, consider visiting a good day-care center for ideas. They often have special arrangements of furniture to encourage independence and exploration while ensuring the highest level of safety.

Play Games with Your Baby

Many parents spend hundreds of dollars buying developmentally appropriate toys, but your baby's favorite toy is you. Infants want to play all the time: They drop a spoon from the high chair to see you pick it up; they hold toilet paper in front of their face to play peekaboo; they press every button on the VCR to see what will happen. Many of these times you will find yourself saying no to your baby, because these aren't games to you. But do remember that these are all just experiments in cause and effect to your baby, while you redirect her interest to other forms of exploration.

Also make sure that you spend ten or fifteen minutes a day playing games where you don't have to say no, but just enjoy the smiles and giggles. Peekaboo, This Little Piggy, Where Is Thumbkin?—these are all time-honored games and songs that will delight your infant. Your child will associate learning and exploration with joy, and nothing could form a more positive backdrop for learning.

Computers Can Help

Whether we realize it or not, computer chips have become ubiquitous in many infant toys. They talk and sing and light up when a baby touches the right button. Recently several companies have introduced computer software for infants twelve months and older. They refer to these as "lapware," since of course the baby must sit in your lap while you work the mouse. These programs require the baby to touch any key to see characters sing songs or play simple games, and they present your baby with a variety of animated surprises. Some developmental psychologists bemoan the premature introduction of computers to children, preferring that they play with more basic toys. But as with any well-designed toy, if a baby enjoys these programs, they will stimulate learning. If they are not well designed, they will be ignored.

TODDLERS AND PRESCHOOLERS

KEY TO PREVENTION: HELP CHILDREN DEVELOP SOCIAL SKILLS AND THINKING PATTERNS THAT ENHANCE LEARNING

In the toddler and preschool years, children develop the thinking patterns and behaviors that socialize them for school learning. However, overindulging in both praise and material rewards can actually interfere with a child's innate internal motivation.

For example, several months ago I was at a friend's house eating lunch when his four-year-old burst into the room excitedly, shouting, "Daddy, come and look at my poop!" After giving me a quick "I know that this seems strange, but I'm sure you understand" look, he took his son's hands and headed to the bathroom to view this miracle of nature. From around the corner I heard my friend, a well-respected psychotherapist and author, proclaim, "Why, that's wonderful, Josh! It's a great poop. You did a great poop in the toilet!"

Perhaps if toilet training had been an issue for Josh, this would have made more sense. But it wasn't. Josh had used the toilet for more than a year. I also knew that Josh received similar enthusiastic praise for pretty much anything that he did. A scribble was treated like a Picasso. Finishing a meal and a glass of milk was reason for calling a national holiday.

Josh's parents (and as if by contagion his grandparents, aunt, uncle, and nanny) mistakenly believed that children benefit from unconditional adulation and praise. They do not.

Infants up to the age of eighteen months need their parents' constant positive guidance, but this changes as children become toddlers and then again when they become preschoolers. Teaching children self-discipline begins with clear limits and greater expectations than those communicated by many of today's parents. A visit to other countries would remind American parents that three-year-olds are capable of picking up after themselves, doing simple chores, sitting quietly in a restaurant without being constantly entertained, and showing respect for others by using good manners. Whining, talking back, and demanding a constant barrage of toys and treats all reflect a sense of entitlement that is not developmentally appropriate in toddlers or at any other age.

Praise is a powerful reward, but it must be used judiciously. It is inappropriate to praise your child for what he can easily do. If he accomplishes something that is moderately difficult, he should get moderate praise. When he accomplishes something extraordinary for him (given his age and natural talents), only then should he get extraordinary praise.

The basic elements of behavioral psychology are the same for children and adults. If you were punished or ignored no matter what you did at work, you would soon be discouraged, irritable, and ultimately depressed. If you received the grateful and heartfelt thanks of your boss just for showing up, it's unlikely that you would be highly motivated to do your best. The combination of appropriate rewards and punishments along with high but realistic expectations is the correct formula for learning and self-satisfaction at any age.

AN OUNCE OF PREVENTION

Use Praise to Reward Effort

As we have seen in our discussion of infants, children develop a sense of mastery by connecting a cause and an effect. But when children receive enthusiastic praise no matter what they do, they can become confused about what is expected of them. They will be unclear about what they have done and unable to reflect on the lessons learned. A good rule of thumb for when to give your child praise is to observe the degree of effort that he is putting into a particular task and reserve your praise for when he persists at learning a new task. Young children enjoy repeating tasks over and over again, because it is soothing to them to do something familiar, but this should not be mistaken for achievement. Hold your praise for when you see your child struggling to do a new task and then accomplishing it. This will help him learn that you value his effort and not just the final outcome, and it will be the first step in teaching him the important habits of patience and persistence.

We know from animal studies that unconditional praise and constant rewards inhibit the motivation to achieve. A rat who gets rewarded no matter which way he heads in a maze has no incentive to find the correct path. Inevitably he will become passive and lethargic. Even more important, this negative habit is difficult to unlearn. When a rat who has learned that he will get rewarded no matter what he does is then challenged with a maze where only his correct responses are rewarded, he has a harder time navigating the maze than does an "unspoiled" rat.

Encourage a Passion for Learning

Between the ages of two and a half and five, many children become entranced, almost obsessed, by a specific field of knowledge. Dinosaurs are a common fascination to young children, but I've also known children who couldn't stop thinking and talking about trucks, dogs, cats, horses, and insects. I've known several bright preschoolers who've been fascinated by geography, particularly maps. One boy of four could name all fifty state capitals, a feat that stirred in his parents both pride in his intellect and a little concern over his quirkiness.

This phenomenon of unbridled passion for learning is common in young children, but it seems to fade in many children with each passing year, and it's a rarity by the time a child finishes elementary school. You can extend the life of this developmental stage by encouraging the current passion with your enthusiastic input and introducing new ones. For example, if your toddler is fascinated by trucks, show him all the ways he can learn about trucks: taking trips to the library, using the Internet, watching movies, visiting a construction site or a mechanic's shop. Make a scrapbook of pictures and photographs and have him dictate comments to you about what he observes and what he learns. But don't stop with trucks. Go to the library, have him pick out another subject area that interests him, and then approach it with the same intensity. Find a way to make the subject accessible to your preschooler, providing as much hands-on experience as possible. Help him see the fun in learning about any subject, and you will pave the way for a lifetime of interest in acquiring knowledge.

Teach Children to Cope with Frustration

Parents often underestimate what their children can accomplish because they don't like to see them frustrated. However, in actuality very little can be accomplished without some degree of initial frustration, and this is an important lesson for all children to learn. Trying to explain to your child to "be patient" is not the answer.

Patience is an abstract concept that means nothing to young children. Children do learn patience, however, when they observe it in you and when you demonstrate to them how they can solve a problem by breaking it into small steps.

For example, James had become frustrated in his attempts to find the jigsaw-puzzle piece he was looking for. He was working on a wooden puzzle illustrating a dump truck that consisted of about ten large pieces. Impatiently, he kept picking up the remaining four pieces and randomly smacking them down. When one didn't fit, he tossed it aside for another.

His teacher said in a soothing voice, "James, you have to try one piece at a time." One by one she picked up each piece and calmly said, "Let's try this way. . . . Now that way. . . ." She modeled a patient rhythm, and when James tried another piece, he copied his teacher's manner. He calmed down quickly and methodically figured out the correct placement of each remaining puzzle piece.

Teach Reading Readiness

One of the great moments in parenthood is seeing your child read for the first time. One of the great mistakes that parents make is pushing a child to read too soon. Sometimes a child will begin to read at three, and sometimes it happens at seven. Most children begin to recognize words and sound out letters when they're in kindergarten, between the ages of five and six. Unfortunately, many parents and even many teachers don't realize that learning to read is developmentally triggered. Expecting that a child should read before he is actually ready can do emotional harm. He could begin his school career with feelings of inadequacy, when in fact he is simply moving at his own pace. He could develop a dislike for books that will be hard to shake. An estimated 20 to 30 percent of school-age children have some reading problems, and since 90 percent of school tasks require reading, this can be a significant factor in underachievement.

It is important for parents to understand that reading readiness is different from reading. It involves providing activities that are fun for young children, without pressuring them to "perform."

There has been a great deal of research on the best ways to prepare children for reading, and most experts agree that encouraging a general interest in language is the most appropriate approach for children under five. Reading to your child every day is helpful, as is encouraging rhythm games and songs. Let toddlers look through their favorite picture books by themselves while you remain close by to give encouragement or comment. When you go on a trip, read out loud all the signs you see. While shopping, encourage your preschooler to find some of the grocery products, and when you're cooking, let your preschooler follow your directions as you follow a recipe. Reading is something that adults do all the time, and young children will certainly want to share in this aspect of growing up.

While it is important not to push a child to read, parents should be able to recognize the signs that a child is ready to read. Here are some to watch for:

- He has an interest in books and will "pretend" read a book.

- She is able to follow two- and three-step directions without difficulty. ("Put away your toys, wash your hands, and come to the dinner table.")

- He has mastered basic directional concepts, such as up-down, near-far, outside-inside, and so on.

- She has age-appropriate visual-discrimination skills. For example, she can see that an M is different from a W.

If you're concerned that your child of five or older is not showing these signs, there are very simple tests that can indicate whether there is a reading or learning problem. Ask your child's teacher to recommend a psychologist or learning specialist who can administer these tests.

Teach Math-Readiness Skills Through Play

Math skills are another fundamental part of school success, but for many children math is a source of considerable frustration and discouragement. Teaching readiness skills will give your preschooler a chance to start school with a positive attitude toward math, which he can carry throughout his school career.

Young children will get limited benefit from being drilled in number recognition or basic addition. These skills will come easily when children are developmentally ready. Instead, find fun ways to use math concepts at playtime as a precursor to formal arithmetic. This will lay the foundation for making mathematics a meaningful skill to your child.

Consider, for example, the mother who set up a "roadway" for her son to play on with his cars. She suggested he line up his cars in different ways, teaching him about shapes, sizes, and sequencing. She asked him to think of how many pieces of track he would need to extend the road to the door, teaching him estimation. At the end of their playtime she helped him to sort the cars by size and then put them in different boxes, teaching him order, neatness, and classification. This is the type of math lesson any child would seek over and over again.

Develop Fine-Motor Muscles for Writing and an Interest in Written Expression

Writing skills are the third leg on which your child's early education will be built. They can be a source of either pride or frustration. Before a child can learn to write, she must build up her muscles and develop her hand-eye coordination. In the preschool years a child may be able to write several letters, simple words or at least part of her own name. Young children primarily acquire prewriting skills from art activities as well as from developing basic spatial concepts (left-right, up-down, front-back).

The following suggestions will encourage your toddler and preschooler to develop writing skills. You should be aware that some children, particularly boys, lag far behind in their fine-motor skills, but with encouragement and practice they will eventually catch up.

- Keep art supplies on low, open shelves so that children can choose what they want to play with and put things away when done.

- Put items that are used together near each other (e.g., crayons and paper).

- Large paper is best for drawing and writing because young children need space to make wide movements with their arms.

- For variety, encourage children to draw in different media and on different surfaces, such as painting at an easel, finger painting, using chalk on a sidewalk, stamping on paper with rubber stamps.

- Provide children with toys that build coordination, such as puzzles, blocks, and pegboards.

Computers Can Help

There are hundreds of computer games available for children in the three-to-six age range that can reinforce the skills of mastery and creativity and encourage a passion for learning. Your child may enjoy "content"-oriented programs like *Jumpstart Preschool* (Knowledge Adventure), which teaches shapes, letters, numbers, and colors. Also try programs like *Thinkin' Things* (Edmark) that teach problem-solving skills.

There are so many programs becoming available for young children that your best bet will be to review what is available on Web sites such as the PEP Registry for Educational Software Publishers (www.microweb.com/pepsite/), which provides ratings for children's software, a list of buying sources, and much more.

SCHOOL-AGE CHILDREN

KEY TO PREVENTION: HELP CHILDREN DEVELOP SELF-MOTIVATION AND SELF-CONTROL

During the elementary school years, children must acquire specific achievement skills, including self-control and self-motivation. As discussed earlier, some children have an inborn temperament that makes learning these skills easy, but other children are naturally more impulsive and must work harder to acquire them. Research suggests that these achievement skills may be at least as important to school and work success as is a child's intellect. Children who do not learn to curb their impulsive tendencies grow into young adults who are easily upset, unable to delay gratification, and easily frustrated. Children who can control their impulses are better able to cope with frustrations, more resistant to getting anxious under pressure, and more self-reliant.

Self-control, the ability to resist internal impulses and external temptations, is a critical part of emotional intelligence, as is the ability of self-motivation. Think of self-motivation as the accelerator and the fuel of a car, and self-control as the brakes and the steering. Without both the "stop" and "go" elements, it is unlikely that you will get where you want to go on time or in one piece.

Parents typically try to control or motivate their children with the use of external rewards. They might reward improved grades with money or privileges. A good mark on a spelling test might mean a trip to a fast-food restaurant or a movie. In school, younger children might get a sticker for staying in their seat or waiting their turn. Older children who perform well will get special attention and perhaps privileges from the teacher. But according to a variety of studies on achievement in children, external rewards will affect behavior only in the short run. Children will soon tire of rewards or expect that new rewards be of greater value. External rewards do not teach self-control or self-motivation unless they are paired with the right type of social approval.

Psychologists use the term "minimal sufficiency" to describe the correct use of external rewards to motivate children or teach them self-control. This means that you should give your children the minimal amount of rewards sufficient to jump-start their natural inclination to succeed in order to please you. A second principle of giving rewards or praise is that it should be done based on effort as much as on the final outcome of the work. Researchers who have studied Japanese families to learn why their children are such high achievers have found that they focus on how hard their children work, whereas American families are satisfied when their children just get the job done.

Finally, research tells us that external rewards are most likely to be replaced by self-control and self-motivation when children (or adults, for that matter) see that they have some influence over how their efforts are evaluated. One example of this is self-grading, in which students are asked to grade their own homework assignments or projects, with this grade then factored into the teacher's grade. Teachers and parents are often surprised that when they give students the opportunity to evaluate themselves, they are typically very realistic and fair about their grading; more important, they begin to see how they can improve the quality of their work.

AN OUNCE OF PREVENTION

If you have ever taken a course on motivation in the workplace, the following recommendations on goal-setting, commitment, self-monitoring, and self-coaching will look familiar. As you teach these new habits to your child, remember the basic principles of teaching any emotional or social skills. Make the instruction fun by having a positive and enthusiastic attitude. Explain and teach the skill at the correct developmental level, using simple language and relevant examples. Encourage your child to master one skill at a time. Reward your child with praise and affection. Let your child see how you use these skills, so that he can model his behavior on yours.

Goal-Setting

One of the most effective ways to teach self-control and self-motivation is to show children how to break down a task into manageable small steps and to take pride in accomplishing each step. Underachievers can quickly become overwhelmed and discouraged by a task. They may procrastinate until an assignment is almost due and then turn in poor work.

You can help your child learn to manage tasks by showing him how to break them into small steps. If your child has a fifty-word spelling test in a week, help him pick a time each day to work, memorize ten words a day, and then test himself on the previous day's memorization. Children love clear signs of progress. This "time management" technique teaches children both responsibility and self-motivation.

Self-Monitoring Skills

Another proven way to increase internal motivation is by teaching children how to evaluate their own progress. The Self-Evaluation Checklist shows a simple way that parents can help their children develop internal motivation by self-evaluation. This form asks children to rate themselves on a 1-to-5 scale on how well they perform tasks like household chores and homework projects. Use this form for children ages eight to twelve for four weeks, and see if your child's performance and cooperation improve.

Self-Evaluation Checklist

Rate yourself from 1 to 5 on the following tasks and chores, with 1=Poor Performance and 5=Great Effort/Great Attitude

Week beginning _____

Task or Chore				Rating			
	M	T	W	Th	F	Sa	Su
_____	—	—	—	—	—	—	—
_____	—	—	—	—	—	—	—
_____	—	—	—	—	—	—	—
_____	—	—	—	—	—	—	—
_____	—	—	—	—	—	—	—
_____	—	—	—	—	—	—	—
Average Rating	—	—	—	—	—	—	—

Self-Coaching

Do you remember *The Little Engine That Could?* The small engine in this story pulled a heavy circus train up the mountain, repeating the phrase "I think I can. I think I can. I think I can. I think I can." Psychologists call this "self-coaching," and studies have shown that when people literally talk to themselves, their concentration and performance increase dramatically. Help your child come up with a motivating phrase that she can say to herself when she feels frustrated. Have her say it out loud several times and then to herself. For example, "I can do this. No sweat. I can do this. No sweat." Explain to her how many top athletes and performers use this exact same technique to motivate them to work through pain and frustration to do their best.

Show Your Children How You Prioritize Time and Effort

How do *you* deal with a busy week? How do you make sure that the really important things get done? Time-management experts tell us to make a "to do" list and then give each item a rating, of A, B, and C. "A" tasks are the highest priority, "B" tasks are moderately important, and "C" are the least important. High-priority tasks are done first, low-priority tasks last. Help your child to make a similar list, prioritizing his tasks, and then doing the "A" tasks first. This simple skill will teach him to self-motivate, and avoid procrastinating. If he can make it a habit, it is a skill that will last a lifetime.

Let Your Kids Know About Your Successes and Failures

You should also take the time to talk to your children about your work, the stresses that occur, and how you deal with them. What do you do when a task seems overwhelming? How do you make sure you meet a deadline? What has happened when you've missed one? Talk about your successes and failures, and never underestimate your influence on your child's approach to her own life. Allow her to see that sometimes you can't do everything you want and that you strive to do better. Help her understand there is no shame in falling short of your goals as long as a sincere effort has been made.

Build Achievement Habits Outside of School

Many underachieving children feel frustrated in school because they cannot be "the best." Most schools become highly competitive environments by the second or third grade, and it is the nature of any group that someone will always be the best and everyone else will line up behind. For this reason it is helpful to encourage children to participate in projects outside school, where they can enjoy achieving in a noncompetitive environment. Hobbies, which developmental psychologist Anna Freud described as "halfway between play and work," provide opportunities for children to become engrossed in a subject where their performance will not be judged. Popular hobbies include crafts, model trains, cooking, photography, collecting, and so on. Older children might enjoy earning extra money by starting their own "small business." Children as young as eight or nine find a rewarding challenge in running their own business, which can involve everything from writing a simple business plan to basic accounting. One ten-year-old boy I know has made a business out of selling baseball cards. A nine-year-old girl provides a pet-walking service to her neighbors. An organization called Kidsway (at www.Kidsway.com) publishes a magazine called *The Young Entrepreneur*, which provides useful information for parents, educators, and kids.

Computers Can Help

Mitch Resnick, a researcher in the Media Lab at the Massachusetts Institute of Technology, has a solution for motivating students to learn that few children would challenge: make learning more fun. Resnick's research team designed *Lego Mindstorms*, a computer program that helps children build robots out of Legos. Resnick's suggestion for keeping children motivated throughout their school career is to make every grade level as hands-on and activity-oriented as kindergarten. Computers can certainly help fulfill this goal.

TEENAGERS

KEY TO PREVENTION: TEACH TEENS THE HABITS OF SUCCESS

Underachievement in adolescence can significantly narrow a teenager's life choices. But even a serious lack of interest in school can change, and the underachieving teen can become a high-achieving adult. You can help your teen by staying focused on the importance of education. You can help him by providing a structured and predictable home life. You can be an advocate for your teen in his school, making sure that he experiences the right atmosphere for learning. Most important, you can help your teenager by showing him how to cope with the many conflicts and stresses that might impede his schoolwork.

History is filled with examples of "slow starters" who didn't become motivated to work hard until they were well into their adolescence or even their twenties. Parents are naturally dismayed if their teenagers bring home poor grades or express a dislike of school, but this does not mean that it is too late to prevent underachievement. Many students who did poorly in high school have gone on to excel in college or in the workplace. Parents should look at this stage of development, no matter how it seems to be going, as an opportunity to instill a sense of the importance of effort and responsibility in their teens.

Entering middle school is a particularly demanding time, when many students first experience real difficulty. The school environment becomes less personal. Moving from teacher to teacher can be unsettling at first. In addition, young teens' bodies are changing, their emotions are heightened, and their hormones are raging. They are simultaneously more self-critical and also more vulnerable to criticism and rejection by their peers. As a result of all these pressures, teens may become demanding and moody at home.

It is also a time when teenagers typically push their parents away. They are vocal about expressing their desire for independence. They test rules and curfews. Since parents have their own busy lives to contend with, and sometimes the needs of younger siblings or their own older parents, it is often easier to give in to the demands of a teen.

During this period parents may also feel pushed away by the schools. Many parents visit their teenager's school only two or three times a year at an "open house," a sports event, or a play or speech ceremony. Most parent involvement in the upper grades is "need-driven." If a child receives a bad grade or gets into trouble with a teacher, a phone call or visit will be made. If a student is college-bound, parents may get involved with the guidance counselor. But most high school students are not thrilled to spot their parents coming down the hall, and most teachers feel that the school is their turf.

Parents often feel that this is a time when they should step back and let their children work out their problems for themselves. In fact, this is not at all what teenagers need. To prevent under-achievement you will need to continue being a reliable and consistent support and presence. Psychologists Jerome Brunner and David Wood have used the word "scaffolding" to describe the correct relationship between a parent and child, as parents support their teen's growth without interfering in it. Try allowing teens to solve their own problems, giving them more guidance in the beginning and then backing away when they've learned the skills they need to truly be more independent. This style of graduated, hands-off guidance will help your teens feel comfortable in times of trouble or exceptional stress, and able to seek your support and guidance when they need it.

AN OUNCE OF PREVENTION

I don't know too many families with teenagers that have a calm and predictable home life. Parents work long hours. Teens have constantly changing schedules of activities. Many teens today are in joint-custody situations. A new boyfriend or girlfriend can cause everything to change. And yet, in the midst of this chaos, you will want to do your best to organize your family life and help your teen prioritize his time.

Help Teens to Stay on Track

Parents must work to provide a predictable schedule for their teens and to make sure that schoolwork is a priority in that schedule. Suggest that your teen make a weekly calendar showing all her planned activities, including study time, and how long each activity takes. Then recommend that she make a list of the activities, starting with the ones that take the most time, descending downward. If schoolwork is not at the top of the list, there is a problem. Sit down with your teen and her weekly calendar and make sure that her schedule reflects the values you're trying to teach her.

Seek Mentors for Unmotivated Teens

Mentoring is a time-honored way to teach young people new skills. It also has been shown to be one of the best ways to teach teenagers the importance of good work habits. The object of any mentoring program is to pair a teenager who is typically not doing well in school with an accomplished professional in a field in which he is interested.

There are hundreds of mentoring programs throughout the United States, but the demand for mentors far outweighs the number of organized programs. There may be mentoring programs available through your school, church, or synagogue, or you and your teenager may have to seek out the right mentor yourselves. For well-thought-out guidelines on helping teens find a mentor, go to the National Mentoring Partnership Web site, at www.mentoring.org.

Make It Clear to Your Teen that Schoolwork Isn't the Only Thing You Value

Teens can be easily overwhelmed by social issues so that school, at least for short periods of time, takes a backseat. Your child is going to need you to keep a balanced perspective on her life, because chances are she won't. Unfortunately, the knee-jerk reaction of most parents when a teen's academics begin to fall apart is to become very centered on fixing that problem instead of taking the time to sort out what else might be going on. A teen who feels that his parents are looking at him as a total person and not just as a "grade machine" is more likely to ask for help when he needs it. A teen who is treated as a complex person with many facets is more likely to be resilient in the face of stress.

Teach Teens to Solve Problems That Take Time Away from Schoolwork

Because underachievement is frequently a symptom of other problems, it is important for you to help your teen learn to understand and manage problems that might infringe on his education. Many prevention programs teach teenagers the benefits of using a specific problem-solving approach, analyzing a problem and then deciding on specific solutions.

Tina had difficulty coping with the changing lifestyles of her parents, who had divorced more than five years before. Tina's father had remarried a woman who was fifteen years younger than he, and they were now trying to have children. Tina's mother had had a series of relationships, causing her to move from one apartment to another nearly every year. Tina never felt at home with either her mother or her father, yet she desired the approval of both and wanted to belong to each family. As a result, Tina paid little attention to her schoolwork and worried constantly about when she would stay with each parent, whom she would go on vacation with, and how she could please them both.

As part of Tina's therapy, she was taught how to analyze each family problem that presented itself by going through a six-step problem-solving process:

Identify and define the problem in a simple sentence: Where should she have Thanksgiving dinner?

Write down all the information about the problem, including the facts, opinions, and other people's possible emotional reactions: My mom and dad each want me. I'd like to go to Mom's but I went there last year. Dad might get angry.

Write down at least four alternative solutions to the problem, including anticipated obstacles: I can do what I want. I can have dessert at my dad's. I can promise to spend Friday with my dad. I can tell my mother it's Dad's turn.

Decide on which is the best solution: Tell them both that I want to see them both and leave Mom's early to spend some time with Dad.

Anticipate what will be the consequences of this solution: No one will be really happy.

Try the best solution and analyze the results. Make adjustments as necessary: It worked out okay. I should have left Mom's earlier.

Teaching teens to solve their own problems is an important part of the counseling process, but there is no reason that parents can't teach this skill. Throughout this process make sure that you listen to your teenager's concerns and give her support and encouragement for her thoughtful decisions, no matter how they turn out.

Computers Can Help

Computers provide many opportunities for parents to stay involved in the education of their teenagers. Spend some time with your teenager on the computer. Encourage him to use educational software to supplement school assignments and to use the Internet for research. Using computers does not have to be an isolated activity when parents are involved in their teenager's learning.

Most schools have Web sites that can help you feel more involved in your child's school experience. On a typical site, teachers can post daily homework assignments or run electronic bulletin boards where parents can voice their comments (rules are posted to make sure this doesn't become a place to gripe or gossip). Many of these sites are run by the students themselves, providing students, parents, teachers, and administrators with a virtual community dedicated to a common goal of student success.

• • •

Underachievement is a problem that can be prevented, contained, and reversed. It begins when children are very young, by encouraging them to develop a sense of mastery and initiative. The toddler and preschool years are times of passionate learning, which must be nurtured by parents and not dampened by overindulgence. The early school years are the best time for children to learn the habits of achievement, including how to persist in the face of difficulty. When self-motivation and self-control are emphasized at this age, they form the foundation for a life of self-reliance. While many forces work to distance parents of teenagers from staying involved in their education, this is not at all what teenagers need. Encouragement, guidance, structure in the home, and high expectations are the elements for success at every age.

5

Overcoming Fears and Shyness

Any parent would be pleased to raise a child who can step out into the world with confidence, courage, and fortitude. Some children, from the cradle on, will do exactly that. They will be relaxed, not easily shaken, curious, and outgoing in almost any social context.

But some children will not come to these traits so easily, if at all. Some babies are simply born more fearful, cautious, and shy. These traits, left unattended too long, can lead a child to move into the world in a cautious and limited way. He may avoid new experiences, find it hard to connect with people, and miss many opportunities to develop his talents. Later in life he may have trouble achieving job success or enjoying satisfying relationships.

As parents, you will want to help your child approach the world, not so much fearlessly but with an interested, considered, open, and excited mind. Whether your child is born with a strong potential for fearfulness or is very social, no child goes through the stages of childhood without encountering some fears. How parents handle their child's fears, however, can have a significant impact on their overall development.

The preventive techniques in this chapter are meant to help

manage and, if possible, eradicate both common fears and other, more serious ones before they inhibit your child's life.

FEARS: THERE'S NO AVOIDING THEM

Between the ages of two and six the average child has about four fears; between six and twelve this number can double. In adolescence the number of fears will usually drop significantly, but they won't vanish altogether. Teenagers might suffer from anxiety about school performance or fear of rejection. And, of course, adults have irrational fears, too. Recently I heard a pilot from Delta Airlines speak to a group of fearful fliers. After forty-five minutes of questions and answers, he confided, "Boy, I'm glad that's over. I have a fear of public speaking."

Fears are so common because they are a basic human emotion, and necessary to the very survival of the species. Fears of the dark, of large animals, of lightning and thunder, and of being closed in are just some of the terrors that we undoubtedly inherited from our prehistoric ancestors. These primitive fears, and many others, appear to be encoded in our DNA—though this coding seems to affect different people in different ways. We do not really know why one child quickly learns that gentle dogs are different from growling ones while another child runs to her parents at the mere thought of visiting a home with any dog at all.

I have included shyness in this chapter because it, too, is a fear, and an extraordinarily common one. Some sources estimate that as much as 40 percent of the population suffers from the problem. Shyness is broadly defined as the fear of being negatively evaluated and rejected by others. It can be triggered by only a few situations (speaking in front of others or meeting someone new), or it can be generalized, rendering a sufferer afraid to be present in almost any social situation. Shyness, too, is likely genetically determined.

Fears and anxieties originate in the emotional part of the brain, called the limbic system. The fear response is designed to call the body to immediate attention if a threat is near, and prepare it for fight or flight:

- The pupils dilate for maximum visual perception.

- The arteries constrict, to maximize blood pressure and allow the heart to pump blood more quickly to our muscles.

- The adrenal gland begins to pump out cortisol, which stimulates the formation of epinephrine and norepinephrine, causing heightened alertness.

- The metabolism speeds up to provide more energy.

Through experience, the emotional part of the brain gradually learns what is to be feared and what is truly not a threat. It learns when to ring an internal warning "alarm" and when just to be a little more watchful. As a child gets older, the thinking part of the brain, the neocortex, also plays an increased role in calming fears. By the time a fearful child is three or four, parents can start to reason with her, and by the time she is six or seven, she should begin to analyze a fearful situation for herself.

Fear becomes a problem in childhood when the innate fear response of the brain cannot be modified. When a fear is encountered, the body is "hijacked" by the emotional part of the brain, causing thought and reason to disappear. Our survival instinct has made our emotional brains much more powerful than our reasoning, which is one explanation for why fears are so common.

An additional problem for many children is the anxiety that accompanies most fears. Not only do they want to avoid a particular situation, but they start to worry about it at other times as well. For this reason psychologists consider fears and shyness (also called social phobia) types of anxiety disorders. It's a matter of degree, though. Children with simple phobias or shyness tend not to worry to the extent that children with other, more intensely experienced anxiety disorders do. A shy child may be perfectly fine, even outgoing, at home. His shyness does not affect him unless he is actually in a social situation. But a child with a separation-anxiety disorder might also worry excessively in anticipation of an event, even when he is with his parents. The other difference is degree of reaction.

Generally a shy child will not have the extreme behaviors (e.g., panic) that a child with a serious anxiety disorder might have.

In this chapter we will look at how to contain or even prevent the entire range of anxiety disorders, from common developmental fears to generalized anxiety. The goal is either to keep a fear from developing at all or to contain it and manage it before it limits your child's life in any significant way.

Because fears and anxieties are so common, there has been a considerable amount of research on the types of fears that occur in childhood and how best to control them. The child with a fearful temperament can be helped most effectively in infancy. Developmental fears, such as monsters and "bad guys," which come and go as the child ages, are best addressed in toddlers and preschoolers. More debilitating fears—including refusal to go to school, and general anxiety disorders—are best treated in the elementary school years, before they interfere materially with other developmental processes. Shyness and social inhibition can be treated early, but it is particularly important and useful to address this in adolescence, when it is most common and when the sufferers are more able to employ techniques to help themselves. Fears that are a result of a trauma should be of immediate concern, no matter what the child's age, but I will discuss this in detail in Chapter 9.

RISK FACTORS FOR SEVERE FEARS AND SHYNESS

Although the vast majority of childhood fears will go away with support and reassurance from parents, some children are more at risk for serious debilitating fears. Some fearful children will develop disorders, such as agoraphobia, which will make it difficult for them even to leave their homes. Others will be afraid of flying, or crossing bridges, or riding elevators. Many may end up living limited lives, and experience less success than their outgoing counterparts.

But the good news is that prevention techniques, applied as early as infancy and as late as adulthood, can make a significant difference. As children grow from toddlers to adolescents to young adults, there are risks that render them vulnerable to developing fearful styles. But there are also different preventive techniques to keep these fears at bay or, at the very least, manage them.

Temperament

Researchers believe that as many as 15 to 20 percent of children are born with an identifiable shy and fearful temperament, putting them at risk for both mild and more serious problems. Fearfulness is such a strong genetic trait that it can be detected in the first few weeks of life. When you put a mobile in front of timid infants or play a tape recording of unfamiliar voices, their heart rates will increase and they will cry loudly with jerky and vigorous movements.

Yet research on animals and humans strongly suggests that, depending on the type of parenting a shy child receives, this trait can be modified.

The Brain

Researchers are now beginning to believe that some children are born with a shy and fearful temperament because of the way that their brains react to the environment. Jerome Kagan of Harvard University believes that an oversensitive amygdala, the emotional control center of the brain, is the main trigger for fearfulness. Kagan's first evidence for this came from his study of cats. About one in seven cats, very unlike its curious cousins, is born timid and reluctant to explore new territory. Defying its predatory instinct, it will attack only the smallest of rodents, too fearful to take on any adversary closer to its size. Direct brain probes have found that the amygdala in these timid cats is unusually excitable, which first becomes evident when a kitten is about one month old, roughly the time that the amygdala takes over its role of emotional control. It is Kagan's belief that timid children, like these timid cats, are slaves to an overactive amygdala, which in humans matures at around eight or nine months, about the time that many infants go through stranger anxiety.

Overprotective Parenting

But the most important and promising aspect of Kagan's work came in a study in which he followed the lives of five hundred children predisposed to shyness for more than seventeen years. According to Kagan's research, shy human babies can also outgrow their genetic predisposition if their parents do not reinforce their hypersensitivity. They will, in fact, develop personality traits that make them indistinguishable from outgoing children by the age of five. Kagan determined that a shy child's personality change comes about from a permanent change in the way the brain deals with stress and heightened emotional states—the taming of an overexcitable amygdala. However, parents who try to protect their sensitive infant from all the things that upset him may be predisposing him to a lifetime of timidity and putting him at risk for a variety of fear and anxiety disorders. Although it is certainly understandable that parents would want to shelter their sensitive babies from distress, in the long run this may be doing them a great disservice, by preventing their babies' brains from biologically adjusting to the more challenging (and realistic) environment.

Shy Parents

As one parent pointed out to me while discussing her shy child, "I was a lot like that when I was her age, I guess, only not so bad. I didn't like to go to school, and I wouldn't raise my hand in class even though I knew the answer. I've always been shy, and I still am, so I'm used to it. I thought my daughter would just be shy like me, but I didn't think that she would be this bad." Since fearfulness and shyness are genetically loaded traits, it is likely that one or both parents of a fearful child will also have this type of personality. As in other genetically determined disorders, parents of shy children may have difficulty in recognizing early signs of shyness and fears, or may have trouble applying some of the interventions that I will recommend in this chapter. If this is the case, you may find it helpful to use some of the same principles of overcoming fearfulness and shyness on yourself first, before sharing them with your child.

INFANTS

KEY TO PREVENTION: NOT GIVING IN TO AN INFANT'S FEARS

All babies are subject to certain common fears. From birth to six months they fear the loss of physical support and loud noises. From seven to twelve months many babies are afraid of strangers, sudden loud noises, and looming objects. But some babies are born with an excessively fearful temperament. Take Sara, for example.

> *Baby Sara could not stand to be without her mother. When she woke up in the morning, she would scream until her mother rushed in. When she was old enough to sit and eat in a high chair, she would eat only on her mother's lap. When a baby-sitter came, Sara would cry and wail until the sitter was sent home. Sara's parents resigned themselves to having a timid baby. They assumed that as she grew older, Sara would become more outgoing.*

If we look at the research on shyness, Sara's parents' assumption that she would outgrow her fearfulness is probably wrong. A fearful and anxious temperament is potentially very stable, and although Sara's reactions to change and her need for her parents will certainly become less dramatic, she will likely remain more fearful and anxious than her peers for the rest of her childhood and possibly beyond. She will certainly be at more risk for serious anxiety disorders, such as phobias and extreme shyness—that is, unless her parents employ preventions that will help Sara not just cope with her fearfulness but also keep it from grabbing hold.

The single difference between a baby who outgrows her fearful temperament and one who doesn't is her ability to calm herself. All infants have this ability. Even in the womb, babies can calm themselves by sucking on their wrists, which they continue to do for the first few weeks of life. Babies also learn at a very early age how to calm themselves by changing their sensory input. By three or four weeks a baby will use his vision to calm herself. If agitated or over-stimulated, he will stare at a plain wall or out a window until he is calmer. By eight or ten weeks, as a baby gets better motor control, he will change from sucking on his wrist to sucking on a finger or a thumb, which feels more like sucking on a nipple.

There are other subtle strategies that a baby may learn to calm herself. Moving her hands in front of her face, kicking her feet in a specific way, or just changing body position—all these may be forms of self-soothing.

Babies with a fearful temperament undoubtedly have similar ways to calm themselves, but these inborn techniques are just not up to the task at hand. Unlike other babies, they are more sensitive to arousal, and, once aroused, the biochemicals that cascade from their brains through their bodies are too much for them to handle. From early on, parents of a fearful infant believe that they are needed to calm their baby, because their baby does not seem to be able to do it himself. They sing lullabies, rock him, walk up and down while rubbing his back, and even take him on long car rides because the motion and the motor soothe him. Eventually parents learn the techniques that work best to calm their infant—even at the expense of their own sanity. These exhausted but highly motivated parents are also quick to learn what upsets their baby. Like their infant, they become hypersensitive to noise, trying to keep their baby's room as quiet as a library. They don't allow their baby to be held by strangers and are wary about any new situation or disruption in the baby's routine.

In studying infants as they grew up, Jerome Kagan observed that about one in three timid babies outgrew fearfulness. He attributed this largely to the way the parents reacted to these babies, being less likely to pick them up at every cry, and when they did pick them up, spending less time trying to comfort them. These parents also felt that their babies needed to "learn to adapt" to their environment rather than have the environment adapt to them. The result of this style of parenting was that the timid infant's hypersensitive amygdala, through dozens and dozens of experiences in self-calming, learned to calm itself, probably by forming more neural networks between the thinking and the emotional parts of the brain.

AN OUNCE OF PREVENTION

If you have an infant who seems to be constantly upset and unable to adapt to new situations, and particularly if you have a family history of anxiety or fear disorders, you should consciously adopt a parenting style that will make your child more resilient.

Don't Be at Your Infant's Beck and Call

To begin with, teach your baby how to calm herself down when she is upset. As pediatrician William Sammons writes in his book *The Self-Calmed Baby*:

"Self-calming creates greater self-assurance and self-sufficiency. Rather than being a helpless baby, your child can finally do something for herself. She feels a sense of accomplishment and is far less vulnerable, because she is less dependent on other people. [Self-calming] provides a level of comfort and flexibility that parents cannot create on their own."

Dr. Sammons insists that every baby can learn to calm herself and that it is a competence she should acquire. He suggests that instead of rushing to pick your baby up, give her five chances to calm herself:

1. First just observe her to make sure that everything is all right.

2. Then wait a minute or two, and softly say a few words.

3. Then step into her view and let her see you; just the sight of you should be reassuring.

4. Again wait a minute or two, and then check her diaper. If she is not wet, talk to her for a few minutes and see if the sound of your voice will help quiet her.

5. Only then pick her up and hold her for a few minutes, soothing her, and then place her back in her crib in her favorite position. If this still does not quiet her, try one of the suggestions below.

Desensitize Your Baby

The second thing that you can do to help your baby become less fearful is to desensitize him to the things that make him upset. The principle of desensitization is a simple one. If a child is afraid of something, gradually expose him to it one step at a time, giving him an opportunity to adapt to the fear at each successive point. For example, suppose your child is terrified to be left alone with a baby-sitter. Invite the baby-sitter over in the morning to talk and play with you and your baby. Have her come back in the afternoon and play with or feed your baby while you watch in close proximity. On the next day have her do the same thing while you watch from another room, but remain in the child's sight. Then have her play with or feed the baby while you are in another room, and finally leave the house for several hours. The important thing is to commit yourself to the outcome. No matter how much your baby wails and reaches for you, you must resist your urge to "protect" him. In fact, rescuing him does not protect him at all; teaching him to be more adaptable will serve him better in the long run. Take one small step at a time, but only go forward.

Provide New Experiences

I know of a couple who did not get a baby-sitter for their child until he was six. Another decided against moving into a larger home because they didn't want their fourteen-month-old to have to adjust to a new room. Parents of oversensitive babies try to keep everything predictable for their children so as not to upset them, but this only increases the chance that they will not grow out of their fearfulness. Instead, parents should seek new experiences— new sights, new sounds, new people—forcing their child to learn to adjust to change.

The most important advice I can give you to help a fearful infant become bolder is to not allow your child's timidity to dictate the way you respond to him or overshadow your day-to-day activities. Rather than keeping him away from new experiences, seek them out. Infants can grow out of their fearfulness, and their predisposition to a life of watchfulness and inhibition can be avoided. Determined and confident parents make the difference.

Make Sure That Your Baby Has a "Transition Object"

Almost every infant has a special "transition object," a stuffed animal or blanket that provides comfort at specific transition times. Children want to sleep with their teddy bear, hold him while they feed, and they may look for him when they are upset. The tactile familiarity is a very important element of the comfort the teddy provides, as is the smell. These sorts of objects "smell like comfort," which is one reason young children don't like to have them washed. The olfactory sense is the most primitive emotional center of the brain, and it can be a very powerful way of controlling emotions.

TODDLERS AND PRESCHOOLERS

KEY TO PREVENTION: USE REASON, REASSURANCE, RELAXATION, AND REENACTMENT

As infants grow into toddlers, they shed some normal fears and acquire others. At one year, common fears include separation from parents, the toilet, injury, and strangers. At two years, loud noises, animals, darkness, separation from parents, large objects, and changes in their living spaces are common fears. The most common fears of three- and four-year-olds involve masks, darkness, animals, separation, injury, and noises at night.

> When his father lifted Barry up into the barber's chair, you might have thought he was placing him into a vat of boiling oil. The five-year-old screamed and wriggled and flailed as if his very life depended on getting back down to the ground. "It's going to hurt!" he shrieked. His father and the hairstylist tried to reason with him, distract him, bribe him, even yell at him, but nothing worked. He was too upset. Barry returned home with the same shaggy head of hair he'd left with. That night, when Barry was in

a deep sleep, his parents trimmed his hair the best they could. It looked a little chopped up, but it was better than going through another traumatic scene at the barber.

Developmental fears are the most common of childhood fears and anxieties, and are considered a normal part of growing up. They come and go as your child ages, lasting anywhere from one to six months. Teaching your child to cope with developmental fears prevents him from generalizing his fears to other people, places, or events.

Developmental fears arise naturally because the child's intellect can't keep up with his ability to perceive the unexpected changes in his expanding world. But as a child's understanding grows, he usually sees that the basis of his fear is unfounded. Take, for example, the common fear that preschoolers have of monsters. Young children do not clearly distinguish that what they see on television or in the movies is different from what they experience in the world. From their point of view having a creature suddenly appear under their bed is not too farfetched. As they grow older, however, children slowly learn that the scary things are "just pretend," and do not exist in the real world.

Unfortunately, for some children this "logic" does not make a difference in the way they feel or behave.

Experience has taught us never to underestimate the power of the irrational mind when it comes to fears. Otherwise-rational adults believe that an elevator will fall down the shaft as soon as they get in, that bridges will collapse if they drive over them, that their heart will stop beating if they leave the house. Have you ever tried to talk someone with a fear of flying into getting on an airplane? All the safety information in the world can't convince such a person that her plane will not be the one in hundreds of thousands of flights that crashes.

Our human propensity for fears makes dealing with common developmental fears in young children a necessity. As Dr. Stephen Garber and his coauthors say in their book *Monsters Under the Bed,* unconfronted fears can last a lifetime. They write, "Although many fears will disappear as quickly as they came, some persist and become ingrained. Fears that continue beyond the usual age that most of your child's peers have overcome them are likely to grow in strength if they are not confronted. . . . Fears that are not confronted not only last, they can also spread." Children who are born with a fearful temperament are naturally more likely to have common fears persist and generalize to other situations.

Special note should be made of the importance of dealing with nightmares, by far the most prevalent expressions of fear and the source of a great deal of anxiety for nearly every parent of a young child. The most common nightmares of toddlers and preschoolers are ones that involve the fear of separation from their parents, such as being taken away by monsters or being lost. Many times nightmares are a reliving of something upsetting that has happened to a child during the day, like getting a shot at the doctor's office or being frightened by something on TV.

Nightmares should not be confused with night terrors, which occur in about 5 percent of children. As the name suggests, night terrors produce extreme fright in children who experience them. The pupils dilate, breathing becomes rapid, and the child may sweat profusely. Sometimes a child may actually get out of bed and run around in a frenzy, screaming as if her life were in danger. Unlike with nightmares, however, children with night terrors are usually fine when they wake up. As Dr. Jodi Mindell writes in her book *Sleeping Through the Night*, "An easy way to distinguish between sleep terrors and nightmares is to determine who is more upset the next morning. If your child is more upset, then it was a nightmare. If you are more upset, then it was a sleep terror."

Shyness is also a common problem for children at this age. Shy children are reluctant to go to preschool and may fight being dropped off. When they are at school, they may watch the other children play rather than participate. They are also usually afraid of physical risks. They may not like to go on a slide or on the jungle gym unless a parent is holding their hand.

This is an important time to help your child work through patterns of fearfulness before it becomes ingrained.

AN OUNCE OF PREVENTION

The "Four R's" of helping children overcome their developmental fears are reason, reassurance, relaxation, and reenactment. As you will see, there are other preventive measures as well, but these are the basic components of dealing with irrational fears at any age.

Give Your Child Clear and Specific Reasons That His Fears Are Unfounded

In a calm and logical manner, explain to your child why his fears are unfounded. Give him factual information, always keeping in mind his level of understanding and language ability. For example, in the case of Barry, the boy afraid of getting a haircut, his father was told by a counselor to explain why a haircut does not hurt. When Barry was in a calm mood, his father explained that getting his hair cut wouldn't hurt because hair consists of used cells that do not feel anything when they are cut. His father demonstrated this by first cutting a piece of paper, then a string, and then a piece of his own hair. Remember that young children are very concrete in their thinking and benefit from visual examples. One mother, whose three-year-old was afraid of being flushed down the toilet, traced her daughter's bottom on a sheet of paper, cut out the drawing, and then compared it with a cutout the size of the hole at the bottom of the toilet. "You see," she explained, "your bottom is much bigger than the hole in the toilet, even if you did fall in."

Give Your Child Reassurance While You Encourage Independence

Reassurance for young children usually comes in the form of a hug and back rub and the comforting words that "everything is all right, there's nothing to be afraid of." This is usually sufficient for most developmental fears. However, some parents go way beyond what is necessary, and their excessive reassurance may actually reinforce a child's fears. Parents who take their child into their bed after a nightmare are setting up a behavioral pattern that will be hard to break, as are parents who promise their child a "treat" if he will stop acting shy or afraid. Just as with infants, overprotecting preschoolers and toddlers from normal fears denies them the chance to develop their own coping mechanisms.

Make Sure That Your Child Knows How to Relax

Teaching your child relaxation skills is considered one of the most important preventive steps you can take. Relaxation skills involve being able to consciously ignore a specific emotion (in this case fear or anxiety) and keep the mind and body in a calm, emotionally neutral state. The simplest way to teach relaxation to your young child is to have him sit in a comfortable chair while you explain that you're going to show him how to stay calm when he is frightened. Have him take three deep breaths, letting out the air slowly. You should do this with him. Then tell him to relax his body with each deep breath. With the first breath have him relax his shoulders and neck. With the second breath have him relax the middle of his body, his stomach and back. With the third breath have him relax the muscles in his lower body and legs.

For the first few times it will help if you touch each part of the body as your child tries to relax it. Since children have to learn how to relax their muscles, you should gently massage each muscle group until you can feel the decreased tension. After a few practice sessions your child will know what it feels like to be relaxed.

Reenact the Fearful Experience

It is not helpful to force a young child to face his fear when he is in a panic. In many cases this will only make the fear worse. One father confided to me he decided to help his five-year-old conquer his fear of monsters "once and for all" by putting on a scary mask and jumping out of a closet to surprise his son. He thought that when he took off the mask, his son would see it was his father and get a good laugh, but this is not what happened. The boy went into a panic and was inconsolable for almost an hour. He then became wary of his father, who he thought might try to scare him again.

This father's attempt to "scare his child into being brave" clearly backfired.

Reenacting a feared situation is helpful only when it is done with the cooperation of the child and follows the principles of desensitization and self-calming discussed above. This approach dictates that children be gradually exposed to a fear, one small step at a time, and then proceed only when the child is calm enough to go on to the next level. It also assumes that the child is taught how to recognize early signs of his fear, such as a rapid heart rate and body tension, and knows one or more relaxation techniques.

Tell Your Child What Will Happen Next

Dealing with separation issues in a concrete fashion makes it easier to reassure young children. Tell your child what you'll be doing while the two of you are apart. If your child is nervous about staying over at a friend's house while you go shopping, say, "I'm going to the grocery store that we usually go to. I'm going to go down the aisles and get things we need for dinner. Then I'm going to get in the car and come home." Paint a mental picture for your child of where you will be when she is away from you. Refer to the things, people, and places that she already knows, so that she begins to develop an image of you in her mind. Avoid going into detail about things she is unfamiliar with or places she doesn't know. This is only likely to raise her anxiety.

Avoid Scary Stories and Movies

If your child has frequent nightmares, you should avoid scary stories and movies just before bedtime, even though, ironically, some children actually request to hear or see exactly that. While you should comfort your child after a nightmare, do not let her stay up for long periods of time. When children try to stay up to avoid having nightmares, they actually increase the chance of having nightmares the next night. This happens because when children don't get enough deep REM sleep, their bodies require more REM sleep the next night, and most nightmares occur during REM sleep.

Protect Your Child During Night Terrors

If your child has night terrors, the most important thing you can do is keep her safe. She may get up and walk around the house, so make sure that the doors and windows are locked and the floors are clear, as she might trip over toys. Don't try to wake your child during a night terror. The general rule is to do as little as possible. Don't even discuss the event the next morning, which will only serve to worry her. As with nightmares, maintaining a regular bedtime schedule is usually the best solution. If the frequency of events continues to increase or if you are unsure of what to do, consult your pediatrician or a sleep-disorder specialist.

To review the Four R's of overcoming fears, let's take a look at Wayne, a five-year-old whom I treated for his extreme fear of dogs. Wayne's parents said that his fear began sometime around three, when they lived next door to a large dog that was penned outside and barked constantly. They couldn't pinpoint exactly when the fear started, but Wayne refused to walk within sight of the dog and would become extremely alarmed when he heard the dog bark, even when he was safe in his home.

I began my work with Wayne by listing all the reasons he didn't have to be afraid of dogs:

- Dogs don't run wild, but are in a pen or on a leash.

- Dogs are pets and like people.

- Most dogs are very friendly.

- When dogs aren't friendly, their owners will tell you that.

- Dogs bark loudly for many reasons. Most dogs who bark loudly are not mean.

We wrote out each sentence on an index card and found pictures of dogs from magazines to place on each card. I asked Wayne to carry these cards around with him and to look them over with his parents several times a day. I instructed his parents to reassure Wayne about his fears, calmly rubbing his back as they viewed the cards.

By the third session Wayne handled the cards easily and without anxiety. Sometimes his parents would catch him sitting and looking at the pictures of the dogs all by himself. In my office I asked Wayne to sit in a comfortable chair as he looked at the cards spread them out before him on a table. I told him to breathe very slowly and deeply. After a few moments I asked him to relax his shoulders, then his chest and stomach, then his arms and legs. Within five minutes he was in a deeply relaxed state. I asked his parents to practice this procedure with him once a day.

At the next session it was time to begin slowly reenacting his fears. As his parents watched, we set up a dollhouse and put a small plastic dog in a "pen" nearby. Wayne then chose a small figure to represent himself. Using this miniature scene, I instructed Wayne to "walk out of the house, as far away from the dog as you like, do whatever you like to do, and then walk back in." We played this scene many times while we also discussed the things that Wayne liked to do. By the end of the session Wayne was enjoying the pretend play, even making comments to the plastic dog ("Hi dog. Good dog. Be a good dog"). After about twelve weeks of treatment, Wayne no longer trembled at the sight or sound of a dog and would pet a small dog if his parents were near.

As you can see, there is no special magic to the Four-R method. It is a straightforward approach to preventing common fears from becoming more serious, one that every parent should learn.

Helping the Shy Child

The Four-R (reason, reassurance, relaxation, and reenactment) approach is also useful in helping the shy child. Assume that all shy children continue to have some degree of separation anxiety. Being away from their parents makes them feel almost as though their parents have disappeared from the face of the earth. Some parents combat this problem by taking their preschooler to work and showing him where they are when the child is in school.

Relaxation techniques will also help the shy child. Teach your child to take three steps forward when she is afraid to do something new and to take a very deep, slow breath after each step. This will have the combined effect of bringing her physically closer to the situation that is making her nervous and also keeping her anxious feelings in check.

Finally, you should rehearse new situations with the shy child, just as you would rehearse a situation with a child suffering from a more specific fear. If your child is afraid of going to a birthday party, have a pretend party first, perhaps using stuffed animals as the guests. Talk very concretely about what will happen. (You may even want to talk beforehand to the mother of the child having the birthday to find out if there will be anything unusual, like clowns or magicians, that might be upsetting to your child.) Help your child organize the time sequence of the party in his mind. Let him think about who will be there. This type of cognitive rehearsal is very helpful for shy children at any age. It stimulates the thinking part of the brain to wrest control back from the emotional part of the brain, preventing fears from escalating.

Computers Can Help

An increasing number of computer programs are described as "virtual" environments, because they mimic the sights and sounds of the real world. But even though they are realistic, they are not real, and so they provide an ideal environment to help people overcome their fears. For nearly a decade, sophisticated computers have been used to create virtual environments allowing psychologists to desensitize patients to their fears of bridges, tunnels, and airplanes, without actually taking them to the site of the feared object.

Although they are designed purely as entertainment, several computer programs for children can accomplish this same trick of the mind, by recreating an environment that has the sights and sounds that trigger the child's fears. A program I have recommended to help children overcome fears is *Pajama Sam and Who's Afraid of the Dark?* (Humongous Entertainment), designed for three- to seven-year-olds. Pajama Sam is a cartoon character who conquers his fear of the darkness by pretending to be a superhero. The child using this engaging program, replete with frightening sounds and visual effects, must help the character of Sam by solving a variety of puzzles and, not coincidentally, face his own fears.

SCHOOL-AGE CHILDREN

KEY TO PREVENTION: STRENGTHEN SOCIAL SKILLS AND KEEP CHILDREN INVOLVED IN ACTIVITIES

The fears of children in this age grroup reflect their growing aware-ness, socialization, and exposure to media. At five years, typical fears include animals, "bad people," separation, and bodily harm. From six to nine years, supernatural beings, darkness, bodily injury, thunder and lightning, and staying alone are common fears. Between nine and twelve, children start worrying about tests, school performance, bodily injury, social rejection, and death.

Fears and anxieties are a much more common problem in child-hood than many people realize. About 13 percent of children between ages nine and thirteen have diagnosable anxiety disorders. We can assume that many more children have subclinical problems, which may not need treatment but will nonetheless affect their emotional well-being. Only a small fraction of these children will get any professional help for their fears and anxieties, so it is up to you to use the interventions that can prevent this common problem from causing any long-term harm.

Fears that occur in midchildhood can have a particularly trou-blesome effect on children's development, negatively influencing their academic studies, social success, and ultimately their sense of self-worth. You can prevent fears from generalizing to your child's school experience or his role in peer groups by recognizing the cause of the fears and working with your child's school to provide experiences that will stimulate his development in spite of his fears.

Tony was a large boy for age six, but in spite of his appear-ance he was afraid of many things. He hadn't had any particular problem attending kindergarten, and in fact seemed to enjoy it, but now that he was in first grade, he never wanted to go to school. His parents thought that he didn't like the structured day or the pressure of the competitiveness in the reading groups (some of the children were much more advanced), but there was noth-ing they could do about it. As the weeks went by, things didn't improve, and Tony would start each day teary-eyed, begging his parents to let him stay home. They considered home-schooling him for a few years, but they didn't know how they could manage without two incomes. Tony's father urged him just to "grin and bear it," but he could see that this advice was meaningless to his son.

There are different reasons that some school-age children are particularly fearful, but most kids who exhibit this behavior tend to focus their fears on the school environment and the hours they spend there as opposed to the time spent at home. Many children are simply over-anxious about being away from their parents. Their fear of separation is much more extreme than the separation anxiety that typically occurs in infants from seven to nine months and again in toddlers from eighteen months to three years. The anxiety younger children feel over being away from their parents goes away after a brief adjustment period, but with older children it does not diminish over time. Younger children experience the fear of being separated from their parents as a "fear of the moment," a fear that sets in only when it is time to actually leave their parents. But fearful older children may worry about being separated from their parents even if a separation is not imminent. Even when they are with their parents, they may worry in anticipation of being away from them the next day.

Not only are many of these children concerned about their own well-being, but they also worry that something will happen to their parents while they are apart. In extreme cases children will even follow their parents around the house when they are home, and resist going to sleep because they cannot keep an eye on their parents. Many children with a separation, anxiety disorder in mid-childhood will complain about physical symptoms (stomachaches, headaches, and so on) when they're away from their parents. As serious as these symptoms are in children, they portend more serious future consequences. Nearly 50 percent of adults who have panic disorders in adulthood report that they had a separation-anxiety disorder as children.

Other children are not so worried about being away from their parents, but rather they are afraid of interacting with other children. Children with social phobias are extraordinarily self-conscious, terrified that they will do something wrong and be humiliated. In the most extreme forms of social phobia, children actually refuse to speak around people who are not family members, because they are so concerned that they will say the wrong thing.

A third group of children have what psychologists call a "generalized anxiety disorder." These children seem to be anxious about almost everything. Although this is not as common a problem in children as it is in adults, it is still believed to occur more frequently than we once thought. A child with generalized anxiety might worry about how she will respond if she is invited to a party, what she will say when she accepts the invitation, and what people will expect of her once she gets there. These children are often bright and perfectionistic, and may have symptoms of other disorders as well.

Unfortunately, many parents see their children's excessive worry as "silly" or "babyish" behavior and try to talk them out of it or simply demand that they "grow up." Usually this just serves to make things worse.

Whatever the reason for a school-age child's fears and anxieties, the most serious consequences are poor school performance and social isolation. Fearful children look for any excuse to stay home from school and are prone to frequent headaches and stomachaches. The time they do spend in school can be constant suffering. Fearful and anxious children avoid contact with both the teacher and other students and will try to fade into the background as much as possible. They dread any activity that will call specific attention to them, such as reading a report out loud or participating in a school play. Many times these children will pretend they don't know an answer to a question for fear of being called upon. As you might expect, fearful and anxious children rarely fulfill their potential in school. They worry excessively about tests and written reports, and as a result often perform below expectations. In trying to avoid attention, they typically don't get their fair share of encouragement from teachers, who are prone to spending more time with more outgoing students. Because they avoid risk, these children may not participate in special projects or extracurricular activities that could enhance their educational experience.

A fearful child's reluctance to being with other children is almost as problematic as his difficulties with school. Psychologists view the ages between six and twelve as an important window of opportunity for children to learn the social skills involved in making and keeping friends. Certainly this is the most important area where shy children need help. As any psychologist will tell you, it is always easier to teach a new skill than to modify a problem, so you will likely be more successful teaching your child how to make a friend than teaching him "not to fear people." This form of prevention is also a much more positive approach to parenting.

AN OUNCE OF PREVENTION

Prevention programs that teach shy children to be socially successful break skills down into specific areas, then further break them down into small steps. What does this mean? Take as an example showing your child how to make a new friend:

- To begin with, have your child think of two or three children her age whom she would like to have for a friend.

- Ask her what she likes about these children.

- Ask her to describe in detail the activities that they might do together.

- Talk to your child about how she might invite one of these children to do an activity with her. Discuss this in great detail, for it gives your child the chance to rehearse in her own mind what she will say and do.

- Probably your child will want to telephone her potential new friend. Help her find the phone number. Talk with her about the times that she could schedule an activity. Think of several alternatives. Rehearse in advance what she might say.

- Now it is time to make the call. Sit near your child for support while she makes the call. Don't be surprised if the call is very short; holding a give-and-take conversation is another social skill that must be learned.

- If your child is successful in making an activity date, continue to talk about it and plan what will happen. This is a tremendously important step for a shy child.

- If your child is not successful, talk about why that might have happened. Don't try to comfort her unduly or let her see it as a failure. Simply encourage her to try again.

You should keep in mind that many shy children are more comfortable with slightly younger children, and with other quiet children. If you can, steer your shy child toward a play date with this type of child.

Outgoing children do not have a problem in picking up social skills, but shy and fearful children seem to lack "social intuition." They may be so preoccupied with their own anxiety or fear of embarrassment that they miss important social cues from others. The important thing to remember is that shy children learn from experience. This is really the only way they will overcome their shyness and prevent it from becoming a lifelong problem. If you give in to your child's stated desire to play by herself and avoid activities with other children, you are denying her the pleasure and stimulation that can only come from a peer group.

Don't Let a Child's Fearfulness Prevent Normal Childhood Activities

It is not an easy task to help shy and fearful children spend time with other children; however, it is an important step in helping them overcome their fears. Encourage your child to spend at least one part of the weekend with other children, even if you have to make all the arrangements yourself. Generally speaking, shy children do better with children who have very similar interests, and they do better in pairs than in groups.

Offer Books on the Subject

Books about children who have overcome their fears or shyness can also be very helpful for fearful children, a technique psychologists call "bibliotherapy." Ask your child's school librarian for recommendations.

Let Your Child See Your Friendship Skills

Be a good role model for your child. Let him see how you enjoy friendships and social activities. This might be particularly difficult for you if you are shy yourself, but there will be benefits for both you and your child. When your child is in the room, arrange to meet a friend for lunch. If a friend is busy or cancels, explain to your child that sometimes things come up and that you don't take them personally. Host a small get-together and encourage your child to invite a friend "for him" or to help you by taking coats or filling water glasses. Allow him to see and hear the pleasures of easy conversation, even if he isn't joining in.

Enlist the Aid of Your School

There are many reasons it is important to communicate with teachers about the needs of your shy and fearful child. Your child's teacher spends much more time than you do in the child's peer-oriented culture. She also has a great deal of influence in terms of encouraging your child to take new risks. Because she is more objective, she is also less likely to see fearfulness or shyness as a solvable problem. Finally, if she is an experienced teacher, she will probably have had many fearful and timid students pass through her classes and should know how best to help them. Here are some of the techniques that teachers and school counselors often recommend for fearful school-age children. You may wish to share this list with your teacher at your next conference.

Peer tutoring

Not only is this a good way to teach social skills, it is a good way to learn them. Shy students typically do best tutoring children a year or two younger or being tutored by students a year or two older.

Either way, peer tutoring provides a structured experience in which students can relate to each other, which is much less threatening to fearful children than unstructured activities.

Changing the classroom environment

The teacher may seat a fearful child with friendlier or quiet class-mates, or assign them together for special projects. Sometimes teachers make the mistake of pairing a shy child with an outgoing one, assuming that the extroverted child will act as a role model, but generally shy children do best with children who are similar to themselves.

Minimize stress or embarrassment

Most teachers are careful, if it can be helped, not to cause additional stress to a shy child. It is often useful to talk to a child about an upcoming activity that might be stressful. Teachers should not, however, excuse fearful students from activities that are difficult for them.

Emphasize cooperative classroom activities

Cooperative learning activities are helpful for all students. In these activities each student has a particular assignment that contributes to the whole project. Cooperative activities encourage groups of children to include every member of the group, and to value each member's contribution equally.

Social-Skills Training

Many schools offer programs for teaching social skills that have proven to be of great benefit to students. Such groups typically work on one or two skills at each meeting. These might include: how to greet others, how to speak on the telephone, and how to make assertive requests (e.g., "Can I play, too?"). Again, it is worth noting that shy and fearful children should be in a group of students similar to themselves to optimize their learning. Talk to your school's counselor or school psychologist to see if he or she will lead a social-skills training group.

TEENAGERS

KEY TO PREVENTION: DON'T ALLOW TEENS TO NARROW THEIR LIFE CHOICES PREMATURELY

Teens fears can range from global to extremely personal issues, including: political or environmental problems, problems in the home, rejection because of personal appearance, and academic and social failure. Shyness is by far the most common expression of fear in the teen years.

As I've said, shyness is a temperament we can see very early in life and throughout childhood, but its prevalence jumps about 10 percent in the teenage years, when shyness may take its greatest toll. Giving shy teens extra help will encourage them to meet the social challenges of adolescence and will aid in their transition into adulthood.

Chronic shyness affects an estimated 35 to 40 percent of children and adults, but that number may rise to as much as 50 percent in the teenage years. Shyness, as mentioned earlier, is broadly defined as the fear of being negatively evaluated and rejected by others, so it should come as no surprise that this is a common trait in the rapidly changing teenage years. Shy teenagers avoid talking because they do not want to reveal their feelings or ideas. They may be afraid of activities in which they think that their behavior will lead to embarrassment. When confronted by situations in which they must talk, a shy teenager may show obvious signs of physical distress, such as perspiring and blushing, and may complain of physical problems like a headache or a stomachache.

Not only do shy children and teens behave differently, but researchers tell us that they also think differently from their peers. It seems to be a part of human nature that most of us take credit for our success but attribute our failure to others. Shy children and teens tend to do the opposite. They discount their achievements, and even if they get good grades or are praised by a teacher, it somehow "doesn't count." Success does little to boost their self-confidence. They can be devastated by an offhand remark or a perceived social slight. They are hypersensitive to criticism and rarely let a negative remark or even a look go unnoticed. It is almost as if these adolescents seek out the cues that could be interpreted as criticism or rejection.

Of course shyness, which is considered a type of social phobia, comes in many different gradations, from the sixteen-year-old boy who is afraid to ask a girl for a date to the eighteen-year-old girl who won't attend her own graduation because she would have to go up onstage to receive her diploma. Shy people tend to have high expectations for themselves and low self-esteem—a combination that virtually guarantees a negative experience.

The typical shy teen is an introvert: quiet, self-deprecating, always trying to direct attention to someone or something else. Shyness has its greatest effect on these teens in the form of missed social opportunities, and a narrowing of their view of life at a time when it should be expansive. Ironically, extroverts can also be shy. Jimmy Carter and Johnny Carson are just two examples of people who have thrived in the public limelight but are self-described shy people. Shy extroverts don't tend to miss as many developmental opportunities as introverts, but they do suffer needlessly with the emotional distress caused by constant self-criticism and a feeling of never being good enough.

The repercussions of shyness for teens are powerful, yet many people view it as an innocuous personality trait. It is not.

When left untreated, shyness has even more serious consequences as teenagers become young adults. Socially shy students have painful thoughts and feelings and experience difficulty with friendships and intimate relationships. Although shyness and grade-point average are uncorrelated in high school, shyness does present many obstacles to later achievement. Shy students are less likely to utilize guidance counselors or other resources for career and college planning. When it comes to interviews, shy students predictably come across as insecure and even uninterested.

Excessive shyness can also be a symptom of serious mental illnesses, such as clinical depression. Since shy people are less prone to seek professional advice or even to ask for help from family or friends, the problem is likely to become severe before it is finally treated.

AN OUNCE OF PREVENTION

The parents of shy and fearful teens may find themselves in an unusual predicament compared to the parents of outgoing teens. They may feel that they are too involved in the lives of their adolescents, because when teenagers avoid social situations and have difficulty making friends, they may become more emotionally dependent on their parents than is typical for this age.

The parents' role in helping teens learn to meet the challenges of the world involves a delicate balancing act, pushing them toward age-appropriate experiences, without creating additional pressure that will cause more anxiety and distress. The suggestions listed below will help you support your shy teen in the short run and provide an internalized value system in the long run. Shyness is overcome slowly—it may take months before you notice even a small change—but you can give your teenager a platform of experiences and values that will guide him for years to come.

Model Friendliness

By definition, shy teens have a hard time making friends. They don't reach out to others, and they give off not-so-subtle messages that they don't want anyone to approach them. It is important to remember that this is not intentional. Shy teens aren't aware of their mostly nonverbal messages, perhaps even wondering why they are never approached. Just as you might for a school-age child, allow your teen to hear you issue invitations to your own friends, or see you in other social situations. Let her hear you make sympathetic remarks to a troubled friend or express joy for another. If you're out in the world with your teen and need directions, walk over to an appropriate person (a policeman or shopkeeper) and ask for help. Let your teen see you take "social risks" and learn that these are not really risks at all.

Shy teens are careful observers and can learn to develop social skills simply by watching. Don't work too hard at this. Just make sure that you are giving your teenager a consistent message through your own behavior that an openness and enthusiasm toward others can bring immediate rewards.

Offer Tips on Basic Communication

Even if your adolescent doesn't ask for it, volunteer some suggestions to make conversations start and flow more easily. Tell her to try the following:

- Use the environment for cues. Comment on something you observe. "This room is way too crowded!" or "Those cookies look delicious."

- Ask open-ended questions. Asking a person questions that require more than a yes-or-no answer will make it easier for you to find something to say back. "You went on the ski trip, right? Tell me about it." or "So how are the play rehearsals going?"

- Carry a prop. Either wear something unusual (a piece of funky jewelry) or carry something interesting (an instrument in its case). That way you give others something to say to you— "Where did you get that necklace?" or "Oh, I didn't know you played the clarinet!"—which will in turn give you a chance to respond.

- Compliment someone. Everyone loves to feel admired. If you say something flattering to someone, he or she will immediately warm up to you, making it far more relaxing to just stand and talk.

Even if your teen manages to use only one of these techniques, it may be enough. Most people are aware of how hard it is for shy teens to make friends and will positively respond to even the smallest effort.

Encourage Activities with People Who Share a Common Interest

The first friendships that children make, usually between the ages of three and five, are based on common interests. From a developmental perspective, this is the context within which friendship skills are learned, so it is a natural place to start with a teenager who is socially isolated. Encourage your teen to find groups that share his interests, whatever they may be (see "Computers Can Help" below).

Since shyness correlates with empathy and altruism, your shy teenager may be motivated to join a community-service group, working for local or national causes. The other volunteers in this group are likely to be just the type of people who will reach out to a shy teen and make him feel included and valuable.

Help Your Teen Practice Dealing with Frightening Situations

Shy teens should not be pushed into social situations in which they feel uncomfortable, but many times these are unavoidable. Teenagers may be required to make a presentation in front of a class, perform a solo on a musical instrument, or share a room on an overnight class trip with someone they don't know. Role-playing situations with your teen may seem a little awkward, but it really helps. As noted earlier in this chapter, rehearsing a feared situation in a protected environment is a form of desensitization, and it's the single most effective strategy for treating fears and phobias. Have your son play his piano piece after you introduce him to your empty living room. Pretend that you and your daughter are sitting on a bus, and help her practice starting up different conversations on varying topics.

Encourage Your Teen to Develop a Special Skill or Talent

Since we know that social phobias are linked to self-worth, anything you can think of doing to build a teen's confidence will also address social anxiety. It really doesn't matter what the skill or talent may be—obviously the choice must be your teenager's—but you should find as many ways as you can to support this interest. Not only will it likely put him in touch with other young people, but it will give him something to talk about and share.

Know When to Seek Professional Counseling

Because shyness is so common, most shy teens will probably not get professional help, but when symptoms are severe, you must intervene. Teens do not outgrow extreme social phobia, and, left untreated, it will develop into a lifelong burden, becoming more entrenched with each passing year. These are some of the symptoms that should be a cause for immediate concern:

- Your teenager has no friends at all and shows no interest in making them.

- Your teenager is bothered by his shyness but can't find any way to deal with it.

- Your teenager rarely smiles or laughs.

- Your teenager shows a genuine fear of people, manifesting physical symptoms and extreme anxiety.

- Your teenager resists leaving the house.

Computers Can Help

Technology has created a double-edged sword in helping children and teens learn social skills. On the one hand, it tempts people to be more isolated than ever. A computer screen cannot convey laughter, a human touch, or all the other nuances that create true human intimacy. Yet for shy people the computer also removes many aspects of rejection. Because computer users communicate primarily in a text-based environment (at least for now), research studies show that shy people don't have the same fear of being evaluated or rejected when they're conversing on the Internet. Some studies suggest that confidence gained by practicing social interaction on the Internet carries over to real-life situations.

There are, of course, thousands of chat rooms on the Internet where teenagers can meet and build cyber-relationships, and this method of communication seems to appeal to teens more than any other age group. As one fifteen-year-old put it, "Before I was on-line, I must say I was a lost child. I've grown so much, because I was able to talk openly to people. No one on-line thinks about your age or eye color or skin color or anything. They see you from the inside." One seventeen-year-old I know participates in three chat rooms: one for teens in her town, one for teens getting ready to go to college, and one "virtual teen mall," where anyone is likely to show up.

As I've mentioned, volunteering for community service seems to be a particularly appealing way for teens to develop their social skills, seeing that there is a higher purpose and reason for what is still a challenge for them. The Internet provides many places for teens to learn about volunteering, but I would particularly recommend a site called Serviceleader.org, sponsored by the Center for Volunteerism and Community Engagement, where teens can find volunteering opportunities, get guidelines for choosing the right volunteering opportunity, and even learn how to be a "virtual" volunteer, performing volunteer service from a home computer. A word of caution: always make sure that you know what Internet sites your teens are visiting. There are dangers on the Internet just as there are in the real world. Your awareness of your teen's activities is the best way to insure his or her safety.

• • •

Fears are a normal part of every child's development, but some children are predisposed to allowing their fears to act as a filter for their experience of the world. The key is prompt action. A fearful temperament can be detected very early in life, but with the right kind of interventions it can likely be overcome. Since fears are so common in preschool-age children, this is a good time to teach children specific ways to master their fears. This will give them a sense of power and control that may ward off many future problems. Above all, parents must guard against allowing their child's fears to carry over from the home into the school and into their child's social development. The earlier that social fears are confronted, the less they will affect a child's sense of competence and self-worth.

6

Preventing Problems in Sexuality, Personal Relationships, and Gender Identity

We are more than thirty years past the so-called sexual revolution. Sexual repression is the exception rather than the rule. Birth control is widely available. Gender discrimination is against the law. But in many ways it seems as if we have traded one set of problems for another. Child pornography is a huge underground industry. Incidents of child sexual abuse are increasing. New forms of sexually transmitted diseases, including the life-threatening HIV virus, endanger our teens.

One thing that hasn't changed very much in the last three decades is that parents are still uncomfortable talking about sex with their children. We know that sexuality is a normal part of life, and that sometimes it can bring great pleasure and other times be part of a serious problem. We know that we are supposed to talk openly with our children in order for them to feel comfortable bringing sensitive issues to us. But that knowledge doesn't seem to help many parents find it easier to talk, much less act, with confidence.

The fact remains, however, that educating our children is the only effective means of preventing both the continuation of problems from generations past and the appearance of new ones.

Parents need to talk to their children about sex, gender roles, and relationships. They need to talk about masturbation, inappropriate touching, menstruation, nocturnal emissions, petting, sexual intercourse, date rape, and sexually transmitted diseases. They need to talk about how to treat others with respect, how to be comfortable with one's sexual identity, how to recognize sexual exploitation, how to show love, how to create intimacy, and much more. When we fail to talk about these issues, we deprive our children of some of the most important information affecting their lives.

Children have lots of questions about sex and sexuality throughout their development, but many parents are so uncomfortable with these questions that they subtly give their children the message that "it's better not to ask." But without a good education and a healthy attitude, children are at risk for many problems, both physical and psychological.

It is difficult to pinpoint why even the most enlightened parents can have a hard time talking about sex to their children. Up until the 1970s American parents traditionally raised their children in a very restrictive environment, where sexuality was treated as a deep secret and every opportunity was sought to avoid the subject. Our culture has become much more permissive around sexual issues in the last thirty years, and some might argue that the pendulum has swung too far. But parents still carry the legacy of being uncomfortable talking about sex with children, a legacy they inherited from their parents and grandparents. In today's complex culture our silence can only be a disservice to our children.

Think about the last time you talked about sexuality with your child or the last time that you talked about your child's self-image as a boy or girl. Consider the last time you talked about how boys and girls—men and women—should treat each other. If you can't remember these conversations clearly, it has been too long. Now is the time to start.

RISK FACTORS FOR PROBLEMS IN SEXUALITY AND GENDER IDENTITY

Like most of the problems discussed in this book, psychological conflicts regarding sexuality and gender roles can be placed on a continuum from the very mild to the very serious. All children have minor problems at some time in their development. They might be embarrassed about their developing bodies. They may feel uncomfortable about their first feelings of infatuation. They might be teased about misconceptions they have about sex. But there are also more serious problems that children or teens might encounter, such as child abuse, early sexual experiences, teenage pregnancy, sexual harassment, and sexually transmitted diseases. Problems having to do with intimacy are abstract and may be hard to recognize, but they are also an important factor in your child's future happiness.

Children can develop difficulties in sharing, loving, respecting, and even simply protecting themselves from hurt. All of our children will inevitably feel the pain of rejection by a loved one or the disappointment of a relationship that is ending. But do you want your grown children to make problems with intimacy a lifelong pattern? The earlier you pay attention to children who lack the skills to build strong close relationships, the better. From a developmental perspective, the years between seven and twelve appear to be critical for children to find their first "best friend," a testing ground where children learn the basics of how to develop an intimate relationship. Children who have not been able to form close one-on-one relationships by the time they enter adolescence will be more at risk for having problems with both same-sex and opposite-sex relationships as they age.

The problems mentioned in this chapter can be life-changing, even life-shattering, but in most cases they are preventable. Parents can begin by assessing whether or not their children are at risk, and if so, take immediate steps to reduce foreseeable dangers.

Permissive Parenting

For the first part of the century, overly punitive and restrictive attitudes about sex were seen as the cause for many sexual problems. Young children were routinely punished for masturbating. Girls who expressed their sexual urges as teenagers were considered "sluts" and a disgrace to their family. Although a double standard existed for boys, they were expected to keep any sexual behavior a discreet secret or face the consequences of social ostracism.

Today the more common risk factor is parents who are too permissive about their children's sexual development. Permissive parents do not act as a buffer between their children and the inappropriate sexual messages that are all around them, nor do they educate their children about potential harm. Permissive parents may think it is cute that their seven-year-old has started to wear makeup and dress in provocative clothes. They may not call to find out if there is adult supervision at a twelve-year-old's party. They may feel that it is none of their business if they find condoms in the drawer of their sixteen-year-old son. But in today's culture, turning one's head and not addressing this not only increases the possibility that children will be exposed to inappropriate sexual behavior, but it will cause parents to miss important opportunities to help their children learn values and appropriate emotional and social skills.

Sex is omnipresent in our society. Daytime talk shows routinely broadcast programs on teenage prostitution, transvestism, underage strippers, and much more. As early as 9:00 P.M., children can watch cable-TV series like *Sex and the City* that show partial nudity and discuss every aspect of sexuality in detail. Attempts to provide ratings for movies and television have been championed by children's advocates but have met with only lukewarm reception by most parents. Movies rated PG-13 are routinely attended by children as young as seven and eight. The much-heralded installation of chips in new televisions that would allow parents to block specific shows have been virtually ignored by parents.

It is not just that permissive parents allow their children to be exposed to sexuality at too early an age, but that many parents have also abdicated their responsibility for teaching children their own values about sexuality. Many parents feel that their children will learn about sex in school or from their peers. But while health-education classes may address the basic issues of sex education, they cannot teach children right from wrong. And while you can rely on the fact that children will hear sexual jokes from their friends, you certainly can't rely on your child's peer group to point out that these same jokes might be offensive to some people and hurtful to others.

Permissive parents may also fail to teach their children about gender respect. In the last few years we have heard many stories about boys as young as five or six harassing girls of the same age or younger. Among teenagers, sexual harassment can become much more aggressive, from teasing and taunting to date rape.

Few would argue that the antidote for these alarming trends must come in the early years. Children must be taught not to call other people names or treat them with disrespect because they look or act different. They must be taught not to touch another person in "private" areas or act in other ways that might be offensive.

They also must be taught to not exclude anyone from play merely because that child is a boy or a girl and to show respect and good manners to everyone. When parents fail to teach their children about sex and gender roles, they create a void in which misinformation can have a devastating influence.

A "Sexualized" Relationship in the Home

On the extreme end of permissiveness, the boundary between adults' and children's sexuality becomes blurred. I'm not talking about overt sexual abuse, but rather about parent-child relationships where the boundaries are not clear, confusing children and almost always creating unnecessary anxiety.

Over the last twenty years I have had dozens of parents surprise me with questions about how to handle their children's sexual curiosity or sexual behavior, questions I would have thought could be answered with a modicum of common sense:

- A mother of a three-year-old boy wondered whether she should stop taking baths with her son because he seemed to be getting aroused.

- A newly divorced father sought my opinion about his seven-year-old daughter, who wanted to sleep in his bed when she came over for weekend visits.

- A mother walked in on her five-year-old son and a six-year-old neighbor simulating sexual intercourse on the bed. She closed the door and then knocked before she reentered, but she wanted to know if she should have said anything to these children.

In each of these cases the parents were confused by their children's natural sexual expression and unsure of their own responsibility to provide clear guidance and set appropriate limits.

Unfortunately, some parents don't see the harm in developing "romantic" relationships with their children. A single mother goes out on a "date" with her eight-year-old son on Saturday night. A father continually takes the side of his ten-year-old daughter against his wife. Children need their parents to draw the line between what is an appropriate expression of love and affection and what is not. When parents treat their children in an overly romantic or sexualized fashion, they set them up for a lifetime of self-doubt and confusion about limits and trust.

Parents need to talk about sex at the appropriate developmental time. But they also need to guide their children toward appropriate sexual behavior and set clear standards about what is and isn't suitable.

Early Puberty

Another potential risk factor for sexual problems in childhood and adolescents is early puberty in girls. The average age of a girl's first menstruation, or menarche, is twelve and a half, but although this is the most obvious sign of maturation, it actually occurs relatively late in the process of puberty. Many girls begin showing signs of hormonal changes as early as eight or nine. Because puberty generally occurs about two years earlier in girls than in boys, a girl who develops a "womanly" figure earlier than her peers may be teased or ridiculed by her classmates, boys as well as girls. Aside from being hurt by the ridicule of their peers, girls who go through early puberty may be drawn to premature sexual experiences, as they seek approval from older adolescents. Researchers have also shown that the physical changes of puberty are accompanied by cognitive changes as well. When compared with girls of the same age who have not had their first menstruation, postmenarcheal girls report thinking more about sex and dating. They even make drawings of themselves with makeup, jewelry, and breasts, in direct contrast to the simple stick figures of the premenarcheal girls.

Poor Role Models for Intimacy and Healthy Relationships

It is very important that parents model relationships that include respect and a willingness to work on problems in an honest, civil, and loving way. Children learn a great deal about what they can expect as they get older by watching their parents interact. Recurring expressions of anger or even subtle disrespect will take their toll on how children perceive a love relationship. Often their later choice of a partner reflects the same pattern they observed in their parents. A girl brought up in a house where a domineering father presides over the family may find herself drawn to domineering men. Similarly, a boy who sees his mother as passive may grow up to expect this kind of behavior in his own wife and feel hurt and betrayed if he doesn't get it. Sometimes men and women consciously look for mates who are the opposite of their parents. But this is far from a guarantee of compatibility, nor is it a good way to start an intimate relationship.

Certainly a divorce can cause a child to question the joys that intimate relationships bring, just as much as observing a hostile marriage can. But whether parents decide to stay together or separate, there are still ways they can prevent their children from suffering from the detrimental effects of their decision. I will discuss this further in Chapter 8.

Gender Orientation

Finally we must examine the possibility that a child's gender orientation may be a risk factor. Although neither parents nor professionals talk much about gender orientation in prepubescent children, scientists are rapidly coming to the conclusion that gender orientation in boys may be linked to a region on the X chromosome, inherited from the mother. This does not mean that there is a "gay gene," but rather that genes could shape the parts of the brain that orchestrate sexual behavior, possibly producing a temperament that predisposes a boy toward homosexuality.

Whatever the exact genetic mechanism, we do believe that a child's gender identity is formed very early in life, probably between the ages of two and four. Psychologists identify children who may have conflicts in gender orientation when they:

- Don't show strong preference for gender-specific toys

- Don't play gender-specific games

- Express the wish to have the physical sex characteristics of the opposite sex

- Have a persistent interest in wearing clothes of the opposite sex

- Have romantic fantasies and dreams about members of the same sex

- Have an attraction to the physical characteristics of the same sex and are uninterested in the opposite sex

In a perfect world, gender orientation would not be considered a risk factor any more than skin color, but no one today believes that we are anywhere close to being either color- or gender-blind. There is still a great deal of prejudice against people who have anything other than a heterosexual orientation, even though gay men and women make up a substantial part of the population. Gender-orientation issues in children raise questions about both values and ethics in parents and professionals, but these issues must be addressed. It is unlikely that parents can influence their child's adult gender orientation even if they want to, but they certainly can help their child learn to understand his or her sexual identity, and possibly prevent the emotional pain that can come when children and teenagers feel "different" from everyone else. Whether gender orientation makes parents uncomfortable or not, ignorance and denial are the true risk factors.

INFANTS

KEY TO PREVENTION: AVOID FALLING INTO PATTERNS OF EARLY GENDER STEREOTYPES

The first eighteen months of life are a time of self-discovery, when your baby will learn about all the pleasures of the senses, including the sense of touch. Babies will "discover" that their genitals are pleasing to touch, just as it is pleasing to put objects in their mouths or fingers in their ears.

Infants don't need to be educated about "sexuality," but it isn't too early to start thinking about your children's sexual identity.

The child's gender is the first thing that parents talk about—often years before conception. In most cultures boys are considered the more valuable gender—though there are exceptions. In Polynesia a baby girl is decorated with shells, and her birth is the occassion for great festivities, while the birth of a boy is not considered a cause for celebration.

In America there is much more initial acceptance of the gender of a child than in many cultures, but there is still a strong preference for boys. Research studies show that when mothers are asked before the birth of their child about their gender preferences, most say that they don't care, as long as the baby is healthy. But according to one study, after the baby is born, 93 percent of mothers of boys said that they were happy with the sex of their baby, compared with 56 percent of the mothers of girls.

Regardless of their initial preferences, parents from very early on go to great lengths to convey the gender of their child to the world. Girls, of course, traditionally wear pink, and boys wear blue. Girls are more likely to be outfitted with some signs of femininity, like a bow in their hair, while boys will usually be dressed in bold primary colors. Toys and room decor also typically reflect a child's gender, both in colors and in themes.

Do these outward trappings really make a difference? Probably. Adults definitely alter their behaviors depending on a child's sex. They talk more to infant girls and bounce and roughhouse more with infant boys.

In one series of experiments adults were asked to make assumptions about a baby they were shown on videotape. Although it was always the same baby, in some experiments the baby was dressed as a girl and in others as a boy. In nearly every experiment the adults viewed the baby as having sex-stereotyped behaviors, drawing conclusions based on their own biases rather than on the behaviors they were actually watching.

The implications of this research are significant, suggesting that most parents unconsciously treat children according to gender stereotypes even though the stated values of our culture are that girls and boys—women and men—should be treated equally. In one study, two thousand mothers and fathers were asked, "What kind of person would you want your son or daughter to become?" Both parents gave responses indicating higher career expectations for their sons than for their daughters, with fathers demonstrating this attitude more frequently than mothers. Parents listed "hardworking" and "ambitious" as traits they wished for their sons twice as often as they listed them for their daughters.

Even if your child is just a baby, it isn't too soon to think about how gender stereotypes might affect his or her development.

AN OUNCE OF PREVENTION

When it comes to the "sex education" of infants, parents have little to do but accept and delight in their children's physical awakening. In terms of prevention, this is a time for parents to think twice about the stereotypes they carry with them and pay more attention to nuance. As we have already learned, babies can be tiny divining rods for a parent's thoughts. Certainly not everything is within your control when it comes to sex roles, but there is a lot you can influence.

I often think of the story told to me by a female psychologist who wanted to raise her son in an environment free of gender biases. When she brought him a doll at fourteen months, along with a toy truck, he immediately threw the doll into a toy chest and played with the truck for the rest of the day and every day thereafter. For weeks she persisted in trying to teach him to rock or feed the baby doll; the most he would do was take it for a ride on his truck. "Eventually," she reported, "I just gave up. I figured that he was going to turn out as nature intended whether I liked it or not." Her early intentions were good, but she neglected to see that while certain types of gender-oriented behaviors, including a young child's choice of toys, seem to be genetically loaded, there are many ways to address gender stereotypes and biases. These opportunities begin when children are very young and continue throughout their development.

Children look to both the same-sex parent and the opposite-sex parent to serve as role models at different times in their development, but the opposite-sex parent is commonly more important. Developmentally, boys "rehearse" their male behaviors with their mothers, and girls rehearse their female behaviors with their fathers.

Be Aware of the Special Influence That Fathers Have on Their Daughters

In his book *How to Father a Successful Daughter*, Nicky Marone urges dads to constantly examine their attitudes about femininity, risk-taking, male superiority, and the kinds of activities and quality of time spent together. Gender roles can be so subtle in our culture that even the most "liberated" father can unintentionally treat his daughter in ways that can affect her adversely for years to come. Marone notes that while fathers understandably cultivate the traditional female behaviors—encouraging their daughters to be sweet, polite, attractive, and emotional—they should not neglect the traits that will later be important for personal and professional achievement, including being competent, taking risks, and mastering skills.

You can fight this tendency to raise daughters along the lines of cultural stereotypes by consciously spending time each day treating them as you might treat boys. Be physically playful with your daughters. Read them books about adventures and science. Teach them how to throw, catch, and kick a ball. Your baby daughter will love your attention no matter what you do, so take this opportunity to give her every advantage you can offer.

Be Aware of the Special Influence That Mothers Have on Their Sons

As discussed in Chapter 1, gender stereotypes can be a risk factor for boys as well as for girls. Boys are more likely to have early learning and behavioral problems, some of which may continue through childhood and adolescence. Mothers can teach their sons how to express and control their feelings. They can read books to their sons about characters who nurture and care for others. As in father-daughter relationships, mothers should be aware of the subtle messages they give their sons about male and female stereotypes. They shouldn't worry about making their sons "effeminate," but rather spend time teaching attributes such as kindness, sensitivity, and attentiveness.

TODDLERS AND PRESCHOOLERS

KEY TO PREVENTION: TEACHING CHILDREN ABOUT THEIR SEXUALITY

Between the ages of eighteen months and five years, children become more and more interested in sexuality and sex-role behaviors. They continue to explore their bodies and are vocal about their interest in the differences between the sexes. They like the pure joy of running around the house without clothes, as well as watching parental reactions. Overt genital stimulation typically begins around age three, after children are no longer in diapers.

Through feedback from peers and adults, children begin to feel that some body parts are okay to talk about and others are "naughty." This is the beginning of sexual taboos.

Children imitate all types of romantic behavior in doll play as well as in dramatic play. They go on pretend dates, have pretend marriages, and play doctor. This is also the age at which children begin to develop more specific gender-role behavior.

It's normal for children to exhibit many forms of sexual behavior at this age, but problems can occur when adults or even older children exploit this normal development for their own purposes.

Although sexual abuse can occur at any age, I will focus on it at this stage because this is when children are most vulnerable, and it is also the time that education about sexual privacy and appropriate touching should begin.

The exact number of children who are sexually abused is difficult to document, because the vast number of incidents go unreported. Most estimates are made long after the fact, when adults feel sufficiently distanced from the event to talk about it. A 1994 review of nineteen studies estimated that 18 percent of female adults had been sexually abused as children, and many experts think that the true incidence of abuse may be even higher.

There is no guarantee that educating your child will protect her from sexual abuse. We all wish that it were that simple. But a child who is taught about her body, her right to privacy, and the warning signs that an adult might be acting in wrong or dangerous ways will certainly be at an advantage over children who don't have this information. Not only will early sex education diminish the risk for sexual abuse, it will give you and your child a foundation to talk about the issues of sex and sexuality that will come up throughout her developing years.

AN OUNCE OF PREVENTION

Only a small percentage of children are sexually abused when they are very young. The most common age for childhood abuse is between eight and fourteen. But their increasing curiosity about sex and sexuality make this the right time to teach children about appropriate and inappropriate behaviors.

The Bathing-Suit Rule

The best-known rule that parents teach young children is the "bathing-suit rule," which states that the areas covered by your bathing suit are "private" and not to be touched by anyone unless you're being washed or examined by a medical doctor. Children should also be taught to talk about their feelings when people or situations make them uncomfortable. The abuse of young children usually occurs in small steps over time, and more serious incidents can often be prevented when children know that they can talk openly about whatever they feel.

Anticipate Problems

Between the ages of two and five, children should be helped to understand that although there are many dangers in the adult world, there is no need to worry if they are aware of them and take certain precautions. Dangers regarding the sexual exploitation of children should be included when you teach the safety rules for traffic, fire, and water.

You should rehearse with your young child the behavioral skills she will need to feel safe and secure. Practice having her say no to pretend strangers. Make sure that she knows who her support people are, so that she can go to them if she is worried or anxious about a particular situation. You should always encourage your child to talk about what worries her, particularly when an adult makes her feel uncomfortable by the way that he treats or touches her.

Be Aware of the Signs of Abuse

As mentioned, child sexual abuse typically happens slowly, over time, but children may be unaware that something wrong is happening. Abuse typically occurs with an adult whom the child trusts, and the adult insists that the behavior should be kept as a "special secret." For this reason parents must be aware of nonverbal signs of child sexual abuse.

Older children may have physical complaints and sudden fears, and they may withdraw from family, friends, and their usual activities, but younger children often have none of these symptoms. They are more likely to reveal that they've engaged in inappropriate sexual activity through their language or through precocious sexual behavior, such as persistent sexual play with other children, with themselves, with toys or pets, or through hints, indirect comments, or statements about the abuse. Remember, however, that sexual interest and play are normal in children and do not in themselves indicate that abuse has taken place. It is worth noting that although an estimated 96 percent of child-abuse accusations are true, this also means that four out of a hundred accusations will be false. Considering the damage that a false accusation will cause—from incarceration to the loss of a job, friends, and family—always seek experienced professional advice when you are concerned.

Know What to Do If Abuse Occurs

If you believe that your child has been abused, remember the following:

- Keep calm. It's important to not act as if you are angry with your child about what happened. Children can mistakenly interpret anger or disgust as directed toward them.

- Give positive messages, such as "I know you couldn't help it" or "I'm proud of you for telling."

- Believe the child. In most circumstances children do not lie about sexual abuse.

- Explain to the child that he or she is not to blame for what happened.

- Listen to and answer the child's questions honestly.

- Respect the child's privacy. Be careful not to discuss the abuse in front of people who don't need to know what happened.

- Be responsible. Report the incident to the Department of Human Services or other appropriate authorities. They can help protect the child's safety and provide resources for further help.

- Arrange a medical exam. It can reassure you that there has been no permanent physical damage and may provide important evidence.

- Get competent professional counseling first for yourself and then, if recommended, for the child.

Help Children Develop "Gender Respect"

The days when a boy pulled a little girl's pigtails and people said that "boys will be boys" are long over. Harassment of girls or boys cannot be tolerated. Many parents teach their children general respect for other people, but remember that young children are very concrete. You must specifically make it clear that using hurtful words to tease or taunt another child is unacceptable no matter what.

Children at this age are more inclined to play with other children of the same sex, but parents don't have to tacitly sit by and let this be the rule. When you make play dates for your child, insist sometimes that a child of the opposite sex be included. Guide your child toward gender-neutral activities like arts and crafts or simple board games. Be clear about your expectations for how your children should treat the opposite sex. If a boy says, "She can't play because she's a girl, and girls don't know how to play this right," say, "That is a mean thing to say to someone. That's like calling someone a name. If I hear you say that again, you will be punished."

Help Children to Understand Sexism

Children need to be taught that sexism is a form of prejudice that cannot be tolerated at any time or in any form. Even at a young age children can be told that as unfair as it may seem, our culture does not treat men and women equally. Ask your child some questions to get him thinking, instead of just letting the gender roles our culture still assigns go unnoticed. Ask your child questions like these:

Can dads raise children just as well as moms?

Should boys and girls get paid the same amount of money for the same job?

Can men cook as well as women?

Are men and women allowed to cry?

Should girls be allowed to play football?

Explain to your child that there are people in the world who might answer these questions differently than he might, because some people really don't see men and women as equally able to do things. Let him know you think it is important to assume that boys and girls can be good at lots of the same things and that they also ought to be allowed to express feelings in the same way. A person's gender shouldn't decide what he or she can or cannot do.

SCHOOL-AGE CHILDREN

KEY TO PREVENTION: TEACHING THE RIGHT VALUES

The ages between six and twelve are the time when children first learn about the details of human sexuality and develop a value system that will guide them through their adolescence. An important part of this value system is the way children treat the opposite sex and those with different gender preferences. Whether your children learn what you want them to is largely up to you.

According to a survey by the Kaiser Family Foundation and Children Now, the majority of 880 parents questioned said that they had discussed drugs, violence, and sex with their children by the time the children had reached the age of twelve. But most parents had not gone beyond the basics. Fifty-six percent of the respondents said they had not talked about relationships or about when their children might become sexually active. Seventy-one percent said they hadn't talked about avoiding pregnancy and sexually transmitted diseases.

Yet these are just the topics that kids want and need to hear about, according to a companion survey of 348 children. Half of the ten- to twelve-year-olds said that they wanted more information about AIDS and sexually transmitted diseases, including how to protect themselves; more than one-third sought additional facts on preventing pregnancy; and nearly one-third wanted to know where to get birth control.

Parents and even psychologists have often underestimated the interest that a school-age child has in sex and sexuality. Until recently, psychologists described this as the "latency" period, a time when a young child's interest in the opposite sex goes underground, not to resurface until adolescence. We now realize that this is not the case. Children at this age are driven by their "need to know." Their increased cognitive abilities make them sponges for facts and information, and they begin to think about sexual issues at age seven or eight. They are also driven by the "need to do." To a large extent a school-age child's self-image is measured by his sense of accomplishment, and if there are things that he knows will happen in the future (like dating or facing sexual responsibilities), he may worry prematurely about whether he is prepared for these tasks. Answering your children's questions honestly and directly (although not always in explicit detail) will simultaneously satisfy their need to know and their need to be prepared.

Studies have also found that children who talked to their parents about tough topics when they were young were more likely to turn to their parents in difficult situations when they were older. It seems that sex education in the grade-school years opens the door for teenagers to talk to their parents about the pressure to have sex and/or concerns about pregnancy. This confirms what experts have been saying for many years: Talk to your children about sex long before they hit adolescence. This will create an atmosphere of open communication in your family. In a study that examined where children go to get important information, children between six and twelve listed their parents as their number-one source of information, but once they hit thirteen to fifteen, friends topped the list, followed closely by television and movies. Among teenagers, mothers were ranked a distant number five as a place to go for information, right behind school and the Internet.

AN OUNCE OF PREVENTION

Unfortunately, many parents don't feel that they are adequately prepared for their role as a sex educator. They dread the time when they will have to sit down with their children and have the "Big Talk," and often they delay this moment as long as possible. Many people say that this is the single most difficult thing they have to do as parents.

To make it an easier task, the first thing you should know is that there is no such thing as a "Big Talk," no one moment when children are suddenly enlightened about sexuality. As discussed earlier in this chapter, children begin learning about their bodies as infants, and they exhibit a sexual interest in others when they are toddlers. They often begin having "sexual" thoughts and dreams at seven and eight—even the boys who make faces when they see men and women kissing on television or the girls who band together in an "I hate boys" club. Your children will learn about sexuality from many sources, but it's your job to provide them with two essential things: clear, factual answers to their questions and an unequivocal explanation of your values regarding sexual behavior. The following are ways you can provide this important information.

Talk About Yourself

Children like to hear stories about their parents and how they handled different situations. Be honest, but give your children examples that teach them the values you want them to have. However, don't feel that your sex life is an open book to your children.

When you think about what you should tell your children, use two guidelines: your comfort level and theirs. If you feel anxious about discussing your early dating experiences, don't. Find other ways to talk about this topic. Look to your child for his or her "comfort cues." Is she fidgety and looking away from you? Is he sitting quietly and looking intrigued? Remember that you always want to be honest, but at the same time you want to be a positive role model for your children.

It's okay to say, "My first boyfriend was really cute, but I don't think he liked me very much. As soon as a new girl moved into our neighborhood, he stopped calling me. But then I just found someone else, too." It's not okay to say, "Boys are really fickle. My first boyfriend dumped me as soon as he found someone he thought was prettier. I cried and cried. I still think about it sometimes." Sweeping negative statements or stories that bring out your own problems with self-esteem can frighten and confuse your child.

Listen for Questions

Children often don't ask direct questions about sex and sexuality. They may talk about a "girl that I know" when they really want to talk about themselves. You don't need to wait until your child asks specific questions. Bring up subjects by talking about TV commercials that give the wrong messages or commenting on a book or magazine that you or your child is reading.

Decide What's Important for Your Child to Know

One of the keys to good parenting is being able to articulate your particular message to your child. You need to be clear about your views and feel comfortable expressing them. Think about the lessons you want to impart. Do you want your child to be aware of sexually transmitted diseases? Start a discussion and make it clear that this is the topic. Don't be vague. Say, "I'm concerned that you may not know all the dangers of unprotected sex. I'm sure they teach you about sexually transmitted diseases in health class, but I wonder if they cover the topic completely?"

If you don't know the answer to a question your child raises, don't be embarrassed or try to fake an answer. Just admit that you have to do a little research and will get back with some information as soon as possible. Cut out helpful articles from newspapers and magazines and share them with your child. For example, "Here is a list of the symptoms of sexually transmitted diseases that I found in an article. Do you want to look at it? It shows what to look for and what can happen if these go untreated."

Talk About the Emotional Side of Sex

Have conversations with your child about the emotions involved in an intimate relationship. These talks will give you opportunities to express your values. Emphasize that kindness and honesty are the underpinnings of every intimate relationship. Don't preach to your child, just give him guidelines on how to respect and care for the people that he loves.

Say, "Anytime You Want to Talk . . ."

Leave the door open for more discussion. Say, "Well, if you think of anything else you want to know, let *me* know." Sometimes children are uncomfortable with a topic and project this discomfort onto their parents. You might hear your child say, "I don't think Mom looked real happy about discussing this stuff." You can put a stop to this line of reasoning by clearly stating your availability. "I'm here. If you want to know something, just ask."

Don't Worry So Much

Many parents worry that they or their child will be embarrassed when sexual topics are discussed, or that they will say the wrong thing. Don't worry. Children appreciate their parents' concern and are probably more comfortable talking about issues of sexuality than you think. When you talk to your children about difficult subjects, it's because you care about them, and children readily understand this.

Be Aware of Your Child's Age and Point of View

Often there may be a "question behind the question." The unspoken question "Am I normal?" is often hiding behind many offhand remarks about sexual development, sexual thoughts, and sexual feelings. At this age, children are very concerned about their developing bodies and their new sexual feelings. Reassure them with both words and deeds that they can always talk to you about their feelings. Make time to talk to your children without being interrupted. It will be time well spent.

Teach Gender Respect

Gender respect should begin in preschool, but it becomes even more important between the ages of six and twelve. Because gender disrespect is such a subtle and pervasive problem in our culture, you must be particularly clear in stating rules of how to treat people with regard to gender issues, and you must show your disapproval and apply appropriate consequences when those rules are broken.

The rules of gender respect should include the following:

- You don't call other people names or treat them with disrespect because they are different from you.

- You don't touch another person in "private" areas (usually defined as between the shoulders and the knees).

- You don't threaten anyone because s/he is a girl, or because s/he behave differently from you.

- You don't exclude anyone from your play just because that child is a boy or a girl.

- You show respect and good manners, particularly to children of the opposite sex.

I was recently told a story about a group of twelve-year-old boys in a suburb of New York City who went around the lunchroom methodically asking each girl if she was still a virgin. The boys thought this was hilarious, until the principal and their parents explained how inappropriate, disrespectful, and hurtful that question could be. They seemed to have had no idea that this question could "upset" the girls at all. To them it was "cool" and, of course, provocative to request this information.

It is crucial to teach children that sexism is a form of prejudice and that prejudice cannot be tolerated at any time in any form. In your own relationships, model acceptance and respect for those who are different from you. Help your children understand that differences make each of us unique.

Computers Can Help—or Hurt

By now it should go without saying that children need to be taught rules of safety on the Internet, just as they are taught how to be safe walking to school or around the mall. There are many software programs that restrict children's access to sexually explicit sites, but no one believes that these can take the place of proper parental guidance and discussion.

A subtler issue is one of computers and gender bias. Because boys tend to be more gadget-oriented and are more often hard-core devotees of video games, educators predicted that they would also embrace computers more rapidly than girls, and it seems that this prediction has come true.

But fortunately there are companies forming every day that see the need for computer programs and Web sites that appeal more to girls. I'm not referring here to the Barbie Fashion software or a program called *How to Be a Model*, but rather to programs that engage girls in the educational and technological aspects of computers by appealing to their interests. My favorite software program specifically developed for girls is called *Let's See About Me*. It features numerous games and activities in which girls get to express their feelings and develop a positive self-concept. A companion Web site allows girls to chat in secure areas and to become cyber–pen pals with girls who have similar interests.

TEENAGERS

KEY TO PREVENTION: HELPING TEENS DEVELOP A COMPLETE AND POSITIVE IDENTITY

Sexuality and gender identity become intertwined in the teen years and will remain that way throughout the life cycle. This is a time when your child will likely experience many "firsts." First kiss, first date, first relationship. The degree to which these firsts build a foundation of self-confidence and responsible behavior can be greatly enhanced by parents.

It is important to remember a basic premise of human learning:

first experiences are the most memorable. We are all likely to vividly remember our first kiss, our first rejection, the first time we met our spouse, our first sexual experience. As parents, we would like to make all of these first experiences positive for our teens, but unfortunately that is not possible.

On the other hand, it *is* possible to give your teenager the emotional tools to handle her first encounters in the important areas of sexuality and relationships, whatever they may bring. Begin by encouraging good communication skills. Give your teen opportunities to talk about experiences before they happen. What does she anticipate? What might be a favorable outcome? What would be terrible? See to it that she is able to communicate effectively to her date. Encourage her to speak directly and to stand up for her rights. Make sure that you are available for follow-up talks.

Of course, you need to walk a fine line between being supportive and prying. Most teens want to keep their feelings private or reserve them for their friends. So let your teen know that if she wants to talk, you'll listen. And if she does want to talk, refrain from giving advice. Let her tell you what she wants, and if she expresses a problem or a concern, guide her toward discovering her own answers by asking questions like "What do you think you should do?" "What would you do differently next time?" "What are some different solutions?"

If you watch MTV or the many popular teen-oriented dramas, you might get the impression that today's teens are sexual volcanoes waiting to erupt. But you'd be wrong. Today's teens are becoming more responsible, more thoughtful, and more knowledgeable about the dangers of unprotected sexual activity than teens have been in several decades. Although it may not seem so from all the media hype, the actual behavior of teens has calmed down considerably since *you* were one.

Consider the following:

- The incidence of sexually transmitted diseases is declining.

- The teenage birthrate, which in 1991 peaked at 62.1 births per 1,000, has dropped by 12 percent, according to statistics compiled by the Centers for Disease Control.

- The number of teenagers now using condoms is three times as high as reported in the 1970s.

- According to the Alan Guttmacher Institute, a leading sex-research organization, 8 in 10 girls and 7 in 10 boys have not had intercourse by the age of sixteen. The average age of first intercourse is seventeen for girls and sixteen for boys. (Seventy percent of cases of sex below the age of thirteen involved rape or abuse.)

Adolescence has gotten a reputation as the most tumultuous stage in the life cycle, but for most teenagers this period is actually less stressful and disruptive than middle age. Extreme behavior is the exception rather than the norm. According to Charles Irwin of the National Adolescent Health Information Center at the University of California, 80 percent of children who enter adolescence do so with normal, healthy backgrounds, and their attitudes and behaviors are the same when they emerge from adolescence. Rather than being alienated, most teenagers feel close to their parents and their families. A national survey conducted by Yankelovich Partners found that 94 percent of today's youth, ages nine to seventeen, say that they trust their parents, and 80 percent ages six to seventeen say that they have really important talks with their parents.

Assume that teenagers want to act responsibly and want their parents to help them do this. Teenagers want to know about the many important issues related to sex and gender rules, and they are anxious for you to discuss these issues with them. They want to know how to protect themselves from unwanted pregnancies and sexually transmitted disease, how to prevent date rape and sexual exploitation, and how to deal with social pressures at a time when cultural mores are vague and the behavior of many adults is questionable.

The real problems that teenagers face may go much deeper than a need for information, and they may require answers that parents find hard to give. How do you find love? How do you form and work on a meaningful relationship with someone? How do you prevent someone from "cheating" on you? How can you handle heartbreak?

Counselors who work with teenagers often say that teens have all the facts about sex and sexuality but have developed a cynical attitude toward intimacy and relationships. Given the role models provided by our national leaders and popular entertainers, this is hardly a surprise. Many professionals believe that today's adolescents are missing the one thing that adolescence is most famous for—the ability to fall in love.

Falling in love can come very early in life, when we refer to it as puppy love. Looking backward, many adults say that they had their first crush at seven or eight years of age, sometimes even younger. Almost always this was a secret or unrequited love—for a girl who was never spoken to, a handsome teacher, or a television or rock star. But it is love all the same—tender feelings, longings, romantic fantasies—the very stuff that adult relationships begin with and try to maintain.

However the clinical emphasis on sex today may have hardened many adolescents against the tender emotions that normally begin a relationship, causing some to say that they feel "old before their time." More important, the courtship rehearsal that is appropriate for this age may be short-circuited, causing teenagers to have to deal with the harder realities of sexual relationships before they've learned to enjoy the softer and sweeter side of infatuation.

If you feel that your teen is developing unhealthy patterns in his relationships, don't hesitate to voice your concern. Don't be judgmental or critical. Just open the door to the discussion and express your observations. "Do you want to talk about what's happening with you and Janice? You seem to be so sad lately." Present yourself as one option for helping your teen explore his personal feelings, but make sure he knows that there are other options as well. There are counselors at school or in the community. Perhaps there's a relative who's easy to talk to. Many teenagers benefit from "peer counseling," which may be offered through your school or through a community mental-health center. Peer counselors are teens who are trained to be nonjudgmental listeners, and they're often a good route for teens who don't wish to talk to an adult.

Will adolescents in the twenty-first century regain some of their lost innocence? Probably not. Will they become less cynical about relationships and develop the skills they need to have fulfilling, lasting relationships? That may be up to you. Here are some suggestions that might help.

AN OUNCE OF PREVENTION

Teach Teens the Elements of Sexual Integrity

Integrity is defined by honesty, sincerity, and ethics. It is a sense of surety that one brings to all social interactions, and it guides us to make the right decisions at the right time. You teach integrity as you teach all other values—through your example, through discussion, and by encouraging teens to pursue responsible behaviors.

Teach Teens How to Say No to Unwanted Sexual Overtures

Assertiveness training can be done in many ways: by reading books and watching movies in which teens are positive role models, through example, and through role-playing.

Many people tell teenagers to "just say no," but often this is not helpful advice. Do you "just say no" if your boss wants you to change a report you've rewritten for the fifth time? Do you "just say no" when your spouse says he wants to change his career and would like *you* to ask for a raise so *he* can take a cut in pay? A better approach is to talk to your teenager about the various forms of negotiation in which everyone can come out a winner. Begin by making sure that your teen knows what she does and doesn't want. Then help her see how another point of view would affect her. Help her see if there's a compromise or, if not, how she can be assertive without being aggressive or making another person feel small. These are skills that are important in all our relationships and ones that parents as well as teens should constantly think about and practice.

Help Teens Form Their Identities

Since many teenagers equate sexual activity with being grown-up, parents should help them find other ways to feel independent and valued for their responsible adult behaviors. As I've said earlier, the most successful teens come from families where expectations are high, so encourage your teenager to find ways to excel in academics, in sports, in the arts, or by working at a job.

Help Teens Accept Their Appearance

In a perfect world the kindest, most sensitive teenagers would be the most popular. The prom king and queen would be elected on the basis of characteristics like honesty, diligence, and community service. But obviously we don't live in a perfect world, and physical appearance counts a great deal. You can keep telling your teenager that appearance doesn't matter, but this won't be true. It matters very much.

Most teenagers make a choice about whether their appearance is a high priority, and you should support their decision. Either they can try to enhance their appearance to fit social norms of beauty, or they can ignore the issue and concentrate on things they deem to be more important. As they grow older, they will see that this is not a black-and-white decision, but that appearance is important at some times and not as important at others.

The majority of teenagers find a way to be comfortable with their choice, as long as their parents support it. Constantly arguing with your teen about spending too much time on her appearance or too little will only add to her apprehension. Trust your teenager to know the right choice for her.

Computers Can Help

There are many Web sites designed to helping teenagers learn and talk about issues related to sex and sexuality. However, if they type a phrase like "sex education" into a search engine like Yahoo or Excite, they will surely get links to sites that will do little to address the issues discussed in this section. So do the homework for your teen. Conduct an Internet search yourself, and then suggest some sites or "bookmark" them in your family computer. Your teenager will have no problem finding inappropriate sites on the Internet if he wants to, but you can at least guide him to the sites you want him to explore.

• • •

Educating children about sexuality and gender roles is difficult for many parents. The things you should talk about to your children will initially seem embarrassing or awkward. Sex education is not just about the "facts of life." It's about respecting others, learning to be safe, and, most important, learning to love. Honest and authoritative communication is the key to preventing problems. It is also the key to helping your child learn to have a life of healthy and happy relationships.

7

Limiting the Effects of Attention Deficit Hyperactivity Disorders (ADHD)

This is not a chapter about preventing ADHD. ADHD is a bio-chemically based disorder, and it is not clear whether prevention will ever be possible. It is clear, however, that this chronic physio-logical problem can be managed and that early intervention can minimize its impact on all areas of your child's life—school, friend-ships, family life, and self-esteem.

The ADHD child may not be exactly like other children his age, but he can be just as happy and successful if you give him the right tools to cope with and understand his problem. This is not, however, a simple task.

Michael's parents placed him in a small private school for kindergarten because they anticipated that he would have a diffi-cult time. He had always been more active and more physical than the other boys his age. Michael was a good-natured but rough-and-tumble child who couldn't walk by a pillow or a cush-ion without wrestling it to the ground. Although tests showed that Michael had an above-average IQ, he seemed to be struggling with early reading and math concepts, and he couldn't recognize even a single number or letter.

Within the first month of school, when Michael's name was mentioned, people heard only the word "trouble." His teacher complained that he couldn't sit in his chair for more than five minutes or get through a single lesson without making some inappropriate comment. Whenever he felt the urge, he raised his hand and told a rambling story about his dog, or his baby sister, or nearly anything that had happened to him that day.

It was a miserable year for all concerned. Michael hated school. He soon found himself teased and taunted by classmates and older children. His parents had daily conferences with his teacher and weekly reviews with the principal. Finally, toward the end of the school year, Michael was diagnosed by a child psychiatrist as having an attention deficit disorder and given a prescription for Ritalin. Michael calmed down almost immediately, but he still hated school and did not seem able to make even a single friend.

Every September thousands of children like Michael start school with a similar experience. Typically they have average or even above-average intelligence, yet they just don't seem able to adjust to the behavioral demands required in a classroom of twenty-five to thirty other children.

Attention Deficit Hyperactivity Disorder is the most commonly diagnosed psychological problem of children, affecting, according to the diagnostic manual of the American Psychiatric Association 3 to 5 percent of children. However, many professionals feel that this is an underestimate of the problem. The Web site of CHADD (Children and Adults with Attention Deficit Disorder at www.CHADD.org), the advocacy group for ADHD children and adults, states that an additional 5 to 10 percent of children may have some of the characteristics that typify this disorder or may have ADHD combined with another disorder such as anxiety or depression. CHADD further notes that another 15 to 20 percent of children may have transient or subclinical symptoms of ADHD, but because these symptoms are only present under specific circumstances, the diagnosis of ADHD is not warranted. Although it is considered an inherited disorder, which can usually be traced back to a child's temperament as an infant, it is most commonly diagnosed when a child is of school age.

There are three basic conditions that define ADHD: difficulty in sustaining attention, hyperactivity, and impulsivity. Researchers generally agree that these conditions are caused by a decreased activity in the parts of the brain responsible for regulating and inhibiting emotions. The effects of these problems can be widespread. ADHD children typically have problems in school adjustment, and they cause a great deal of stress in their families. Although they are usually outgoing and friendly, they have a hard time "reading" social cues, and typically they experience difficulty making and keeping friends. Because they receive so much negative feedback, ADHD children may have a low self-esteem, which can later lead to depression.

But the fact that ADHD is considered to be a neurological and biochemical disorder does not mean that a child is doomed to have lifelong problems. Each of us has a unique neurological makeup consisting of a variety of intellectual and emotional factors that affect the way we learn and behave. Our success in life is determined by the way we utilize these factors together, relying on our strengths and abilities to cope with our problems.

According to researchers who have studied ADHD children as they've grown into adults, about 60 percent continue to have ADHD symptoms, and about half of these adults have moderate to severe problems. But what about the 40 percent of adults who do not continue to have ADHD symptoms and the 30 percent who have only mild problems? How do these people learn to cope with this neurologically based problem? What are the experiences and tools your child needs to mitigate the effects of ADHD?

According to Dr. Lillian Hechtman, who has reviewed dozens of longitudinal studies on the long-term effects of ADHD, there isn't a single specific symptom that can predict whether a child with ADHD will have serious long-term effects from this disorder. Instead, it appears that there is an additive and interactive effect between a child's personality, his social background, and the support of his family that determines whether he will have a lifelong problem. While some of these factors cannot be changed (such as economic status), other factors can be influenced, including some aspects of a child's personality development.

If you are the parent of an ADHD child, you have opportunities throughout your child's development to provide the experiences that can minimize the effects of this disorder. Medication will help with the ADHD symptoms, but it will not cure ADHD or prevent it from having wider developmental consequences.

Your job of preventing ADHD from being an overwhelming influence on your child and your family is not an easy one, but it can be accomplished. I have known many successful adults who still have some symptoms of ADHD, but they have turned them into strengths rather than weaknesses. They do two or three tasks at once. They have boundless energy and enthusiasm. They are curious about everything and have a playful attitude about their work. They are good fathers and husbands (although they often need some extra understanding). When I ask each one about his childhood, I hear the typical story of an ADHD child: difficulty in school, testing the limits at home, high-risk behaviors. But I also hear another common denominator—loving parents who never gave up.

RISK FACTORS FOR ADHD BECOMING A CHRONIC PROBLEM

Temperament

Few people who work with ADHD children doubt that this disorder has a biological base. Symptoms tend to run in families. It is also three times likelier to appear in boys, suggesting that it is linked to inherited gender traits. One study found that if a parent has ADHD, his or her offspring has a 57 percent chance of having it, too. On the other hand, there is no evidence of a single ADHD gene.

At this time we cannot say precisely that there is an ADHD temperament, but research relating brain activity to temperament suggests that in the future we may reach new conclusions. The fact that children with ADHD seem to share certain temperamental traits and tend to grow into adults with similar personality characteristics does seem to suggest inherited biochemical traits. It is assumed that these children are born with a predisposition to impulsive personality development. Still, we can also assume that even when children are born with a temperament that might cause them to develop ADHD, under certain conditions they might also outgrow it. Some researchers say that infants born with a difficult temperament also are born with strong "self-righting" tendencies. The influence of these self-righting tendencies, combined with a natural desire to change as a result of parental involvement, suggests that a child's fate should never be seen as fixed.

The Brain

While most psychologists believe that ADHD is a brain disorder, the exact mechanisms that determine why children develop these behaviors are far from clear. According to Dr. Phyllis Anne Teeter in her book *Interventions for ADHD*, there are more than eleven prevailing theories as to the specific brain processes associated with ADHD.

Since ADHD is primarily a problem of self-control, the likeliest explanation is that there is a dysfunction in the higher areas of the brain, the frontal lobes of the cortex, which give us the ability to control our impulses and plan our responses to a particular situation. Most psychologists also feel that this brain dysfunction is expressed by an imbalance in certain neurotransmitters, the biochemical equivalents of emotions. The neurotransmitters dopamine and norepinephrine are known to affect specific aspects of ADHD, including attention, motor activity, and motivation.

To understand this better, let's examine what happens to a child as he watches an ad on television for his favorite ice cream. The sight of the ice cream triggers a sense memory of the pleasures of eating ice cream, and he begins to anticipate this event as if the ice cream were sitting in a bowl right before him. The emotional centers of his brain send out the message "I WANT ICE CREAM—ICE CREAM IS GREAT!"

The task of actually getting the ice cream is then handed off to the "executive" center of the brain, the part that solves problems, and the decision of how to act is based largely on past experience of what works and what doesn't. A child without a problem in impulse control, even as young as two or three, might ask his mother for some ice cream, but when told that he will have to wait until after dinner, he accepts this and continues watching TV. His brain tells him that he will get the ice cream if he waits, and he is satisfied with this answer.

But the brain of the child with ADHD doesn't seem to process this information in the same way. He isn't satisfied with waiting for the ice cream. It is as if the possibility of getting ice cream were gone forever. Perhaps more important, his brain doesn't tell him that if he throws a tantrum or makes a fresh remark to his mother, he'll be in a much worse predicament. Whether his mother gives in and gets him some ice cream or stands her ground and lets him be unhappy, he doesn't learn from this experience. He is unable to delay gratification, nor can he access the "memory" that the ice cream will come after dinner. Also, he doesn't have the self-control of a child without ADHD. Angry about not getting what he wants, he may have a tantrum or storm into his room and slam the door. It doesn't occur to him that good behavior is the best way to get a reward.

Parenting Style

Parenting styles have a significant effect in determining whether a child with ADHD successfully learns to cope with this disorder. Parents who are most successful with an ADHD child are able to set clear limits and respond immediately to misbehavior, and they are simultaneously able to maintain warm and nurturing relationships with their child.

Recalling the parental styles I've talked about earlier, it should not be surprising that it is the permissive parent who will likely have the most problems with an ADHD child. They find it difficult to provide a structured environment or set limits, which of course is exactly what ADHD children need. One might think that ADHD children do better with authoritarian parents, who make clear and constant demands and rules etched in stone But authoritarian parents typically do not give their ADHD child the extra nurturing that is needed. Life for ADHD children with authoritarian parents can be one negative experience after another, making it hard for them to develop a sense of self-confidence and self-worth.

As with other problems discussed in this book, authoritative parents who balance limits and emotional support have the best chance of raising a well-adjusted ADHD child. But this is not as easy as it sounds. ADHD children require more of everything: more attention, more limits, more love, and more self-awareness on the part of their parents. It can be a trying and exhausting job, even for the most dedicated parent.

Parents of ADHD children frequently need a great deal of support. CHADD, the Association for Children and Adults with ADHD, mentioned earlier, is one of the most active parent self-help groups in the country, with over four hundred chapters. The involvement and passions of the parents in this organization testify both to the difficulties involved in raising an ADHD child and to the commitment it takes.

Family Stress

It should come as no surprise that any type of family stress, such as a divorce or marital fighting, can cause an almost immediate reaction in an ADHD child. Even a child without ADHD will feel helpless and out of control during trying circumstances. But these feelings are multiplied in an ADHD child. Of course, this can be a chicken-and-egg problem, since parenting an ADHD in itself causes stress in the home. Many such parents describe themselves as "emotionally bankrupt." They relate exhausting stories of the constant need to attend to the behavioral demands of these children. It is easy to see how these overactive and inattentive children can affect not only an individual's sense of self-worth but the marriage, the siblings, the extended family, and even neighbors and family friends. In addition, parents may experience a great deal of frustration in working with their child's teachers, who themselves are having a problem with the child and consciously or unconsciously blame the parents.

Some researchers have found that ADHD children are more responsive and better behaved with their fathers. In some cases this can be a positive factor, and in other situations it can be an added risk factor, since fathers typically spend much less time with their children than mothers. A frequent scenario is that a father criticizes his wife for not being more successful with their son, while the wife resents her husband for not spending more time with the child. As a result, marital discord becomes a part of the family profile, creating a cycle of unhappiness for all. Often the ADHD child will then experience a worsening of his symptoms as the tension in the household mounts and focus on his needs decreases.

Delayed Language Development and Learning Disabilities

A high percentage of children with attention deficit disorders also have learning problems. They may be slower to develop their speech and language skills, have poor short-term memory, and may be prone to having difficulties in other aspects of learning.

Delayed speech and language skills are likely caused by the same pattern of brain functioning that causes ADHD, but it is hard to say which comes first or whether they both occur together. We do know that besides having a general lag in language development, ADHD children characteristically develop internalized speech much later than other children do. Internalized speech, or "inner speech," is a term used to describe what we colloquially call "talking to ourselves." A three-year-old child might see a piece of candy on a table and say out loud, "Candy! No, don't have candy." But by five or six that same child thinks, "I won't take the candy. That would get me into trouble." This "inner speech" helps a child control his behavior. An ADHD child, who does not use inner speech to control his actions, would be more likely to just take the candy and gobble it down, than would a child who uses inner speech to augment his self-control.

It is understandable that children who have both behavioral and learning problems will see school as an unhappy place to be. ADHD children will typically experience negative reactions from their teachers as well as their peers and meet with significantly fewer successes than the average child. When a child fails, the school often blames the parents and the parents blame the school. This begins a vicious cycle that benefits no one in the end.

A Lack of Praise and Positive Attention

Praise and criticism are symbolic but powerful forms of rewards and punishments. Constant punishment will eventually result in feelings of helplessness, lethargy, and depression. Praise has the opposite effect. When given appropriately, it builds a sense of self-worth and belonging. There is even evidence that praise and criticism have biochemcial effects on the brain. Praise causes the release of dopamine, the "pleasure" biochemical. Constant criticism causes the release of a group of biochemicals called catecholamines, including cortisol, the stress hormone.

Children with ADHD typically inspire too little praise or positive attention. Parents and teachers may be so caught up with the child's difficulties that they forget to note the child's smaller, but significant, successes.

Medication

About 70 percent of children diagnosed with ADHD are referred for medication for some period in their development. Although many people believe that drugs are overprescribed, there is no question that medication is helpful for most ADHD children, when combined with psychological and behavioral interventions.

But medication in itself may present a risk factor for children. First, there are side effects. A small percentage of children will develop tachycardia (an increased heart rate) from psychostimulant medication. Sleeping problems and appetite loss occur in an estimated 15 to 20 percent of children. The most serious effect is a decrease in growth rate in children following a prolonged use of medication. All of these side effects seem to go away, however, with lower doses or discontinuance of the medication.

The psychological risk factors associated with taking medication to control behaviors may be more of a concern. Some professionals, as well as many media reports, have raised parents' anxiety about whether taking medication affects a child's self-esteem and makes him more prone to later drug abuse. To date, there is no conclusive evidence that this happens. Pro-medication professionals argue that unmedicated ADHD children would be even more at risk due to the increased chances of school failure and peer rejection.

The stress of the actual drug-taking procedures, however, can pose a problem in itself. Ritalin must be taken every four hours. This means that most children on Ritalin must go to the school nurse during the middle of the day for their second pill. Children, of course, don't like to call negative attention to themselves. They don't want others to see that they have a problem, since they are aware that their peers can be very cruel in singling out and teasing children who are different. Peer acceptance or rejection is a powerful determinant of a child's sense of self-worth.

Some psychologists worry that children on Ritalin or other medication may develop a form of "learned helplessness." They receive the message from their parents or from other adults that they aren't able to behave well unless they have a pill to help them.

INFANTS

KEY TO PREVENTION: EARLY BEHAVIORAL INTERVENTION

Even though we recognize that a predisposition to problems with attention, overactivity, and impulsivity may be inherited, there is no such thing as a baby with ADHD. This diagnosis is never made until a child is at least three or four, and even then it's questionable whether this label should be applied to children at such a young age. Most commonly the diagnosis of ADHD is applied only after a child begins formal schooling at age five or six.

Yet when we look back at the history of children with ADHD, we find that, compared to other infants, they were fussy and irritable and often had colic in their first three months. Children with ADHD were often "difficult" babies, hard to soothe, with irregular sleeping and eating habits, and they were often described as excessively active.

At this time we cannot accurately predict whether or not an infant will grow up to be diagnosed with ADHD, any more than we can predict whether an infant will grow up to excel in math or be a great athlete. But we can make a calculated guess. If a male infant is considered to have a difficult temperament, and if at least one parent has had symptoms of ADHD, then certainly that child will be predisposed to have this disorder. In any event, the techniques for diminishing the potential effects of ADHD will help all difficult babies. The two elements of this prescription are teaching babies to soothe themselves and helping them become more responsive to simple parental requests.

AN OUNCE OF PREVENTION

The following suggestions are designed to have both immediate and long-term effects in making life easier for your difficult baby and for yourself. They will help you to mold behavioral habits that may theoretically have permanent effects on the brain and neurochemical makeup of your child. Equally important, once you feel confident that you're taking reasonable steps to help offset long-term problems, it is easier to focus on developing stronger emotional bonds with your child. All of us like to be successful in what we do, and very few things give us the pride and self-satisfaction of feeling like a competent and successful parent.

Teach Children to Self-Soothe

Unfortunately, there are no easy ways to teach a baby to calm herself. While babies typically find a way to do so on their own, a baby predisposed to ADHD will have a tougher time. In his book *365 Ways to Calm a Crying Baby*, physician Julian Orenstein recommends everything from decreasing sensory overload, to using a device that makes the crib feel like a car going at fifty-five miles per hour, to reciting repetitive nursery rhymes and singing games. What's important is finding one or two things that will quiet a cranky and irritable infant and to expand these activities gradually as the child gets older. Write them down so that you'll remember them. Look for things they have in common: Do they all involve touch? Sound? Do they work better at night or during the day? As your child develops a repertoire of ways to calm herself, she should become less dependent on you for this task.

Make Teaching Compliance a Priority

A mother of a seventeen-month-old recently complained to me, "My baby learned how to shake his head no when he was nine months old. He has yet to shake his head yes." By the time babies are a year old, they should be able to stop a behavior when a parent firmly says, "No" or "Stop that," and they should also be able to comply with simple parental requests, like "Give me the keys, please." Difficult babies, on the other hand, may refuse to comply with parental prohibitions or requests. They understand what their parents want, but *they* want something else, and that takes precedence. When a parent becomes more insistent or intervenes physically, a difficult baby will likely cry. If he is picked up, he may pull away in defiance.

You can, however, teach your infant the "game of listening." Don't wait until it's time to clean up. Make a game of putting the toys in the toy box. Do this three or four times in a row (babies love to repeat activities), and then when it is really time to clean up, they will have rehearsed this behavior and it will be more automatic.

If your child still doesn't comply with your simple requests, you may need to demonstrate what you mean. "See? I'm putting a toy in the box. Now you put a toy in the box." If you find yourself putting away all the toys, this hasn't worked. When all else fails, you may have to guide your child physically to comply. In this example, you would put a toy in his hands and, holding it there, take him over to the toy box and guide him to putting it in. Then, in the future, take out only one or two toys at a time.

Don't Reinforce or Ignore Negative Habits

Difficult babies are also prone to picking up and holding on to negative behavioral patterns. One little thirteen-month-old I know was holding her father's keys as the two of them climbed the stairs. When she reached the top, she threw the keys down the stairwell. The father retrieved them patiently, to the child's delight, and when he handed them to her again, she immediately threw them back down the stairs with a giggle. This was repeated nine or ten times, until the father grew tired of this strenuous game. At that point the baby burst into tears when her father said, "That's enough of this game." The next day the baby wanted to play "drop the keys" again, but her father refused. She burst into tears. The next day the same thing happened, and this continued for a period of about two weeks, until the child finally forgot about the game.

The lesson of this story is to stop negative behavioral patterns with difficult infants as soon as you spot them. Of course, all young children like to explore, and they will sometimes do things that annoy or trouble us. That's just part of the task of raising a baby, and you certainly don't want to criticize them for every negative thing they do. But you do have to set clear limits. Take, for example, the baby who decides that her dinner of spaghetti makes an interesting pattern on her high-chair tray. You could calmly say, "Well, that's a pretty picture you're making, but we don't play with our food. After dinner we can make pictures with crayons." Then state the rule: "Your food has to stay on your plate."

The problem with difficult babies is that they do not easily learn the lesson at hand. They will typically continue to misbehave, out of both curiosity and willfulness. If you allow a child like this to continue to misbehave, you're setting up a pattern of "resistant" behavior, a pattern that will be very hard to break in the future.

Reinforce Early Signs of Self-Control

True self-control doesn't emerge until children are about two years of age. This is the time when children should be able to control their behavior without constant reminders. But ADHD children may not learn self-control as easily as other children, so parents of children at risk for ADHD will have to pay more attention to teaching this important skill when their children are even younger. Make sure that you praise your baby for following your directions and in particular for his patience. If he stays in his high chair after he is done eating and watches you while you finish eating, say, "Good boy! Thank you for being patient and sitting there nicely!" If he sits down when you ask him to and waits while you put on his shoes, say, "Thank you for doing that! Thank you for being patient."

This may seem like a simple recommendation, but, as I've noted, parents of ADHD children tend to focus on negative behaviors and not pay enough attention to positive ones. Praise is a powerful reinforcer, even for very young children. Indeed, praise is the most effective tool you have for shaping your child's behavior.

Pay Attention to Your Child's Language Development

We know that children with ADHD often have delays in their language development, which will later exacerbate their behavioral problems. Read to your baby often, even if he has an attention span of only a few pages at a time. Talk to your infant constantly throughout the day, verbally labeling objects around the house and watching for his understanding. When your infant uses gestures to express his needs, respond by describing his gestures with words and then articulating your response to his request: "Oh, you want me to get you your juice? Okay, here is your juice." These activities will encourage overall language development and communication skills, which will play an important role in helping your infant learn to control his behavior as he matures.

TODDLERS AND PRESCHOOLERS

KEY TO PREVENTION: EARLY DETECTION AND EARLY INTERVENTION

With the increasing public awareness of ADHD, parents and professionals are more sensitive to the early symptoms of this disorder. The most common and most serious symptoms are a combination of overactivity with the failure of the child to develop age-appropriate behavioral controls. We must of course take into account that children between the ages of eighteen months and five years, particularly boys, are expected to be very active and also to have frequent episodes of willfulness. The difference between ADHD children and other active and rambunctious children at this age is one of degree and persistence of their behavioral problems. For example, one study of four-year-olds found that 40 percent displayed problems in inattention and noncompliance, based on the reports of preschool teachers. The majority of these problems didn't last more than three to six months. But 10 percent of the children continued to have problems until the second grade, significantly impairing their early school adjustment.

Another indicator that there is something more serious going on is the attitude of parents (particularly of mothers) to the child. Young children who later develop ADHD have a history of battling with their mothers throughout the preschool and toddler years. Observation of the interactions between an ADHD child and his mother frequently reveals more negative feelings expressed by the mother, more reports of stress, less overt affection shown, and far fewer positive interactions. As a result of this gradual emotional separation between parent and child, mothers also report that they have a lowered self-esteem.

Behavioral problems of young ADHD children usually peak between ages three and six. At this stage we expect children to be easier to manage and more responsive to adults, but ADHD children show more difficulties. Aaron, at age four was a case in point. Aaron's parents had started potty-training him when he was two and a half, but he wore a diaper at night and had accidents nearly every day. He would sit and watch television for a half hour or so, but he couldn't concentrate on any other activity for more than a few minutes at a time. Aaron was enrolled in a preschool, but there were complaints from his teachers almost daily: "Aaron hit Melissa and wouldn't say he was sorry." "Aaron had a bad day today. He wouldn't come in from recess and had to be put in the time-out corner." "Aaron has a problem playing cooperatively with the other children. He takes their toys, and they don't want to play with him."

Some children have behavioral problems at school but not at home, or vice versa. Since these children are able to control their behaviors at least part of the time, it is less likely that they have ADHD, though they may have some other type of behavioral problem.

There is controversy about labeling young children with a diagnosis of ADHD. On the one hand, professionals argue that an early accurate diagnosis means that a child will receive the right kinds of treatment before the problem gets more serious. Others are concerned about children getting the wrong diagnosis at this age and then having to live with this "label" for the rest of their childhood years. In my opinion, what matters most is to treat and alleviate the symptoms and make sure that parents and children are developing a positive relationship. If a child is making consistent progress in learning to control his behaviors, and if his parents acknowledge this progress and feel closer to their child, then having a diagnostic label is not important.

Relatively few children need medication at this age unless they have severe symptoms that don't respond to any behavioral techniques. Psychostimulant medication is not as effective as it is for older children, and there is more concern about side effects with younger children.

Children at risk for ADHD should be carefully observed in kindergarten and first grade for early learning problems or difficulty adjusting to a structured classroom. Whether your young child is eventually diagnosed with ADHD or not, the following recommendations will help him establish behavioral patterns that will work in all areas of his development.

AN OUNCE OF PREVENTION

The key parenting concept is "encouragement." The more opportunities you have to be approving, the more confident your child will feel and the better able he will be to meet the challenges before him. Look for and encourage his positive behaviors, rather than dwelling on the negative ones.

Make a "Special Time" for Your Child

Psychologists are naturally concerned about teaching parents to manage their child's difficult behavior, but they are equally concerned that parents maintain a positive relationship with their willful or noncooperative child. Many recommend that parents set aside five or ten minutes a day to play with their child, when criticism and negative comments are not allowed. During this "special time," your child can do whatever he wants: play with action figures, make things out of clay, or romp in an active game. Give your child your undivided attention and play along with him, even trying to imitate or "mirror" what he does. As long as he doesn't harm anyone or anything, there should be no rules or expectations. Just enjoy your child's activities from his point of view. As simple as this may seem, this technique conveys a very important message to your child: "I have rules for your behavior, but I also have time just for you. You are very important to me and I will always make time for you."

Teach Your Child to Control His Anger

A frequent complaint about young ADHD children is that they cannot control their anger. They throw tantrums or hit or bite other children.

The Traffic Light game is one of my favorite techniques for teaching young children to control their impulsive and angry behavior. By the age of three or four, most children understand the meaning of traffic signals: red means to stop immediately, yellow means to look both ways and then proceed with caution, and green means to go. The intent of this simple game is to teach children to "catch" their first movement toward an impulsive behavior (this is called a behavioral trigger), stop the behavior, consider the consequences, and then go on to do something more appropriate.

To prepare the game, take a three-by-five index card and draw a picture of a stoplight—a rectangle with one green, one yellow, and one red circle. Then sit with your child and go over the meaning of each "signal." Explain how the traffic light keeps cars from running into each other and keeps pedestrians safe. The next time your child misbehaves, give him the traffic-light card. Have him put his finger on the red circle while he slowly breathes ten times. Then have him put his finger on the yellow circle on the card, and give him some choices of positive things he could do. For example, if he's angry because you turned off the TV, say, "Think of two other things that are fun to do besides watching TV." Suggest two choices if he can't think of any. Finally, have him put his finger on the green circle and then go and act on the best choice. After practicing this a few times, you should be able simply to give your child the traffic-light card when he is angry and watch him go through these three steps on his own.

Teach Your Child to Play Cooperatively with Others

For over twenty years I've recommended that parents teach their children cooperative games that emphasize working together rather than competing with someone else. In a cooperative game everyone wins by achieving a common goal. There are no individual winners or losers. The benefits of this type of game to a child prone to anger and oppositionality should be obvious. Cooperative games teach children teamwork, reliance on others, and selflessness. There are hundreds of cooperative games, many of them borrowed from other cultures. For younger children try the game of Balloon Attack. Get the whole family together (or three or four children), and give each player a balloon. Then set a three-minute egg timer and have each player throw his or her balloon into the air. The object of the game is to prevent any balloon from hitting the ground before the timer goes off. To do this, all the players will have to help one another. Play a cooperative game every evening instead of watching an extra half hour of television (see Terry Orlick's *Cooperative Sports and Game Book* for dozens of fun ideas). Then watch how family members start to get along better as you make this a priority in your home.

Find a Discipline Technique that Works

As a general rule, the simplest discipline techniques are usually the most effective. This is probably because they are easier for parents to remember and to use consistently. This is the case with the Count 1-2-3 technique. When you want your child to comply and either stop a particular behavior (e.g., arguing, whining, or demanding) or start one (e.g., pick up toys, turn off the television, make the bed), begin with a simple directive. Just say something like "Turn off the television, please." If your child doesn't do what you want within five or ten seconds, hold up a finger and sternly say, "That's one." Let another five seconds go by (without saying anything else), then hold up a second finger and say, "That's two." If another five seconds pass without a response, say, "That's three. Now take a time-out." Then immediately escort your child to a time-out corner, where he must sit quietly for three minutes. If your child still refuses to comply, repeat the procedure again. According to Dr. Thomas Phelan, author of *1,2,3, Magic,* who has refined this technique for working with ADHD children, the main mistake parents make in using this technique is getting angry at the child, which then reinforces the delaying behavior. When parents use the "no emotion" rule and carry out the 1-2-3 technique without variation, children quickly learn that it is much easier to comply in the first place than to stall.

Catch Them Being Good

This is another simple technique used to help young children learn to behave. The principle is simple: Praise children for their positive behavior and ignore their negative behavior as much as you can. It is also called "behavioral shaping." Many parents of ADHD children find themselves constantly nagging and criticizing their children about their behavior. Not only does this make their time together unpleasant, it also tends to make the child's behavior worse. Understanding that every child behaves appropriately at least some of the time will help you pay attention to the times when your child is doing exactly the right thing. Catch him being good, with a word of praise or a gesture, and you will have begun to reverse the cycle of negative behavior followed by negative response leading to yet more negative behavior.

Give Positive Directions

When I tell some parents to catch their child being good, I've sometimes heard this sarcastic retort: "You come over to our house and try it! My child is never 'being good.'" When I hear this, I suggest another behavioral technique called "positive direction." In this technique, parents must refrain from criticizing their children, but instead tell them exactly what they want them to do. Let's say that your child puts his feet up on your couch. Don't say, "Get your feet off the couch now!" Instead say, "Please put your feet on the floor." Describe exactly what you want him to do. It's very likely that he will listen to your simple direction, and then you can quickly "catch him being good" by saying, "Thank you for listening!"

Point Systems

Some parents resist giving rewards to children for good behavior, thinking that it amounts to "bribing" children to be good. To me this is only a question of semantics. The fact is that ADHD children typically respond well to earning points and getting rewards. To begin, identify two or three behaviors you want your child to change. You might be able to name fifty behaviors that really bother you, but you must prioritize and start with the ones that are most important. State your goals in such a way that you can easily determine whether a given goal is accomplished. For example, if you want your child to clean up his toys without being nagged, the goal would read, "Ronald will clean up his toys when he is asked just once." If your child meets a goal, he should get a "token" (poker chips work well) or a sticker. Then make a rewards "menu" for your child to cash in his points at the end of the week. The better the reward, the greater number of points that must be earned. Research tells us that ADHD children respond to this kind of system best when there are negative consequences as well as rewards. There should be a "cost" for misbehaving. Every time your child breaks a rule, a point should be taken away. Many parents find this difficult to do, but it is the best way to teach children cause and effect, and it makes a behavior-management program much more effective.

Consider Enrolling in a Parenting Program for Hard-to-Manage Children

All of these techniques *sound* easy, but I've heard too many parents of ADHD children bemoan that "nothing works with my child" to think that there are any easy answers. If you've tried several techniques and nothing seems to work, don't despair. You're not alone. Consider enrolling in a parenting course aimed at teaching effective discipline. These courses usually consist of four to six evening sessions and are offered through your school or local community-service agency, by parenting experts. Not only do these courses present sound information, along with video demonstrations of how the techniques work, they also give you a chance to talk to other parents and learn what works (or doesn't) for them. To find a course near you, call your local elementary school and get a recommendation from the school psychologist, counselor, or school nurse.

Computers Can Help

Children with ADHD are typically drawn to computers because they provide the high interest and continuous feedback they crave. Parents must take a firm hand, however, and guide their children toward the wealth of fun and educational programs now available for children, and away from games that promote violence. There are many arcade-style games that require similar skills as the popular violent games but don't have destructive and aggressive themes. Two of my favorites are *Pocahontas* (Disney Multimedia) and *Freddie the Fish* (Humongous Enertainment).

In an earlier chapter I mentioned two computer programs on learning appropriate behaviors that might also be helpful to your ADHD child. *The Lie* teaches children the consequences of not being honest with your parents and *Life's Little Lessons with the Berenstain Bears"* teaches helpfulness and cooperation. As with all computer programs, the repetition and multimedia stimulation are particularly beneficial to the child with ADHD.

SCHOOL-AGE CHILDREN

KEY TO PREVENTION: HELPING YOUR ADHD CHILD FEEL THAT HE CAN SUCCEED

In the elementary-school years, ADHD children can be very difficult to teach. Besides their problems with attention and impulsivity, a high percentage of children with ADHD have reading and other learning problems. But despite these problems, many are good students and motivated to learn. Your job in this stage is to make sure that your child feels that he is successful in school and thinks of himself as a person who can achieve his goals.

Children at this stage begin to define themselves by the "pecking order" of their class. Children with good grades are at the top. Children with poor grades are at the bottom. Studies tell us that children tend to find their position at school in the first or second grade, and, all things being equal, they hold it throughout their school years.

> Sam was a very bright eleven-year-old who tested in the gifted range. He had all the symptoms of ADHD, but was not diagnosed. In spite of his intellectual gifts, he got below-average grades. His teachers in grades one to four unanimously considered him a pain in the neck and difficult to teach. Sam considered himself an average student. In the fourth grade, when he was finally diagnosed with ADHD, he was put on Ritalin and given academic and psychological support. But the biggest challenge was raising the expectations of his teachers and having them work to make him one of their top students, as his natural abilities would dictate.

Children with ADHD are particularly susceptible to underachievement because of the constant negative feedback they receive from their teachers. For many ADHD children, the legacy of underachievement extends far beyond the school years. An estimated 50 percent of ADHD children grow up to be adults who are less successful at their work than are others with the same natural abilities.

Because ADHD children typically have problems both at home and in school, parents need more support during the school years. They need to be educated about this complex disorder and helped to understand that the many problems their children encounter are not anyone's fault. They also need to know what they should and shouldn't do to help their children. There are dozens of books on helping the ADHD child, yet many parents feel they don't have enough information, probably because parents need emotional support even more than they need facts and techniques.

Something else that makes it so difficult for parents is the fact that these children frequently have other psychological problems as well, such as Oppositional Defiant Disorder or ODD (see Chapter 2). In addition, ADHD may sometimes lead to depression in older children and teens, as they repeatedly experience problems in school as well as peer rejection.

So what can be done? It boils down to one simple adage: Nothing succeeds like success. With rare exceptions, children who are successful at learning become motivated to learn more. Children who are successful at making one friend will learn how to make another. Conversely, children who fail repeatedly will eventually feel helpless and pessimistic no matter how much encouragement and support they get from adults. Their enthusiasm and efforts in school will be diminished. Similarly, children who are socially isolated and experience constant teasing and peer rejection will be vulnerable to many other psychological problems as they grow older. They may be more at risk for drug and alcohol abuse, antisocial and criminal acts, and dropping out of school.

AN OUNCE OF PREVENTION

Helping children succeed in school is a tall order if you are the parent of an ADHD child. But you're not alone. Work collaboratively with teachers, with school counselors and psychologists, and with your pediatrician. Educate and involve family members about the particular needs and problems of your ADHD child. ADHD is not your child's fault, nor is it yours. It is a biochemically based disorder that we are learning more about every day. Your child's behavior

will improve as he gets older, but you must avoid letting small problems escalate into larger ones. The following are some preventive
suggestions.

Encourage Your Child's Teacher to Adapt the Classroom to Fit His Needs

Experience has shown that ADHD children can succeed in a regular classroom, but they typically benefit when some specific adjustments are made. Teachers may resist doing this, but children diagnosed with ADHD have a legal right to "reasonable" classroom
accommodations.

When an ADHD child is having trouble in the classroom, the
teacher should request a multidisciplinary meeting, which is usually
attended by the school psychologist, the principal, and other support personnel. This meeting should identify specific educational
goals and recommend classroom adjustments to achieve these goals.
Some of the techniques used to help ADHD children succeed in
school include:

- letting the child sit in the front of the class so he can get some
  extra attention

- tape-recording lessons

- special seating arrangements (usually near the teacher)

- study carrels to block out distractions

- untimed tests, including standardized achievement tests

- support from a resource-room teacher or aide trained to work
  with children who have different learning requirements

If a child has an additional learning problem, he might also
qualify for more intensive services as a special education student.
Call the principal or school psychologist to find out the procedure
for having your child evaluated.

Provide Tutoring

ADHD children have difficulty learning in a group, but they do much better when they get individualized attention. Your child's school may provide some individual tutoring, but your child is likely to need more. The most important element of tutoring is the consistency and one-on-one attention it provides; the specific teaching methods are usually secondary. There are tutoring centers in most cities, and many teachers will work after school as tutors, but this can get very expensive. Parents can certainly help with homework, but they usually do not work well as tutors for ADHD children. In fact, it usually just ends up as something else to argue about. High school students or teachers-in-training from a local college often make good tutors, but they may need a little supervision from you or your child's teacher.

Teach Learning and Organizational Strategies

ADHD children don't just have to learn; they have to learn how to learn. Traditional school learning comes easily to the average child, but not to the impulsive ADHD child. As a result, most educational specialists who work with ADHD children coach them in how to approach each academic task so as to heighten the chance that the child will be successful. There are many ways to teach ADHD children simple organizational skills. Give your child a list of what needs to go into his book bag in the morning, and have the teacher make a similar list for the afternoon. Have your child check off each thing he puts into his book bag; then you or the teacher should go over his list. Being on time can also be a challenge for an ADHD child. Give him an inexpensive digital watch with a timer. Tell him that he needs to be in his seat for his first class when the timer goes off. Make it into a game. See if he can be in his seat when the timer goes off, every day for a week. If he can do it, give him a small reward.

If you are highly organized yourself, you might already be a good person to coach your child in learning strategies. But if you are more like your child and had difficulty in school yourself, pick up a book on study skills, like *13 Steps to Better Grades* by Ruth Fallon, and take the tips from an expert.

Promote Home-School Communication

It goes without saying that the more you can communicate with your child's teachers, the more you'll be able to support and supplement his learning. But this is easier said than done for parents with a child who has ADHD. Parents of children with behavioral problems often feel that "no news is good news," and when they don't hear from the teacher, they assume that things are going well.

Unfortunately, this is not often the case. Teachers are uncomfortable giving parents a constant flow of negative feedback, and they may wait until it is absolutely necessary—such as when report cards are handed out—to break the bad news. By this time a negative pattern has already been established. Like so many other aspects of an ADHD child's life, the focus is put on what is wrong rather than on what is right.

A much more productive approach would be to set up a communication system from the first day of the school year, in which daily notes are written from the teacher to the parent. The teacher may note positive and negative behaviors, and you as the parent can discuss them with your child, praise him, or give him appropriate consequences. This technique has been shown to be very helpful in improving overall classroom behavior.

Teach Children Self-Management

Children with ADHD lack the skills to monitor and control their behaviors, but these skills can be taught. Give your child a set of index cards with the numbers 1 to 7 printed in sequential order. The number 1="out of control" and 7="in total control." Ask your child to rate himself on a card several times a day just by circling the number that describes him best at that given time. This will help him be more aware of the things he can do to control his behaviors, and it will reinforce the fact that he, and no one else, is responsible for what he does.

Another technique that teaches self-management is to have children learn to reinforce their own improved behaviors, rather than to depend on adults. In the above example a child could give himself a point for each card that had a 7 circled on it. *He* would be the judge of whether he deserved the point. When he had five "7" cards, he could then cash in the cards for a special privilege. Unlike reward systems in which adults hand out the rewards, this system reinforces a child's sense that he is in charge.

Help Your ADHD Child Make and Keep Friends

From the ages of six to twelve a large part of a child's identity is formed from his ability or inability to make friends. At this age we expect children to have a series of "best" friends, then later be able to identify with a group of friends. But children with ADHD frequently have difficulty achieving either of these goals. Social-skills training has been advocated for ADHD children, but recent studies suggest that the skills children learn in a clinical setting don't often transfer to the real world. For this reason parents are in the best position to help their ADHD children make friends.

Begin by trying to find a child who is like your own child: the same sex, the same interests, even the same activity level. Encourage play dates for an hour or two at a time, and be close by if any problems occur. Don't provide too much guidance, as ADHD children generally do better in unstructured play. Encourage communication between your child and this friend through short phone calls or e-mail.

Finding a group of friends will be more difficult for your ADHD child, but organized sports may at least give a sense of belonging to a group, even if he is not friendly with the other team members. Also remember that your family, although not made up of peers, is an important "group" for your child. Family meetings, for example, will help your child learn important skills, like waiting for your turn to speak, group problem-solving, and compromise.

Use Medication Only as Part of a Comprehensive Treatment Plan

Thousands of studies have made it clear that psychostimulant medications, such as Ritalin or Dexedrine, work in reducing the short-term behavioral symptoms of ADHD. As discussed, the side effects of these drugs are usually minor and typically go away when the medication is stopped. The problem with these drugs is that they may work *too* well. Anyone who takes them, whether that person has ADHD or not, will likely have the beneficial effects of increased attention and memory and better emotional control.

Because the drugs work so well, some parents have adopted a very cavalier and arbitrary approach to using them with their children. For example, one parent recently told me, "Normally I give Matthew his Ritalin only on school days, but I'm going to a family dinner on Saturday night and I want him to behave, so I'll give him medication then, too. I don't know about Sunday. I have to go to the mall for two or three hours, so Ritalin might be a good idea."

These parents aren't lazy or intentionally manipulative. They just become dependent on the relief from their children's troublesome behaviors provided by the medication. But it is important not to fall into this habit of making medical decisions for your children. A pill may be a convenient way to get instant cooperation, but clearly this is not the way any type of drug should be used. Medication should be used only as part of an approved treatment plan and in conjunction with other intervention techniques. Its effectiveness should be constantly evaluated, with an eye toward weaning the child away from the drug if at all possible.

Computers Can Help

Children with ADHD have particularly benefited from the explosion in computer software designed to help with their school learning. There are so many software programs that teach academic skills in a systematic and fun way that it is difficult to recommend one or two. To date, my personal favorites are the *JumpStart* programs available from Knowledge Adventure. These programs, available in home and classroom versions, present an entire year's currriculum on CD-ROM. Using entertaining games, they keep continuous track of your child's progress in every academic area.

It is also important to point out, however, that while computers are wonderful learning aids, they're not substitutes for parental involvement. You should become involved with the learning that your child is doing on the computer and coach his progress just as you would if he were learning in a more traditional, noncomputerized fashion. Children with ADHD love the computer, but when compared with their peers, they tend to be less organized and systematic in exploring its possibilities. Your own computer literacy, whether in exploring the Internet or understanding the programs your child is using, will be a critical factor in the success of this approach.

TEENAGERS

KEY TO PREVENTION: SELF-ACCEPTANCE AND REALISTIC PLANNING

Twenty-five years ago, when I first began treating children with ADHD, psychologists held the mistaken belief that this was a disorder only of childhood. It was widely thought that the cognitive development and hormonal changes that accompany adolescence would diminish the activity and impulsivity that characterize this disorder. Now we know that ADHD is not confined to childhood, but rather is a chronic problem that can have lifelong effects if left untreated.

Stuart's parents were very involved with their ADHD son as he was growing up. They took him to a neurologist, a psychiatrist, a learning specialist. They hired tutors. They had constant meetings with his teachers. Stuart was their only son, and they were committed to his well-being and success.

Their efforts were rewarded. Stuart made B's and some A's at school. He was well liked by his teachers. Everyone applauded his parents' herculean efforts. But as Stuart became a teenager, his parents were unprepared for a new set of problems, ones even their intense commitment couldn't alleviate. Stuart had been lonely in middle school, but his loneliness deepened in high school. He had trouble making friends. He felt awkward and embarrassed around girls, and he didn't want to date. He preferred to stay home and play video games and watch television. Just at the time that his parents felt he'd "conquered" his problems, he seemed unhappier than ever.

Certainly there are many teenagers other than just the ones with ADHD who experience difficulty in school, problems in making friends, and awkwardness and frustration in dating. But ADHD teens are typically far less resourceful in meeting their own needs than others and far less resilient when they experience failure.

Studies of ADHD children as they become teens show that in most cases overactivity significantly diminishes but problems in self-control persist. ADHD teens continue to need help in many areas of school as the subject matter gets harder and the need for independent study increases.

From a social perspective, it helps to think of your ADHD teen as two or three years less "mature" than his peers, so you can readily understand his disadvantage in forming friendships or in dating. (Think of yourself when you were sixteen years old, and envision yourself hanging around with a thirteen-year-old?)

The ongoing problems that ADHD teens had as children now combine and interact with the common problems of adolescence. Teenagers have a particular form of egocentrism. Psychologists sometimes say that teens see themselves as the "star of their own movie" and feel that no one really understands the unique experiences they are going through. They also may act as if there is always an audience for their "story" and they are continuously being judged on everything they do.

This type of self-consciousness can be particularly problematic for ADHD teens, because they often feel like the victims rather than the heroes of their stories. They are now more aware of how others view them than when they were young and may be more affected by criticism or complaints about their behavior. When we add impulsivity and poor judgment to this mix, it is easy to see why

ADHD teens may be more at risk for all the problems common to adolescence.

As the parent of an ADHD teen, you will have to be much more involved in guiding his choices. Understandably, your teen may resent this. But you will have to stay on top of your teen's developmental progress regardless. Just as in earlier stages, your emotional bond with your teen will be an important part of your success.

AN OUNCE OF PREVENTION

It is critical that the ADHD adolescent be helped in active contexts. He needs to learn to "work" with others by being with them, whether it is the family, friends, or just a group of kids on a shared mission.

Consider Family Counseling If Your ADHD Teen Has School or Social Problems

By the time an ADHD child has reached midadolescence, he's probably been exposed to numerous forms of counseling and behavioral-management techniques. Some of these may have been positive, others negative. But if problems still persist ADHD teens may benefit more from family than from individual counseling. Family counseling will help you look at new ways to provide structure for your ADHD teen that are more appropriate to his age. An experienced family counselor will also be aware of the special risks that face ADHD teens.

Give Your Teen Adventure Experiences

Adventure Camps, also called Wilderness Camps, are very popular with ADHD teens and can give them a new sense of self-worth in social situations. The programs at these camps can last from a weekend to a whole summer, and they involve a variety of outdoor challenges from rope climbing and kayaking to wilderness camping. They promote self-confidence in individuals as well as interdependence among group members. Always make sure that you choose an accredited camp with trained counselors and safety procedures. To find accredited therapeutic wilderness programs, call the Association for Experiential Education at (303) 440-8844.

Help Your Teen Develop a Responsible Attitude Toward Medication

The majority of ADHD adolescents continue to show a positive response to medication. Studies suggest that teens on medication enjoy improved academic performance and more rewarding social lives. However, many teenagers don't want to be on medication anymore, and of course they are now at an age when they can make their own choices. Some teens are more sensitive to the side effects of the medication, others don't like feeling that they have a "disability," and some report that "the pills don't help anyway." Still other ADHD teens are just so disorganized and forgetful that they are unable to follow the prescribed medication regimen, and thus it has diminished therapeutic benefits. Parents often want a teen to take total responsibility for his medication as he enters midadolescence, but this may be unrealistic. (Parents may also worry that by encouraging one drug they'll be somehow inviting experimentation with other drugs, but there is no evidence to support this fear.)

The more teens understand about their medication, the likelier they are to comply with a doctor's prescribed usage. Make sure that your teenager understands why he is on medication and that this isn't a sign that he is stupid, nor is it a drug that gets people high. Explain how the medication helps him and other people with the same problem. Help him understand what the side effects are. There are several books available that explain ADHD from a teen's point of view, such as *ADHD: A Teenager's Guide* by James Crist. These can be very useful in helping ADHD teens feel that they aren't alone with this problem.

If a teen wants to try going without his medication, it should be an "experiment" that his parents, teachers, and physician are aware of. If he can function well, that's great. But if his schoolwork and behavior start to suffer, the medication may have to be reinstated.

Find Small Steps That Lead to Success

ADHD teens are often initially enthusiastic and optimistic when confronting a new situation, but this optimism can fade quickly. As mentioned, most ADHD teens don't have the same self-control and self-management skills as their peers, so persistence remains a problem. You can help your teen by showing him how to break down a task into small steps. He will learn to take pride as each substep is ticked off. For example, if he has a term paper to write, show him how to divide it into sections, and write a specified amount each day. If he has trouble dating, encourage him first to attend open dances. Let him correspond with other teens through e-mail or by phone. Help him enjoy these small social interactions as he develops the skills for deeper relationships.

Consider Early Career and College Counseling

Thinking about what an average teen will do after high school is worrisome for most parents, but it's even more of a concern for parents of ADHD teens. Many ADHD teens have difficulty in a structured home life and a highly supervised high school setting, so parents naturally wonder what will happen when they are on their own, without those stabilizing forces. Will they get to class on time—or at all? Will they keep their rooms a mess? Will they be tempted by drinking or drugs? Will they be able to keep up with the work?

ADHD teens do best when college and career issues are confronted early, even in the ninth or tenth grade. Parents should talk to a school counselor about the various post–high school opportunities, which range from community colleges to colleges specifically designed for learning-disabled students. Perhaps for some teens, higher education isn't the answer at all. Some ADHD teens might be better off guided toward early career training. These are important decisions that need to be discussed many times throughout your teen's developing years. Ultimately, everyone wants the same outcome: a happy and successful teen.

Computers Can Help

ADHD teenagers, like other teens, are drawn to the Internet chat rooms, and these can be a good opportunity for them to learn communication skills and to feel part of a group. Chat rooms force an ADHD teen to be more patient and thoughtful as messages are typed back and forth.

Of course, time on the Internet must be budgeted and monitored, just like time on the phone, or time watching television. This can be a problem for all teens, but particularly for ADHD teens, who may not have good judgment or the ability to prioritize their time and activities. Using a simple timer can help. Set it for a half hour or forty-five minutes, and when the time is up, so is the Internet session.

There are hundreds of chat rooms on the Internet that are appropriate for teens and thousands more that are inappropriate. Parents need to set rules and limits on using the Internet, just as they do for other activities where teenagers can encounter dangers. There are computer-software programs, like *CyberPatrol,* that can restrict access to certain areas of the Net and keep a record of the sites your teenager visits, but most enterprising teens can get around such safeguards with just a little effort. The best approach is to make sure that Internet safety is a regular topic of conversation, along with discussions on alcohol, cigarettes, and safe sex.

• • •

ADHD is a biochemically based disorder and must be faced head-on as early as possible. Although we cannot really diagnose a child accurately until four or five, preventive efforts can begin in infancy, by teaching "difficult" infants to self-soothe and to be more compliant. By the time a child is a preschooler, there are many important tasks that parents can help their active and impulsive children achieve. Parents should particularly work on finding a discipline technique that is effective and on continuing a positive emotional bond with their child even in the light of those difficult behaviors.

By the time he is six or seven, the focus on helping the ADHD child shifts to the school. Helping him feel successful in academics as well as in his social interactions is the key to developing a sense of competence and self-worth. Although we once believed that teenagers would grow out of their ADHD, this is usually not the case. ADHD teens are typically less hyperactive, but they still have problems in self-control. Parents of ADHD teens will continue to be involved in making sure that their sons and daughters achieve appropriate developmental milestones in spite of their chronic problem. It is important to remember that at least half of adults who had ADHD as children report that they have successfully coped with this disorder, and many have focused their energy and enthusiasm into highly successful careers and satisfying relationships. This is the goal to keep in mind as you work with your ADHD child. Take satisfaction in every step your child makes toward achieving it.

8

Preventing the Long-Term Effects of Divorce

In the 1960s and '70s the divorce rate soared from just over 10 percent to nearly 50 percent of marriages. Trying to be optimistic in the face of a social crisis, psychologists and parenting groups promoted the belief that enduring divorce could often be better for children than living with parents who had a bitter and loveless marriage.

Now, more than three decades later, with the children of this divorce explosion having their own children (and getting their own divorces), we can look back and see the naïveté of this assumption.

The simple truth is that divorce is never "good" for children. Children of divorce frequently suffer from both an interruption in their normal social and emotional development and from specific psychological symptoms. Researchers estimate that when they grow up, nearly half the people who experienced divorce in their childhood are less successful in their work and in their relationships, and they are more prone to emotional problems, including depression and substance abuse.

Of course, growing up in a home beset by constant discord, amid a loveless marriage, can also be harmful to children. They certainly will not have good role models for developing intimate relationships later in their lives. As they grow older, they might even ask their parents, "Why didn't you get a divorce if you were so unhappy?" and they may fantasize that their own lives would have been better if this had happened.

No counselor can look into the future to tell parents whether getting a divorce or staying together in an unhappy marriage would be better for any particular child. All we can do is point out what children need as they grow in order to prevent problems from developing, and urge parents to do their best to make these needs a priority.

On the positive side, if 50 percent of the children of divorce experience long-term problems, this also means that half the children of divorce *don't* report serious long-term effects. They may have their complaints and regrets, but when we examine these grown children of divorce from a psychological or sociological point of view, we cannot distinguish them from adults who didn't experience a divorce when they were young.

THE STAGES OF DIVORCE

Psychologists recognize three major stages that families go through when they divorce, with each stage having its pitfalls and opportunities. "Opportunities" may seem like an odd choice of word considering the emotional pain that divorce inevitably brings, yet from a purely developmental point of view, any challenge in life can spur emotional growth.

The three stages include the Crisis Stage, lasting up to three months; the Reorganization Stage, which lasts up to two years after the divorce; and the Adjustment Stage, lasting from two to five years.

If you've gone through a divorce, or you know someone who has, you will know that "crisis" aptly describes the initial reaction to divorce. It is a period of extreme emotions for the couple, typically characterized by swings between anger and depression. Children are not usually as emotionally reactive as their parents are to an impending separation or divorce. They may be very upset at first hearing the news, but shortly thereafter they may be eerily calm.

Younger children don't really understand all that a divorce implies. It is an abstract concept, like death, and they may choose not to think about it. Even older children and adolescents may initially react with a surprising amount of composure. Most children and teens have much better psychological defenses than parents give them credit for, and they will typically rally these defenses at a time of crisis.

Children of all ages, however, are more reactive in this initial stage when their parents have emotional difficulties. They are not used to seeing their parents this upset, and it can be frightening for them. Although most children will be able to continue their lives with a minimum of difficulty, their ability to handle prolonged stress is fragile, and it depends on continued support from their parents. If this support is not forthcoming, they may soon become emotionally vulnerable, with problems ensuing. The most significant danger of this stage is what psychologists refer to as "diminished parental capacity." Children need their parents to protect them, guide them, and support them throughout their developing years, but when parents are preoccupied with their own pain and suffering, children can suffer as well.

The second stage of a divorce, the Reorganization Stage, generally begins three months after the initial separation and lasts from twelve to twenty-four months. It should be characterized by the beginning of a return to normalcy for both children and their parents. Custody arrangements should become consistent and predictable. As children adjust to the changes in their lives, they can begin to explore their feelings and conflicts about what has happened. In this stage, parents should strive to stabilize their lives so that their children will feel as secure and confident as they did before the divorce. This is also a period when many parents seek help. Now that the crisis is over, parents may turn to friends, a support group, or a professional counselor.

A common mistake that parents make in this stage is to turn to their children to fill an emotional void. Sometimes it is subtle, like when a mother finds herself confiding to her son about the details of her problems at work, as if that child were another adult. Sometimes it is more obvious, like when a father has his daughter dress up for a Saturday-night "date," and they go to a high-priced restaurant as if they were a couple. It is not the job of children to cheer up their parents or to be a companion. When I hear a parent say, "Oh, my child is my best friend," I know a problem exists.

It is also not unusual in this stage for parents to seek their children as allies against the ex-spouse. Since anger and hostility are often still present, some parents make the mistake of asking their older children and teens to choose sides. One ten-year-old I treated said that her mother "grilled" her about every visit to her father's new apartment. This mother would ask detailed questions about the arrangement of the father's furniture, what he served for each meal, and whom he was dating. The daughter said that her mother made her feel like a spy.

The third stage of divorce, the Adjustment Stage, might not actually start until two years after the initial separation, sometimes even later than that. You know you are in this stage when your life feels "normal." Although most parents and children report that they never feel exactly the same after a divorce, by this time there should be a sense of calm and predictability to a child's day-to-day life, permitting her to deal with developmental issues that have nothing to do with the divorce. Yet even this stage can present problems for parents, problems that get passed on to their children. Frequently parents in this stage don't "let go" of the ex-spouse. Hostility isn't usually as intense as it was, but the bitterness and resentment still colors the family life. A few years ago I worked with a man who had been divorced from his wife for over ten years. His two children were in their mid-teens. Both he and his ex-wife were remarried. Yet he talked about problems with his ex-wife in every conversation we had. They wrote venomous letters back and forth on a weekly basis. Both still retained lawyers who contested the terms of the divorce. I could only imagine the effect all this had on his children.

While the divorce process is considered over when life gets back to normal and the divorce issues cease to be a daily concern, children of divorce live with it as an important part of their identity for the rest of their lives. This is critical for parents to understand. No matter what age the child was when the divorce occurred—infancy through adolescence—the event is part of a child's history.

In a "successful" divorce children see their parents as having made a mistake but having had the courage to correct it. As adults they learn that we all make mistakes, but when we deal with them well, they are certainly forgivable. When children develop understanding and forgiveness as they grow, the effects of the divorce are usually of a limited nature. But a difficult divorce that has caused unresolved pain for parents or their children can have a powerful effect on their futures. Children grow up feeling that something "bad" happened when they were young. The divorce is never fully accepted and understood, and instead it remains an unhappy filter through which all future relationships are viewed.

Of course, any divorce will bring some pain and sadness, but it need not be a major influence on your child's development or your own.

RISK FACTORS FOR DIVORCE BECOMES A LIFELONG PROBLEM

Reducing the risks that your children will have lasting problems as a result of your divorce takes a special kind of commitment. Many parents understandably find it hard when they are in pain to make decisions in the best interests of their children. But this is exactly what is required. Unfortunately, there are few immediate rewards for parents of children going through the intensity of a divorce, so it is important to keep the long-term picture clearly in mind. This is what prevention is all about.

Psychological Vulnerability

As we saw in Chapter 1, some children are simply less resilient than others. They may be temperamentally more sensitive to change and stress. They may have fewer of the skills that we refer to as emotional intelligence, making them less able to express, communicate, or control their feelings. They may have learning difficulties or be predisposed to some of the other problems that have been covered in this book, like ADHD, shyness, or underachievement.

Any of these factors may compound the effects of a divorce, making children even more vulnerable to emotional and behavioral problems. If this describes your child, you will have to be even more vigilant than the average parent in protecting him or her from the complex stresses of divorce. Read this chapter carefully, and consider a professional consultation if you are concerned about how your child is reacting to the divorce. Don't wait for symptoms to appear. We now know that many children who didn't seem to have problems when they were young developed them late in adolescence and even as young adults.

If you're going through a divorce and your child is also at risk for other problems, you might want to investigate a divorce-counseling group for children, usually run at school, through a community health center, or other mental-health agency. These programs are particularly helpful because they allow children to meet and talk to peers who are going through a similar situation.

Gender

Boys and girls react differently to divorce. For example, school-age boys tend to have more problems than girls when dealing with the initial parental breakup. At this age some boys develop an intense attachment to their fathers and feel great pain at the void left when the father is out of the home. A boy who develops behavioral problems as a reaction to stress may then begin battling with his mother, who now must be the chief enforcer of household rules. School-age boys who withdraw emotionally as a reaction to a divorce may have difficulty allowing themselves to seek others who might provide solace or support

School-age girls, on the other hand, are less likely to show immediate problems after a divorce. Girls aren't as likely as boys to have behavioral problems, nor are they as likely to have their concerns at home spill over into their performance at school. However, girls *are* more likely to have problems in their teenage years, even if the divorce occurred years before. Rather than acting out these problems, girls most commonly internalize them, suffering from depression or physical problems. They may also have trouble with dating and in forming healthy relationships, patterns that can last well into adulthood.

Disruption of Routine

When parents get a divorce, everything a child knows and takes for granted is suddenly changed. One of the most significant initial stress factors on children is the change of routine. Children thrive on predictability: going to bed at the same time with the same nighttime ritual, viewing a video with the whole family every Friday night, even knowing that there's a specific time and place to do homework. A divorce interrupts all this. Suddenly there is concern over the simplest of matters: "Who'll pick me up at the bus stop?" "Who'll make dinner?" "Who'll take me to baseball practice, or piano lessons, or Sunday school?"

In 90 percent of all divorces, children initially remain with the mother and visit the father on weekends. Now weekends that were once a time to "unwind" become a ritual of ambivalence. Most children want to see their father, but visiting him also means coping with being in a new place, often away from friends, certainly without all the familiar books, toys, and other paraphernalia of everyday life.

With sensitive and cooperative parents, most children adjust to a new routine fairly quickly. Problems may continue, however, when parents don't make a reasonable effort to keep life consistent for their children. If children have different bedtimes, different eating habits, and different rules in each household, the stage will be set for continued confusion and conflict.

Parental Fighting and Parental Blame

Intense arguments and family violence can be traumatic to children, and these occur with a high percentage of divorced couples. I remember counseling one couple, both of whom were college professors. In their initial session they collaboratively described a scene where the husband yanked his wife out of the car during an argument. She proceeded to kick him in the groin, then throw their three-year-old child into the car and drive away. Nearly ten years later I can still vividly recall dozens of therapy sessions with this couple and their loud arguments, bitter accusations, and uncontrolled sorrow. I can't help but think that if this fighting made such an indelible impression on me, what did it do to their child? Too many times a child's brain records these memories like a handprint set in concrete. And once set, the memories cannot be erased.

A subtler form of aggression comes with parental blame. In some families the parents are careful not to fight in front of their children, but one or both have no qualms about complaining to their children about the ex-spouse with undisguised anger and meanness. No doubt the parent thinks that this anger is deserved. Perhaps an affair precipitated the divorce. Maybe the husband isn't keeping up with his support payments. I've heard dozens of stories about an ex-spouse who had committed some "unforgivable" act. But blaming the other spouse to your child doesn't hurt the ex-spouse; it only hurts your child. You may succeed in turning your child against your ex-spouse, or you may succeed in turning her against you. In either case everybody loses. In study after study we find that children who are alienated from a parent are much more psychologically damaged than children who stay connected to both parents, no matter how great their faults and weaknesses might be.

Asking a Child to Be a Parent

Just as children shouldn't be asked to join the battle against another parent, they also shouldn't be asked to tend to a wounded parent. In my experience very few people "bounce back" from a divorce, even though the other partner may think that this is so. But help with an adult problem should not come from a child.

Girls seem to be most frequently put in the role of having to "parent a parent." Often they accept this role easily and gracefully, and it makes them feel wanted. Because girls tend not to have as many immediate adjustment problems as boys, they may appear to be emotionally strong to a parent who is in acute distress. But this appearance is deceptive. Long-term studies that have followed the children of divorce for decades show that girls tend to have a delayed reaction to divorce, often looking back with resentment at the time it took to care for their parents and the opportunities they missed when they were asked to be more than a child.

Paternal Absence

In the initial stage of divorce, most children must cope with the absence of the father. But many mothers are surprised that children are so affected by not seeing their father on a daily basis. As one newly divorced mother complained to me, "My husband came home from work late, fell asleep on the couch after dinner, and on weekends he was out with his buddies. My kids hardly ever saw him, so nothing has really changed." But this isn't true from a child's point of view. Even though a father might not spend nearly as much time with his children as the mother, children are used to the "atmosphere" of the father. Just having the father around—even sleeping on the couch or engrossed in a ball game—provides children a sense of security and belonging that becomes lost when parents separate.

Children suffer tremendously when a father disengages himself from them, yet this seems to be the rule rather than the exception as the months and years go by. One national survey found that only one in six children from a divorced family saw their father on a weekly basis, and a high percentage hadn't seen their father for an entire year. Part of the reason that fathers become less involved in their children's lives is remarriage. Men are twice as likely than women to remarry in the first three years after a divorce, and the majority will either start a new family or inherit a family.

Whatever the reason that fathers become emotionally detached from their children, they should be aware that this presents a very serious risk factor, potentially causing emotional problems that may never be remedied.

Remarriage

Remarriage, as we've just seen, is a contributing factor to parental estrangement from children. Few children handle the remarriage of a parent without conflict, which often leads to renewed bitter feelings between the child's primary parents. There are competitive feelings toward the stepparent, conflicted loyalties to the parent "left behind," and anger that remarriage has ended all chances at a reconciliation. In the new family, children may resent a stepparent who is assigning chores or handing down discipline. And then of course there are the stepsiblings who create endless excuses for arguments and hurt feelings.

The stress caused by remarriage when children are involved is clearly reflected by the number of second marriages that end in divorce. In a twenty-year project, the Virginia Longitudinal Study of Divorce and Remarriage tracked 450 families who experienced a divorce. Among the project's findings were that remarriages involving children were five times likelier to end in divorce than other second marriages.

Change in Standard of Living

With all our concern about the psychological factors that can hurt the children of divorce, we cannot ignore how a lowered standard of living can affect a child's life. According to one study, out of one hundred families divorced for more than five years, sixty-three of the households where the children resided had a substantially lowered income. This resulted in a range of problems. The study concluded that divorce frequently has an economic impact on children, causing a move to cheaper housing, a change of schools, and other disruptions to a child's life.

Children often feel insecure, resentful, and even scared by the loss of familiar comforts. They can also become depressed and anxious as they watch a parent cope with financial stress. Since mothers are the custodial parents 90 percent of the time, and since women are already likely to have lower wages than their husbands, appropriate child support is a necessity to maintain the same standard of living that children had before the divorce. But according to the Federal Office of Child Support in the 20th Annual Report to Congress, only 54 percent of the families headed by a woman divorced from the father receive regular and full payments, and only 24 percent of the families headed by a woman never married to the father receive regular child-support payments.

Underestimating the Effects of Divorce

It is understandable that parents want to put their divorce in the background as soon as possible. Once they are through the Reorganization Stage, they may have a new job, a new home, a new spouse. They want the pain of the divorce to be a thing of the past. But this is not possible for a child. The divorce is part of her history, part of her identity. Parents who try to pretend that the divorce is a dead issue are doing a disservice to their children and putting them at risk for serious emotional problems later in their lives. Parents who understand that a divorce is never really over for their children will best be able to foresee and prevent such problems.

INFANTS

KEY TO PREVENTION: KEEPING LIFE PREDICTABLE AND FATHERS INVOLVED

Infants, of course, are not consciously aware of their parents' divorce. They don't have the cognitive ability to perceive that their parents are suddenly not eating meals together or sharing a bed. They haven't yet developed a sense of time, so they can't quantify how extensive is one parent's absence. But they do have an acute sensitivity to their parents' emotions. They will pick up on a parent's sadness and on the angry words and gestures that frequently pass between divorcing couples. They may react to their parents' changing emotions and moodiness, particularly since these are likely to be intense. In many cases a single mother of an infant is understandably overwhelmed and overstressed. Combine this with the constant demands of raising a baby, and it would seem unusual to find a person who *wasn't* on emotional overload in this situation. And naturally, any emotional problems that affect a mother, particularly depression, will have an adverse effect on an infant.

Babies will also be affected by the changes in routine that accompany the initial stage of a divorce. Infants (and older children as well) thrive in a home that is stable and predictable. They are happiest when the same thing happens every day: mealtimes are the same, bedtime is the same, parents play the same games with them in the same way. But divorce will surely upset their routine. One woman I know let her baby sleep in her bed when her husband left. Another started spending every other night at her own mother's house, dragging her baby in tow. Even when parents try their best to keep their baby's schedule the same, it is often impossible. There may be a new baby-sitter coming at a different time, or a new day-care arrangement because of a move or a mother's new job.

Another notable problem that affects infants whose parents are divorcing is the danger of losing their father altogether. As we've seen, a high percentage of divorced fathers emotionally disengage from their children as they grow older, even though they start out with every intention of staying involved in their children's lives. But the fathers of infants are more apt to rationalize their absence sooner. They may feel that they hardly know this child, and that after a short time the infant will not even recognize them. They may feel that it is better to just step out of their child's life now, before a permanent attachment is formed. They mistakenly feel that this is better for the child—and for themselves.

The significance of a parent's emotional state on an infant's well-being and the effect of changes in a baby's routine will vary according to the temperament of the baby. Easy babies are by definition more adaptable. Difficult and fearful babies are more sensitive to change. By this reasoning, a child who is already at risk due to his temperament will be even more so if his parents divorce. Some of the preventive measures that I will suggest here may seem difficult to manage for parents in the throes of a divorce. But when a baby is at risk, no sacrifice should be too great.

AN OUNCE OF PREVENTION

Keep the Father Involved

There are many reasons that fathers may feel they should just stop seeing their baby. The most significant is the ongoing hostility with the baby's mother and the common request of mothers to "just stay away." There are obviously significant reasons for a couple to choose to divorce at a time when they are surrounded by pressures to stay together, and it isn't surprising that mothers of a very young child may want to avoid all of the anger that accompanies a divorce by asking the father simply to bow out of the picture. Another factor is that many men feel uncomfortable with the jobs required in taking care of infants. They may not like changing diapers or dealing with messy eating habits. Many men say that they prefer being with older children, whom they can talk to and play with in a more conventional way.

Although it may go against all their natural instincts, mothers should work to keep ex-husbands involved in the lives of their children. Children need their fathers. Fathers need to be with their children. Certainly a father can form an attachment to his child when the child is older, but it's always more beneficial for him to remain an important part of his baby's life from the moment of birth.

Keep to a Routine

This is easier said than done. Divorce is a very disruptive influence on a family, particularly in the first few months. Yet routine is what your baby needs. Write down your baby's schedule: the time he eats, sleeps, plays, listens to a favorite audiotape, and so on. Try to keep to that schedule. Post it on the refrigerator or in another obvious place, where you will see it several times a day. This will help you make your baby's routine a priority, even when there are many pressures and problems fighting for your attention.

Avoid Shared Physical Custody of Infants

Many parents seek shared physical custody as the most equitable and reasonable way to raise children. In trying to keep the child's time equal with both parents, they might split the week in two, or have their child with them every other week. While this can work with older children, it is not advisable for infants.

Most experts agree that infants do best when they have a single home: one room, one crib, one place to eat and play. Although it may be awkward, a father should try to visit with his baby for regular periods of time in the mother's home. Remember that this is only for a relatively short period of time. When your baby becomes a toddler, she will be much more adaptable, and will enjoy spending time at her father's home as well.

Parents Should Live in Close Physical Proximity

Since shared physical custody is not recommended for infants, try to work out an arrangement in which parents live near each other. When a father has to drive a long distance to see his baby, this will eventually be a disincentive for him to visit. Similarly, you would want to avoid having a baby take long car rides on a regular basis.

Make a Shared-Parenting Agreement

A shared-parenting agreement is an informal contract to create a stable and predictable environment for a child immediately after a divorce. There are many forces that will work against the parents of infants making the required sacrifices. That is why a shared-parenting agreement will be particularly helpful. This agreement is not legally binding, nor is it used as the basis for a divorce decree. But it is a commitment that carries important psychological weight.

If possible, the plan should be worked out in a single session with a neutral mediator. The session will probably last at least three hours, but it could go on for six hours or more. It should be understood from the beginning that neither spouse will be happy with the plan—that is the nature of compromise. It is the mediator's role to look after the best interests of the child and to stress the importance of adhering to the plan for the designated six-month period. Minimally, the plan should spell out a visitation schedule that will be predictable for the child and at least a temporary financial arrangement. The overriding principle of the plan is to reduce the "shock" to all members of the family and prevent a difficult situation from becoming much worse. It is hoped that after six months both parents will have stabilized their lives and developed the habit of making their young child their very first priority.

TODDLERS AND PRESCHOOLERS

KEY TO PREVENTION: HONESTY AND CONSISTENCY

In some ways toddlers and preschoolers are similar in their needs to infants when their parents get a divorce. They are still very sensitive to their parents' emotions, particularly to their fighting. They still rely on a predictable schedule to make them feel secure and to use as a base to venture further out into the world. But this stage also presents new problems for parents. Preschool children are much more aware of what their parents do and say, and this can be a mixed blessing. You can explain to your preschooler about the divorce and why it is happening, but this explanation can temporarily raise more anxiety in the child as he grapples to understand the true meaning of your words. Preschool children are also much more aware of the changes in their parents' habits and behaviors. An infant won't be concerned when a strange man comes to pick up his mother for a date, but a three- or four-year-old will certainly take note. He'll be aware that his mother is getting dressed up, or that she's wearing perfume. He'll be aware that this man going out with his mother may be a threat to him and to his father.

Even the most amicable divorce can be a traumatic experience for young children. Children want to see their parents together. This gives them a sense of safety and security. When parents of young children separate, it can raise fears of abandonment in a child. A four-year-old might think, "Daddy has moved out of the house. Maybe Mommy will, too!" Preschool-age children, from three to five, have a very active fantasy life, and they are likelier to elaborate a negative event (fear of abandonment) than a positive one (a trip to an amusement park). This is why fears are so common in the preschool years (see Chapter 5).

Young children begin to worry about a particular situation or event, and the more they think about it, the more it is embellished. A cartoon monster becomes a monster that could exist in real life, and then a monster that lives in the closet. Using a similar line of thinking, a child might illogically reason that if her parents are separating from each other, they might soon separate themselves from her, too. If they're mad at each other, they may be mad at her, too. If they're sad and unhappy, she may be the reason they feel this way.

This type of excessive worry is common in young children, even in families where there is no divorce. Divorce, however, tends to cause a particular problem because it involves prolonged intense emotions, that are not really comprehensible to a young child. It can cause a cycle of worry and anxiety that both adds to and feeds off the stress of adjusting to all the real-world changes that accompany a divorce, such as having two homes and meeting the new people that parents date.

Some young children react to the trauma of a divorce with obvious changes in their behavior, such as manifesting fears and anxieties, having nightmares, staging angry outbursts, or retreating into periods of sadness and lethargy. Other children have a subtler reaction. They may be intensely watchful of their parents to see if anything is wrong. They may cling more to one or both parents, and want to sleep in their parents' bed. Many young children regress to earlier behavior. They may wet the bed again, or even wet themselves during the day. They may want to have a bottle again, even though they haven't had one for years. They may cry more and use baby talk. Some symptoms are common in young children during the initial crisis stage of divorce, but if they last more than a week or two, they serve as a signal that the child isn't able to muster more age-appropriate coping skills, and early professional intervention might be indicated.

In the preschool years both boys and girls can be much more dependent on their father, and may suffer more from his absence. A boy seeks his father as a role model and as an active participant in "male" activities. He will miss his father's physical way of playing or his interest in sports, and he can become very upset about this loss. Between three and five, girls often become "romantically" attached to their father, and they may interpret his absence as a personal rejection.

As in every stage of a child's life, many of these problems can be addressed by sensitive parents who are willing to put their own needs on the back burner so that they can focus on the developmental needs of their children. The first three to six months are critical as children adjust to the crisis of the divorce. But the next year or even two can be equally important. Parents must find a way to reorganize their lives and balance the needs of their growing children with their legitimate desires to move on to the next stage in their own development.

AN OUNCE OF PREVENTION

Tell Your Preschooler About the Divorce in Simple Language

Many young children don't want to talk about the divorce. They often find it easier to cope with their feelings by trying to ignore the situation altogether.

Parents should tell their children about the divorce in the simplest terms possible: "Mommy and Daddy are very unhappy living together. When this happens, sometimes mommies and daddies decide to live in different places and not be married anymore. This is called a 'divorce.' Mommy will be living here with you, and Daddy will live in a new place, which you will visit. Mommy and Daddy will always love you and take care of you, and we will all be fine."

Parents often worry about the exact words they will use to tell their children about the divorce, but the specific words are much less important than the way you impart this information. Be calm and reassuring. Be truthful. Have a series of conversations about the divorce for several days, repeating some of the important things from the day before.

Some young children refuse to hear about the divorce once it has been announced. It's simply too upsetting for them. Often it will be easier for them to listen while the two of you are doing an activity together, like taking a walk or baking cookies. Don't force your child to talk if she doesn't want to, but do talk about your own feelings in realistic and positive terms. Remember that your non-verbal communication is as important as what you say, and just being with your child and expressing affection says a lot.

Reading books can also help you convey the right message to your child. Ask your local librarian to suggest age-appropriate books about divorce, and then read them to your child. My favorite book is *The Dinosaurs Divorce*, by Marc and Laurene Brown, a colorfully illustrated cartoon book that starts out by explaining, "If dinosaurs got married, then some of them would also have gotten a divorce." When you find an appropriate book, leave it out on a table when it is not being read. This will help make the divorce a concrete reality. It will also make it easier for a child to look through the book herself, or ask to have it read.

Explain the Reasons for the Divorce

Young children are famous for asking "why?" and you can be sure that you will hear this question at some time during the divorce process. Give simple but honest answers. Even if an answer is embarrassing and one you wish the child didn't know, it is always better to be honest. As child psychiatrist Richard A. Gardner explains in *The Parents Book About Divorce*: "Parents do best when they describe to their children the basic reasons for the divorce. It is surprising how frequently parents do not provide their children with this important information. I believe that some of the disturbances that children of divorced parents suffer results from the fact that parents, often with the best intentions . . . are not appropriately truthful about the divorce."

Being "appropriately truthful" does not mean that your life is an open book to your child. Children need honest answers, but not all of the details. Information that might cast a bad light on a parent should be balanced by positive statements about the parent. Something like "I can't live with Daddy anymore. He is always so angry at me. But he is a good man and he loves you very much."

Communicate with Others About Your Divorce and Your Child's Reactions

Even though divorce is so common, many parents of young children feel ashamed of their inability to keep their marriage going. This shame is amplified when one parent feels at fault, say, for having an affair. But even though you may be embarrassed, the important people in your life need to know about the divorce, about how your child is reacting, and the details of what will happen to your child. Will there be a change in where he lives? What is the visitation schedule? Will there be a change in his day care? By keeping others involved, you will also be developing an important support network for you and your child. Encourage other adults in your child's life to share their observations about how he seems to be adjusting to the divorce. The best way to prevent problems from becoming serious is to be aware of the early signs of trouble.

Address Symptoms Immediately

When young children have emotional reactions to their parents' divorce, these usually come in the form of disruptions to eating and sleeping habits. A child's appetite may decrease or increase. She may demand more foods high in sugar and fat, what we call "comfort foods." A child may sleep more or less. Most often a young child won't want to go to bed at the usual time, or will wake up in the middle of the night wanting to be soothed by her parents and to sleep in the parental bed. Most children respond to continued reassurance. They want you to hug them and hold them and tell them that everything will be fine. Though they may want to change their eating or sleeping habits, try as much as possible to help them keep to the usual routines.

Spend Time with Your Child

This may seem like very simplistic and obvious advice, but in reality children not only spend much less time with their noncustodial father after a divorce, they spend less time with their mother as well. As Barbara Dafoe Whitehead writes in *The Divorce Culture*, "By their own reports, divorced mothers are less likely than married ones to read to their children, share meals with them, and supervise their school activities. Compared with married mothers, single mothers exercise less control and have fewer rules about bedtimes, television watching, homework, and household chores."

The changes that occur in most homes after a divorce are gradual ones. In the beginning, most parents work hard to keep everything the same, but as time passes and the heightened emotions start to subside, parents typically change their work schedules, seek new child-care arrangements, and begin to think about a social life. Gradually, as the months go by, new demands on a parent's time translate to less predictability in a child's life, and even the most basic routines, like dinnertime and bedtime, can become inconsistent. A benchmark in the process of coping with a divorce is your success in reorganizing your life so that it is consistent and predictable for your child. The sooner this happens, the better for all concerned.

Consider the Effect of an Earlier Divorce on Your Young Child's Development

If the divorce occurred when your child was an infant, he won't remember it. If either or both spouses have remarried, he'll accept the new "binuclear family" as perfectly normal. Since he isn't cognitively mature enough to compare himself to children his age who haven't gone through a divorce, there is no stigma attached to the fact that he has two homes. On the other hand, if a child has been raised primarily by his mother and visited his father only on weekends, he may not have the same level of attachment to his father at this age. Since he is still very egocentric and vocal about his wants, he may sometimes say, "I don't want to go over to Daddy's house. I like it with Mommy better." This can be hurtful to a father, particularly one who has tried hard to remain in his child's life, but it's important to remember that this is just a stage. Continued visitation is the only way to build on the emotional attachment between a father and his child.

Remarriage can also have a significant effect on a toddler or preschooler. In most cases the child has spent a considerable amount of time alone with her mother, and a new man in the picture may be greeted with the same wariness as the announcement of a new sibling. In most cases this can be easily worked through. Attention to the child's needs and an understanding that her jealousy is normal will pave the way for a relationship with her stepfather, who can go on to become a very important person in the child's life.

SCHOOL-AGE CHILDREN

KEY TO PREVENTION: CREATE AN ATMOSPHERE OF OPEN COMMUNICATION

The sense of loss that accompanies a divorce is much more acute in a school-age child. This child will have developed a clear notion of family and will go through a grieving process at the loss of a family structure that once seemed inviolate.

School-age children are also much more aware of the reaction of their peers to a divorce. They may be embarrassed to tell their friends and may try to keep the divorce a secret for many months. One eight-year-old explained to me, "None of my friends have parents who are divorced, and they won't like me if they know that my parents are divorced. Girls don't like it when someone is different. I don't like it either."

School-age children may have a variety of emotional reactions to their parents' divorce. Anger and sadness are the most common. They may also have symptoms such as problems sleeping or new fears and anxieties. When symptoms last for more than the initial crisis period of three or four months, professional consultation should be sought. One of the most serious problems occurs when a child's emotional reaction to the divorce spills over into school. When a divorce occurs, children often seem dreamy and preoccupied at school. They may not be overly sad, but they can appear removed and uninterested in both their schoolwork and their friends. It is important to let the teacher know if you are going through a divorce. She will be the best person to alert you to early signs of school problems.

AN OUNCE OF PREVENTION

The best message you can give to your child is that you are always available when he or she needs to talk and that you are willing to talk about anything.

Make Conversations About Your Divorce a Two-Way Street

Very young children probably won't have too much to say about your divorce. You will do most of the talking. But things will be different with a school-age child. By six or seven, children become very articulate about their feelings and may not hesitate to express them. Some of these feelings may be difficult for you to hear, but remember that expressing emotions is part of the healing process. Communicating is the first step in learning to understand and accept one's feelings, and it is the best way to prevent troubling emotions from developing into behavioral and psychological symptoms at a later date.

It is also important to explain to your children that it is normal for them to have both negative and positive feelings at the same time. Children as young as five or six can understand that you can have two different feelings about the same thing or the same person, that you can love someone and yet be angry at that person, too.

Help Your Child Adjust to Living in Two Homes

Even if your child is with his father only on weekends, he is likely to feel that he has two homes. Feeling that he has a home with his father is his way of staying connected to him. But going between two homes can cause many problems for school-age children. They may miss activities with their friends if the father and mother live a significant distance apart. They may not have the toys they like to play with at their father's house, or they may forget to bring over the homework that's due on Monday. You can help your child by anticipating these problems and helping him be organized. Go over what he'll need for a weekend visit with the noncustodial parent, and make sure that your ex-spouse is aware of any activities that are important to your child. Generally speaking, if parents are committed to making visitations go smoothly, all these problems can be worked out. But if parents are still angry and uncooperative, the stage will be set for prolonged difficulties and unnecessary pain for your child.

Correct Misperceptions

Counselors who work with children of divorce have identified specific misperceptions that crop up at this age. These ideas occur in children so frequently that parents can anticipate them long before they are voiced. The following are some common misconceptions children have and ways you can respond to them.

Children Are to Blame for the Divorce

Parents get divorced because they can't agree and can't get along. The one thing they can agree on is their love for their child. Children are never the cause of a divorce.

One Parent Is Bad

Everyone makes mistakes in a marriage, or in any relationship. Even if one parent wants the divorce and the other doesn't, that doesn't make either parent bad. Try to talk about your child's own friendships to help her understand that relationships consist of actions and reactions, not of good and bad.

Divorce Is Something to Be Ashamed Of

Nearly half the children in the country are affected by divorce. This makes it very common. All families and all people have problems at some time. Divorce is not something to be embarrassed about.

Parents Getting a Divorce Never Really Loved Each Other

Parents wouldn't have gotten married unless they were in love. Many parents still have loving feelings for each other at the time of a divorce, but they don't want to live together anymore.

Parents Might Get Back Together

This is a universal fantasy of children, but it rarely comes true. Help your children understand that there is nothing they can do to bring their parents back together.

Children Can Help One or Both Parents Feel Better

It is not a child's job to take care of a parent, but the other way around. Parents who are sad or angry about the divorce need to get help from other adults.

Make Sure That Children Have Special Times with Both Parents

School-age children are activity-oriented. If both parents try to do one regular activity alone with a child each week, it will help the child trust in each parents' commitment. The activity should be one that both you and your child enjoy, and it should become a fixed part of the weekly schedule. It is usually more beneficial to children if the same activity is done every week.

Don't Be the Only One in Your Child's Life

In some families one parent becomes totally involved in a child's life, to the exclusion of all other adults. This is particularly likely if the father moves far away and the mother is living at a distance from her own family. Your being the only adult in your child's life, however, will ultimately make her more vulnerable to emotional conflicts. If you begin a serious relationship or remarry, you can expect that she will have a very hard time sharing you again. Keep other adults involved with your children. If grandparents or aunts and uncles are not available, then recruit neighbors or close friends. Children need to know that they can get love from many sources.

Prepare Your Child Well in Advance for Your Remarriage

Children at this age are less accepting of remarriage than either younger or older children. They may feel that they have "paid the price" for your divorce, and why should they now have to adjust to a new family? This is particularly true if there will be stepsiblings.

In spite of the impression you might get from TV sitcoms, blended families are almost always difficult for children, but there are a few things you can do to make the adjustment easier. Begin by preparing your children well in advance. Give them plenty of time and opportunity to get used to this change. Continue to spend time alone with them, without the new spouse. Reassure your children that you still love them and that this love cannot be replaced. Encourage them to spend time alone with their new stepmother or stepfather. See if they can find things in common and can develop their own relationship. Don't expect a stepparent to replace a parent in your children's eyes. When a stepparent tries to act as a disciplinarian or as the sole authority in the house, children often rebel.

Consider the Effect of an Earlier Divorce on Your School-Age Child's Development

When children start school, they are eager to fit into their peer group and to be like the other children. In many places divorce is so prevalent that it is not a stigma to children, but this isn't always the case. In communities where divorce is rare, the school-age child may feel as if she has a secret to hide and be very embarrassed by her special status. Sometimes children of divorce are teased by their classmates for not having a daddy or a mommy at home, and this can lead to social rejection. You can anticipate this problem and make it easier on your children. Emphasize that they are not different. They come from a divorced family or have a stepfamily, a fact that makes their life story different from others', but all families have some differences, and difference is not bad.

There are many factors that can affect the adjustment of school-age children of divorce, such as whether the mother has remarried and whether the father is still close to his children. At this age boys may start to seem more and more like their biological father, which can become a source of friction between a boy and his mother, particularly if she is still single. One mother told me, "It's like I'm married to my husband again. They're exactly the same, and my son annoys me in exactly the same ways as my husband did." Of course this is an exaggeration, brought on by the boy's behavior problems. Behavior problems in school-age boys occur fairly frequently, particularly in an all-female household.

Girls are usually better adjusted at this age. Whether the father is absent or present, girls normally adjust pretty well if the divorce occurred a number of years ago. Problems with girls are seen more when a mother remarries. Girls are typically more attached to their mothers than boys are at this age, and they may resent having a stepfather intrude on this emotional bond. If the biological father is still in the picture, a girl may look to him for new support when her mother remarries. A sensitive stepfather can also make it easier for school-age girls, particularly if he is respectful about the importance of the mother-daughter bond.

TEENAGERS

KEY TO PREVENTION: CONTINUED EMOTIONAL SUPPORT AND GUIDANCE

Many people expect that teenagers will respond better to the news that their parents are divorcing than younger children. They assume that teenagers have been aware of the problems in the marriage for some time. Since teenagers are moving away from the family, seeking to be more independent, parents anticipate that the announcement of an impending divorce won't significantly influence a teen's day-to-day life.

But all of these assumptions are usually wrong. Teens more typically respond to the announcement of divorce with a mixture of shock, anger, and disappointment.

Jane, for example, was sixteen years old when her parents told her that they were going to get a divorce. Her mother said they wanted to wait until after her sixteenth birthday to break the news so they wouldn't ruin the party that had been planned for almost a year. Her mother further explained that she and Jane's father had "grown apart." She noted, philosophically, that "these things just happen." They didn't hate each other, but they didn't love each other either. They just decided that it was best not to stay married.

Jane reacted to this reasoned explanation with rage. "You're disgusting!" was her only remark as she stormed out of the room, slamming the door behind her. Jane's mother wasn't expecting this kind of reaction. She'd always had a close "grown-up" relationship with her daughter and assumed that Jane would understand her point of view and the fact that the divorce wasn't intended to hurt her.

Parents who are divorcing frequently misjudge the passion that teenagers have for their families. They look at a teen's adultlike exterior—the clothes, the interests, the grown-up problems—and assume that their teen will respond to the news of a divorce as a friend might. But teenagers are typically very dependent on their families for support and protection. While they may be critical of their parents at times, they also hold them up as role models. But as Neil Kalter notes in his book *Growing Up Divorced*, "When parents separate, this process can be derailed as adolescents begin to perceive their parents in extremely negative terms. Divorce can bring a lasting, bitter, and demeaning view of parents."

Kalter also explains that teenagers are prone to personalize their parents' divorce. Their tendency to have an egocentric view of the world is even further exaggerated. They may complain, "Why are they doing this to me?" or "If Dad loved me, he wouldn't do this." Rather than being objective and dispassionate, a teen may react to the news of her parents' divorce as if her world has just exploded—and in a sense it has.

Still another misconception among parents of teens is that custody won't be an issue. In some cases parents fight for custody of a teen just as they would for a younger child. Teenagers are more apt to be drawn into the legal process and can be put in the unenviable position of having to testify about the personal life and "qualifications" of their parents. This can cause a great deal of resentment in a teen who feels that he is being asked to take sides against his own parent.

Parents of older teens sometimes decide that it is not worth battling over their teen, assuming that he knows his own mind and can make his own decision about where he wants to live. As one father rationalized, "I hardly see my son anyway. I get up early and go to bed early. He gets up late and stays out late. I'm thinking of getting him a car so that he can just visit me whenever he wants." But this cavalier attitude doesn't sit well with teens. They want to be wanted. A teenager needs a home and a sense of family, just like younger children.

Aside from the normal problems that teens have in adjusting to a divorce, it is difficult to predict if they are more vulnerable to psychological problems at this age. There is certainly no shortage of ways for teens to avoid thinking about their problems or to call attention to their conflicts. Some teens, when confronted with their parents' divorce, are more inclined to experiment with or abuse drugs and alcohol or to suddenly show a complete lack of interest in school. Girls in particular can be very vulnerable at this age to depression and eating disorders. But there is no evidence that divorce per se pushes a teen to have a psychological problem. In fact, many teens react very responsibly at the time of their parents' divorce, often showing more maturity than the grown-ups. It is s probably best to look at divorce as an extreme stress to teenagers, which comes at a time when they are dealing with many other issues. If a particular teen has already shown that she copes well with stress, then she'll probably be fine. But teens who have other problems that make them psychologically vulnerable will likely be more at risk with their parents' divorce in the background.

AN OUNCE OF PREVENTION

Like younger children, teenagers adjust better to a divorce best when parents are open and honest about what is happening. Routines and rules should remain the same. Also like younger children, teens should be kept out of the middle of the divorce, and they should not be used as a replacement partner or an ally against the ex-spouse. But teenagers also have special needs as they seek to form their own unique identity. Here are some ways to help teens stay focused on their own developmental issues rather than on the problems presented by the divorce.

Take the Time to Talk Through Your Teen's Emotions

Be respectful of your teen's emotional needs when you tell him about the divorce, and take the same thoughtful precautions you would with a younger child. Preferably both parents should be present. The talk should occur a few weeks before the physical separation is to take place, providing enough time for the teen to process what is happening but not so much time so that he'll be anticipating the event for many weeks or even months. Don't burden your teenager with your ambivalence, giving him the idea that the decision is still up in the air. Just tell him what you have decided and why. Tell him in detail what your plans are and how his life will be affected. Each parent should take a turn talking.

It's okay to discuss your feelings and to invite your teen to share his reactions. But don't press him too much. Remember that this is a shock, the same as if you'd told him about a serious illness or death in the family. Give him time to react.

After the initial conversation, set a time for the teen to be alone with each parent. This will surely be emotional for you as well as for your teen, but try to focus on his feelings, not yours. Give him support and reassurance. If you're concerned about how your teen will react, consider seeing a counselor for guidance. This will give you an opportunity to rehearse what you will say and to anticipate the various outcomes. The more at ease you are with this process, the more you can support your child. Contacting a counselor in advance will also give you a valuable resource if problems arise in the future for either you or your teen.

Don't Go to War with Your Spouse

If there is a single measure of a successful divorce, it is that the children feel that they have two loving and committed parents. This becomes more difficult, however, when teens see that each parent's emotions are still tied up with hostility toward the other parent. Few, if any, of the basic components of parenting can be accomplished if parents continue to harbor overt animosity toward each other. Anger and bitterness can hijack reason and make otherwise responsible parents become preoccupied and unavailable. Of course this is easy advice to give and hard to take. If you are in a bitter struggle with your spouse, try to see a mediator before you talk to your teenager about the divorce and impending separation. The more issues that are settled between you and your spouse before the physical separation takes place, the more available you can be for your teen.

Focus on Issues Other Than the Divorce

Your divorce may be the major concern in *your* life, but it doesn't have to be the number-one priority for your teen. She has schoolwork to worry about, friends, boyfriends, college, and career planning. Keep her focused on these matters. Make them the topics of your conversations just as you did before the divorce. Your teen looks to you for guidance and support. A divorce shouldn't change this.

Read Your Teenager's Nonverbal Cues

Some teenagers are articulate about their feelings and needs and some are not. But your teen's body language and other nonverbal cues will always communicate the truth. He may say that "nothing's wrong," but he slouches in his chair, sits half turned away from you, and avoids eye contact. The message is clear, so don't ignore it: he is unhappy and doesn't want to tell you. It is not difficult to read nonverbal cues, but we aren't used to doing this or trusting what we see. Have confidence in your ability to read your teen's behavior, and put words to what you see. Say something like, "You look unhappy to me. It's in the way you're sitting and your avoidance of talking to me. I want you to know you can say anything that's on your mind, and I want to help you if you have a problem."

Confront Issues Regarding Sex and Relationships Honestly

One subject that is almost certain to arouse ambivalent feelings in teens is their need to confront the fact that their parents are sexual beings. Again, it is important to deal with this issue openly and honestly and see it as part of the reorganization process. It is important also to see this from a teen's point of view. While parents often expect teenagers to understand their desire to date again, this expectation may be unrealistic. Uncomfortable with their own sexuality, teenagers may react with open disgust when their parents show an interest in dating. Your only comfort may be that it is much healthier for your teenager to deal with these feelings now than to harbor resentments that will emerge later. Boys in particular may have a hard time accepting that their mother has begun dating, and they may feel betrayed. This is a normal reaction, and one that should be talked about. Do not, however, allow teens to be rude or express their anger in inappropriate or discourteous ways. Your teenager will have many opportunities over the course of his life to feel hurt and disappointed; this is as good a time as any to teach him how to work out these conflicts.

Fathers: Stay Involved in Your Teen's Life—Mothers: Help Make This Happen

The noncustodial father must make a concerted effort to stay involved in his teen's life. He must provide for his teen financially, even though he may have other pressing demands on his income. The mother, no matter what has happened in the past, must work to help make this easier. She must support the ongoing relationship between teen and father, no matter how personally vexing this might be. Support groups can help parents vent their feelings in an appropriate manner, while keeping their behaviors in line with the best interests of their teen. Divorce is the end of a marriage, but it isn't the end of the family. Parents' responsibilities to do what is right for their children continue past the divorce—at least until the children are grown.

Consider the Effect of an Earlier Divorce on Your Teen's Development

Many adolescents whose parents divorced when they were young, and who have a good relationship with both parents, don't have problems related to the divorce. If the mother remarried when they were young, they will look on this as a stable family, with good and bad aspects, just like adolescents from an intact family. But if there's not been a remarriage, the problems of alienation from the noncustodial father or continued hostility between the parents can take a severe toll. As Neil Kalter notes in *Growing Up Divorced*, many teenagers and even many mental-health professionals don't realize that the problems of an adolescent may be related to an earlier divorce. They may think, "That was so long ago. How could it be an issue now?" Kalter notes, "The implicit assumption is that divorce is a circumscribed event consisting of the parental separation and/or the legal finalization of the divorce. Ongoing stresses stemming from the divorce are not recognized."

Subtle effects from an earlier divorce can also influence a teenager who is experiencing the normal range of adolescent problems. Issues can become more intense. Girls and boys who grow up without a father around can have identity problems. A boy may reject his mother as not understanding his needs. A girl may look to boyfriends to take a fathering role, only to be disappointed time and again when they are unable to meet these needs.

When fathers stay involved in their children's lives, both teenage boys and girls are less apt to have serious problems. When this does not happen, a male counselor may be able to address many of these issues, particularly if he is sensitive to problems that teens bring along from the divorce.

Computers Can Help

Scientists have argued that computers can never think like humans because they can't follow the "illogical logic" of emotions. But a computer's lack of emotionality is exactly what is called for in a time of emotional distress. An interesting example of how the cold-hearted reasoning of a computer can aid a teen in getting past the initial trauma of divorce is an Internet site called Kidshare.com. This site was originally developed as a software program by two divorced parents, both of whom had gone through painful custody battles. The software was used by judges throughout the country to plan visitation schedules for children, based on dozens of factors extracted from a questionnaire filled out by the parents The site does the same thing. It is designed to help parents work out a visitation schedule for their children or teens, printing out schedules and calendars for kids and encouraging divorced parents to e-mail each other rather than have verbal confrontations.

There are many Web sites that can help parents learn about the complex problems they will face in the divorce process and benefit from solutions that others have found. DivorceCentral.com, for example, provides a wealth of practical information, from individual state laws concerning divorce, to financial advice, to referrals to local mental-health professionals. It also has chat rooms and bulletin boards that allow divorcing parents to support each other.

E-mail is an easy way for parents and children to keep in touch, providing an opportunity for communication whether a noncustodial parent is ten miles away or ten thousand miles. It is not the same as being together, nor is it the same as a phone call, but it is a simple, instant, and fun way for parents to stay connected to their children. It is a habit well worth developing.

• • •

Many of the key factors in preventing divorce from becoming a long-term problem for children remain the same from stage to stage. Schedules and rules should be kept consistent. Issues should be dealt with and discussed openly and honestly. Children should be protected from the anger of their parents, and they should not be used either as allies against the other parent or as substitutes for the spouse.

Above all else, noncustodial fathers should continue a close relationship with their children and should make a commitment to give them emotional as well as financial support. All families eventually survive a divorce and move on with their lives. Most children grow up to be happy and healthy adults in spite of the breakup of their family. When you make a commitment to keep their interests a priority, this is much more likely to occur.

9

Preventing the Long-Term Effects of a Trauma

Let us hope that your child will not experience any major trauma in his or her developing years. But even if a trauma should occur, it doesn't have to be a "life-shattering event." More than fifty years of research, beginning with the study of children who experienced the London bombings in World War II, has shown us that children can adapt surprisingly well to most of life's hardships. They may not bounce back immediately, but they can adjust to a wide variety of stresses and go on to live satisfying and successful lives.

Childhood trauma comes from many sources. Sometimes it can occur over an extended period of time, as with cases of neglect or maltreatment or repeated family violence. But for most children a trauma is a single event, such as the death of a parent, a hospitalization, a natural disaster, or a severe accident.

Although the majority of children exposed to a trauma do well and have only mild, transitory symptoms, some develop significant problems, which can continue to affect them many years after the trauma is over. These problems come in different forms, from symptoms that look like ADHD, to depression, to psychosomatic problems like headaches and stomachaches As we shall see, there are many risk factors that can predispose a child to short- as well as long-term problems, and many of them are within your control.

Most parents may feel they are not trained to help children who have been through a traumatic event. In many cases the parents are in distress themselves and coping with their own psychological reactions. However, traumas bring out the "hero" in all of us. Parents can reduce the risk of trauma as well as utilize interventions that can make a difference in helping their children overcome even the most unimaginable circumstances.

To understand exactly *what* parents can do, it is helpful to think in terms of four stages of prevention that apply to children from preschool age through adolescence. (They don't apply to infants and toddlers, but there are other, more general preventive techniques that should be considered for them.)

STAGE ONE: TRAUMA PREPAREDNESS

Your first job of prevention begins even before a trauma occurs. If you are in a part of the country where natural disasters are common, you have probably already taken steps to prepare for the possibility of that kind of trauma. You may have talked to your children about where to stand and what to do if an earthquake strikes, or shown your teenagers how to help you prepare your house in the event of a hurricane or tornado. But there are other types of traumas that children can be prepared for. Children as young as three can be taught to dial 911 and ask for help in an emergency. At this age they also should know what to do if a fire breaks out in the home. Older children can learn about first aid, and adolescents can learn CPR.

The Federal Emergency Management Agency (FEMA) suggests that you develop a "Family Disaster Plan" by taking four simple steps. First, learn what hazards exist in your community and how to prepare for each. Then meet with your family to discuss what you would do in each situation. Next, take steps to prepare for a disaster, such as posting emergency phone numbers, designating an out-of-state family contact, assembling disaster-supply kits for each member of your household, and installing smoke detectors on each level of your home. Teach your children how to recognize danger signals.

Make sure they know what smoke detectors, fire alarms, and community-warning systems (horns, sirens) sound like. Finally, practice your Family Disaster Plan so that everyone will remember what to do if a disaster does occur. Contact your local emergency-management or civil-defense office or the local Red Cross chapter for literature about how your family can create a disaster plan.

Children can even be psychologically prepared for unforeseen events, like a sudden illness or a family death. Not a day goes by that the television news doesn't report a story of a tragedy that affects some child. Understandably, most parents don't see these stories as topics they want to discuss with their children, but protecting children from the real misfortunes that befall people all around them only leaves them psychologically unprepared. Children don't mind talking about difficult subjects. They usually find it comforting when they see their parents calmly and directly confronting even the most serious events. When a parent asks questions like "What do you think would happen if Dad or Mom got sick and couldn't work anymore?" or "What would you do if there was a shooting in your school?" children learn that problems and their solutions can be anticipated.

STAGE TWO: RESPONDING TO THE TRAUMA

Obviously, the first step to take when children experience a trauma is to see if they have been physically harmed. Sometimes children may be able to tell you if they are in pain, but since shock is a common initial reaction to trauma, they might not be able to communicate even a serious problem, and an immediate medical examination may be required.

Depending on the type of trauma that has occurred, parents should next be concerned about their child's safety and psychological security. Shelter may have to be found and other steps taken to "normalize" a child's life as soon as possible. Above all, the family should be kept together and children should remain with their primary caretakers.

Experts advise parents to remember that normalization is a direction, not a destination. When a child's environment and routine go back to being predictable, this is a chance for healing to begin, but it may be many months and even years before it is complete. Parents should be aware of the many psychological symptoms that can indicate that a child is working through the effects of a trauma:

- refusal to return to school and "clinging" behavior, such as shadowing the mother or father around the house

- persistent fears related to the catastrophe, particularly fears about being permanently separated from the parents

- sleep disturbances, including nightmares or bed-wetting, that persist more than several days after the event

- irritability and loss of concentration

- behavior problems not typical for the child

- physical complaints (stomachaches, headaches, dizziness) for which a physical cause cannot be found

- withdrawal from family and friends, listlessness, decreased activity, preoccupation with the events of the trauma

STAGE THREE: EMOTIONAL HEALING

The emotional healing process begins after the child's outward routine has been reestablished. The exact nature of this healing will of course depend on the extent of the trauma. In every case, however, parents can help their child to be aware of her feelings and learn to communicate them effectively. Healing will also involve correcting misconceptions or distortions that children typically have about the event, such as self-blame. It will include empowering the child or adolescent so that she doesn't feel like a victim.

Emotional healing should also include educating family members and even close friends of the child who has been traumatized. Participation in self-help groups and exposure to inspirational literature can be useful for older children and teens. Most experts recommend a holistic approach to healing, which includes attention to diet, exercise, and other lifestyle habits, as well as to spiritual issues.

In the case of very serious trauma, or when a child has several different risk factors, counseling may also be indicated. Counseling focuses on building a relationship of trust with a traumatized child and helping her to express her feelings and conflicts in words, via symbolic play, or through one of the different art therapies. Counseling sessions may involve a symbolic reenactment of the traumatic event to help the child fully master her painful feelings and memories. Sometimes, if symptoms of fearfulness and anxiety are severe, medication is recommended.

This phase of emotional healing ends with the elimination or significant reduction of any psychological and physical symptoms. The child should once again have an age-appropriate sense of mastery and control. There should be an observable shift from a "victim" status to a "survivor" status, reflected in the way the child speaks and behaves. The child should once again be able to confront the normal developmental challenges of family, school, and friends.

STAGE FOUR: POST-TRAUMA AWARENESS

It wasn't very long ago when clinicians thought that Post-Traumatic Stress Disorder (PTSD) was only an adult problem. Now we know that children and teens can suffer from the same disorder, unable to "put the trauma behind them." Symptoms of PTSD in children can come in many different shapes and forms, often mimicking other disorders. When children are diagnosed with PTSD, psychotherapy is usually recommended.

Many children don't develop the severe symptoms to warrant a diagnosis of PTSD, yet the trauma continues to have long-lasting effects on their development. As we shall see, there are many things parents can do in this stage to reduce the aftereffects of a trauma.

RISK FACTORS FOR LONG-TERM EFFECTS FROM A TRAUMA

The two factors that can help us predict whether an individual child will suffer long-term problems after a trauma are the nature of the trauma and the circumstances surrounding it. The most common traumas are discussed below, along with advice on how to reduce the emotional impact in each situation.

Death of a Parent

The death of a parent is probably the single most significant traumatic event for a child, but the psychological effect of this loss can vary with the circumstances. A sudden, unanticipated death typically has the greatest impact on a child. When a parent dies after a long illness, as painful as this may be, at least the child has time to work through some of grieving issues with the parent still present.

The age of the child will also be a factor. Preschool children usually see death as temporary and reversible, a belief reinforced by cartoon characters who "die" and "come to life" again. Children between five and nine begin to think more like adults, yet they still may have a hard time believing that death is irreversible. Children at this age frequently think that their deceased parents are waiting for them in heaven, very much as if they were waiting in another city.

As time passes and these children begin to understand that their parent's death is permanent, they may display profound feelings of anger and sadness. We tend to think of the grieving process in adults as occurring in distinct and sequential stages (denial, anger, bargaining, depression, acceptance), but these stages aren't nearly so well defined with children. Their grief often comes at unexpected moments. Children are also likelier to reveal their feelings in disguised ways. For example, anger may be revealed in aggressive play, nightmares, increased irritability, or willful behavior toward surviving family members.

Allowing children to express and understand their feelings about their loss and supporting the process of their grief will eventually help them put their loss into perspective and go on with their lives. *How Do We Tell the Children?* by Dan Schaefer and Christine Lyons is a particularly useful book to guide you in helping children and teens cope with death. The Dougy Centers, with eighty chapters around the United States, are another resource which can give children support. The Dougy Centers run self-help groups for children who have experienced a significant loss, and they also provide parent resources. For information, visit their Web site at www.dougy.org.

Abuse

Sexual or physical abuse will certainly be perceived as traumatic for children, but again the severity of the trauma will depend on the circumstances. The child's pain and suffering, the unpredictability of the abuse, and of course its duration will all be factors in the psychological damage caused. To reduce the effects of this type of trauma, professionals must consider the total developmental and psychological needs of each child, as well as the strengths and weaknesses of the child's support system.

Hospitalization or Disfigurement

Generally speaking, the older the child, the more traumatic the effect of a chronic illness or physical disfigurement. Again, the psychological implications can be better or worse, depending on extenuating circumstances. When parents are able to spend considerable time with the child on a daily basis, the psychological trauma will be significantly reduced. The pain and discomfort of the medical treatment will also be an important factor. Older children will miss their friends and may be particularly susceptible to the "stigma" of being different from their peer group. They worry that they won't be attractive to members of the opposite sex and that they are doomed to be "outcasts " or "freaks."

Understanding the psychological needs that occur with each age will help diminish the risk that a physical problem will become a psychological trauma. For example, Ronald McDonald House (www.rmhc.com), sponsored by McDonald's restaurants, is a home away from home that allows families to stay near their hospitalized, seriously ill children for little or no cost. This is an extremely important preventive measure for young children. The Starbright Foundation (www.starbright.org) has developed a network of interactive computers, now placed in hospitals across the nation, that allows kids to talk and play with other hospitalized children. This helps them cope with the daily realities of living with a grave illness and also makes them feel a part of their own special community. The Starbright Foundation has also developed a videotape series for teens called "Videos with Attitude," helping older children and adolescents to understand what it's like to be ill by listening to teens who have been there. The MTV-style videos focus on common problems such as how to communicate with hospital staff. Tapes are free to seriously and chronically ill teens and their parents.

Accidents or Disasters

The difference between an accident and a disaster is a matter of degree. One crucial distinction is that a disaster has a wider impact, affecting the community as well as an individual child or family. As in other types of traumas, the conditions surrounding the event will play the most important part in determining how much it will traumatize a child. Being separated from the parents is the single most significant factor that can contribute to a trauma. Second is the loss of a home. Often it isn't the physical loss of the house and its contents that affects a child, as much as the parents' reaction to that loss. Many parents, understandably react with an acute depression. Their emotional unavailability to their children then presents a serious risk factor.

Suicide and Violence in the Student Community

Community violence is becoming an increasingly prevalent source of trauma for older children and teenagers, and one that can have significant emotional impact on children and teens even if they were not directly involved in the incident. For some children, the perceived threat of violence is enough to cause psychological symptoms. Shootings such as the one at Columbine High School in Colorado are the most visible form of community violence, but they are not the most common.

Suicide among teens is a much more frequent occurrence, and therefore more apt to affect your child in some way. Suicide ranks third as the cause of death for teens between fifteen and nineteen years old, killing teens at four to five times the rate of homicides. As tragic as this is for the family of a teen suicide, experts in prevention are becoming just as concerned for close friends of the victim and worried about the effects on the larger community as well. For example, in October of 1999 a senior at a Connecticut high school hanged himself in the school gym. He had been treated for psychological problems for some time, but the suicide seemed to have been triggered by a breakup with his girlfriend. The two school psychologists immediately went on crisis alert, visiting classrooms and talking about suicide as well as counseling the boy's friends. But even with their quick response, they estimated that another six to eight students began talking about committing suicide themselves, and several actually made suicide attempts.

Suicide- and violence-awareness programs have proliferated in recent years, and most schools have crisis plans in place to allow rapid responses to any serious problems. The Internet is playing a particularly useful role in awareness, which you can see for yourself by viewing the violence-prevention site sponsored by the American Psychological Association (http://helping.apa.org/warningsigns/index.html). This site advises teens on how to recognize the signs of violence in others and on how to control their own anger. Visit the Yellow Ribbon Suicide Prevention site (www.yellowribbon.org) to get similar advice about suicide prevention in teens.

Family Factors

When a child experiences a trauma, other family members may also be profoundly affected, even though they were not directly involved in the event. Unfortunately, a family's negative reaction to the trauma can then be an additional stress to the child. Family therapists have given us a profile of a family environment that will be most beneficial for a child recovering from a trauma:

- The trauma is recognized by the family, rather than denied.

- The family understands the effects of the trauma on all family members, rather than just focusing on the victim(s) of the trauma.

- Family members actively seek solutions to the various problems caused by the trauma.

- There is tolerance and a sense of togetherness among family members.

- There is open communication and expression of affection.

- Family members make use of resources outside the family.

- Violence or intense arguing is absent.

- Drug and alcohol use is infrequent.

If moderate to severe family problems existed before the traumatic event, the odds are that they will only get worse afterward. Seeking immediate family counseling can be very useful in creating a family environment that will reduce the short- and long-term effects of a trauma.

Duration and Chance of Repetition

If a trauma occurs over an extended period of time, such as in the case of abuse or a prolonged illness, this can add additional risk to the child and the family. This is also the case when a child perceives that a trauma may be repeated, such as during hurricane or tornado season or when a series of violent threats occur in a school or community. Even when there is ongoing support for a child, the effects of prolonged stress can be very debilitating on both psychological and physical development. Prolonged stress can trigger many types of psychological reactions, but most commonly it will lead to depression and anxiety disorders.

INFANTS AND TODDLERS

KEY TO PREVENTION: EARLY STIMULATION

Very young children aren't going to be susceptible to the same types of traumas as older children, nor will they go through the same psychological stages after a trauma has occurred. This is not to say, however, that infants are immune from the stress of a trauma. If there is the loss of a family home or the prolonged illness or death of a family member, a baby will certainly be affected by any change in her environment or routine. She will be most affected by the absence of an important caregiver or the heightened emotional states of the people around her. But although this stress can have negative effects on a baby, it isn't the same thing as a trauma. Infants don't have sufficient emotional or cognitive development to be affected by a trauma in the same way as an older child.

The notable exception, however, is maltreatment or neglect. There have been many studies of babies adopted from poorly run orphanages or from highly dysfunctional families that reveal the devastating psychological and physical problems that occur when infants don't receive sufficient stimulation and basic care. Some research shows that babies who were neglected or mistreated have brains that are much smaller than normal. Other studies, which have followed these children as they grow, have found that even when they are later placed in loving homes, many children suffer from significant learning, emotional, and behavioral problems.

Toddlers are at the crossroads in this issue, which is why I mention them both here and in the next section, on preschoolers. Because of their lack of cognitive awareness, they don't go through the stages that older children go through, but, like infants, they are still sensitive to their parents' distress and to changes in environment and schedule. Also, much like infants, they are still subject to the psychological effects produced by lack of adequate attention and care.

AN OUNCE OF PREVENTION

Because an infant's brain is highly malleable, early intervention can make a significant difference in later development, even in cases of severe neglect. The following recommendations apply to all at-risk infants when early problems are known or suspected.

Consider a Developmental Assessment

Your pediatrician will be on the watch for any specific developmental delays, but you may also wish to consider a more extensive evaluation. Most states offer an early-developmental screening through their departments of health and education. This screening will determine whether further evaluation is indicated, to identify problems in physical, cognitive, emotional, and social development.

Provide Stimulation and Enrichment Programs

If a developmental assessment finds that an infant has specific problems, an infant-stimulation program will be prescribed, specific to your child's needs. This program could require medical specialists like physical or audio therapists, but more likely it will involve instructing the parents to do simple and fun activities with their baby. These activities, along with a caring and nurturing environment, can make a significant difference in mitigating the effects of earlier problems.

Give Your Baby a Consistent Routine

All babies do better with a predictable routine, which includes feeding time, changing time, nap times, and of course regular play, story, and cuddle times. Babies begin to anticipate certain activities at certain times, and this expectation provides an organizing structure to their developing awareness.

Have a Support System

Taking care of a high-risk baby is an emotionally and physically demanding job. Ideally, parents should have their own support system of relatives, friends, and self-help groups to aid them in giving as much as they can to their infant.

PRESCHOOLERS

KEY TO PREVENTION: UNDERSTANDING THE TRAUMA FROM YOUR CHILD'S PERSPECTIVE

By the time children are two and a half or three, they are cognitively aware enough to be affected by many traumatic events, from family violence, to parental absence or loss, to a natural disaster. However, their reactions to the situations may be subtler than older children's, and certainly different from those of teens or adults. The normal moodiness of preschoolers may be exaggerated. They may get upset over the loss of a favorite toy, blanket, or teddy bear, even though these objects were previously not that important to them. Their general temperament may change and even be completely reversed. A shy, obedient child could become more reticent and withdrawn, or he could suddenly be noisier and more aggressive. Fears of all kinds are common in preschoolers after a trauma, but children of this age are particularly prone to night fears. They may be afraid to sleep alone and may insist on sleeping with their parents. They may be afraid of wind, rain, or sudden loud noises.

In more severe cases young children may show extreme withdrawal, even from their parents. A trauma causes some children to lose trust in adults, because the adults could not prevent the traumatic event. This is usually accompanied by a "numbing" of the emotions and behaviors, so that they appear still to be in shock. These symptoms may be accompanied by a reversion to younger behaviors, such as bed-wetting or thumb-sucking, as children try to recapture the safety of an earlier time in their lives, before the trauma occurred.

Toddlers and preschoolers are particularly sensitive to their parents' behaviors after a trauma. As one mother explained after a fire had burned down their home, "My four-year-old doesn't take his eyes off me. He wants to follow me wherever I go. I often catch him staring at me and listening to every word I'm saying to my husband. It's kind of spooky, but it seems to calm him down."

When parents aren't able to cope with a trauma, a young child may become more frightened. He may see his parents' new behaviors as proof that the danger is real and still imminent. If parents seem overcome with a sense of loss, the child may feel his own losses more strongly.

On the other hand, when parents talk calmly and realistically about what has happened and what will happen, children usually find that their anxiety is manageable. Having children participate in the family's recovery activities will help them feel that their life will soon return to "normal." A parent's response during this time may have a lasting impact.

Parents need to be aware that even though their young children may sometimes seem unaffected by a traumatic event—playing with their toys or watching TV as if nothing has happened—their imaginations may be hard at work. Even though they can't usually articulate their fears, looming in the back of their minds is the possibility that a trauma might reoccur, that someone will be injured or even killed, or that they will be separated from the family and left alone. These fears may have no basis in reality, but they are still very real to the young child. The following suggestions can help you take important steps in preventing even the most serious trauma from having lifelong consequences for your toddler or preschooler.

AN OUNCE OF PREVENTION

Most young children recover very well, even from a major trauma. Understanding the different stages of prevention will help make this process easier for your child.

Stage One: Trauma Preparedness

Teach Your Preschooler How and When to Call for Help

Young children can be taught to call for emergency assistance as soon as they are old enough to work the phone. If they cannot yet recognize numbers in order to dial 911, put a colored sticker on the phone so they can call the operator, who will then assist them. You will also need to teach your preschooler to recognize emergencies and to give his name and address out only in an emergency situation. Rehearsing emergency procedures will be the best way to assure yourself that he understands what to do.

Teach Your Preschooler to Be Aware of Safety Issues

Young children need to be alerted to dangers around the home. You probably do this already as different situations come up, but occasionally take a tour of your home and point out all the things children should know about. A glass left on the edge of a table could fall and break. Toys left on the stairs could cause someone to trip. It's important for your child to recognize unsafe situations and how to remedy them.

Stage Two: Responding to the Trauma

The most important thing you can do is reassure your young child that things will be all right, and the best way to do this is by keeping your family together. You may be tempted to leave your child with relatives or friends while you seek assistance after a trauma, but it is almost always better to keep the child with you, letting her see that you are taking steps to return things to normal. When children are separated from their parents after experiencing a trauma, even if it is for a short time, they begin to worry that something else will happen to their parents to keep them from returning.

There are many other ways to reassure your child that things will be all right again. Hug her often. Spend extra time with her at bedtime. Play with her to show that most aspects of life can go on just as before the traumatic event.

Here are some additional practical suggestions.

Talk Calmly and Honestly About What Happened

Children may want to hear you tell the story of the trauma over and over again. Be patient. This is how they begin to sort out the chaotic events and feelings they've just experienced.

Use Art Activities to Help Your Child Express Himself

Art activities can help younger children to express themselves. Since children have limited skills at this age, simple techniques work best. Take a small box of crayons and say something like "Different colors can mean different feelings. Let's say that red is angry, and blue is sad, and green is afraid. Do you know other feelings that can be other colors? Now draw your feelings on this paper, and we can talk about them."

A child may draw a picture related to the trauma. You can help most by simply commenting on what you see. Don't try to interpret the drawing. Don't judge it. Don't ask your child what something means. Just let him say what is on his mind.

Give Information Your Child Can Understand

Talk to your child about what is happening as a result of the trauma. Be specific and be honest. For example, if a parent is in the hospital, say something like "Daddy is sick, and he has to be in the hospital for a long time. We will go and visit him every Wednesday and every Saturday, but because he is sick, we can only visit for a short time. He can't get out of his bed and play with you, but you can hold his hand and talk to him."

It is also helpful to talk about and label your own feelings, showing your child that it is normal to have many feelings after a traumatic event. But try to be positive as well. Continuing the example from above, you can say something like: "It makes me very sad that Daddy is in the hospital and that he hurts. But the doctors are trying very hard to make him well again, and that makes me feel better."

Allow Children to Grieve

No parents like to see their children suffering from a loss, but grieving is part of the healing process. As a reaction to a trauma, young children often express tremendous grief over losing a small "treasure," like a particular toy, a blanket, or a favorite book. Sometimes they may seem inconsolable about this loss. Remember that children are very concrete in their thinking, but their feelings represent a much larger sense of loss. Don't diminish what they are feeling by telling them that a toy or a book can be replaced. Instead, let them know that you understand how they feel: "It's very sad to lose your favorite doll. It's okay to be sad about losing things that are important to you."

Stage Three: Emotional Healing

Use the "Body Scan" Technique

Young children are particularly prone to develop psychosomatic symptoms, to "feel things with their bodies." You can help them understand that they are now safe and secure by occasionally using a technique called the "body scan." Say to your child, "Let's see how our bodies are feeling today. How do your feet feel today? Okay? Mine, too. How about your legs? Are they good? Mine, too. How about your stomach and your chest? Your arms?" Continue in this manner until you've reached the head, and then say, "Well, I guess we feel okay today! That's great."

Of course, if your child doesn't respond that things are "okay," you should determine if there is really a physical problem. Repeated complaints should be checked out with a physical examination.

Communicate with Your Child's Teacher or Other Caretakers

Make sure that other people in your preschooler's life are alerted to symptoms and problem behaviors. You should communicate with them at least on a weekly basis at first. This will help you learn about your child's reaction to the trauma, even if she doesn't appear to be having a problem. It will also help you straighten out any misconceptions that could be troubling her. For example, one three-year-old announced to her preschool class, "My daddy went blind and died because he was watching too much TV." In reality her father had lost his sight from an AIDS-related neurological disorder and died of cancer. He was blind for a period of four months before his death. Sometime before her father's death someone had said to this young girl, "You know you can go blind by watching too much television," and she mistakenly put these two facts together. Her mother immediately sat her down and corrected this misconception.

Stage Four: Post-Trauma Awareness

Be Aware of Delayed Symptoms After a Trauma

Young children typically recover quickly from a trauma, but not always. As mentioned earlier, recovery can depend on a variety of risk factors, and symptoms can occur many months later. Periodically give your child a chance to talk about the trauma by looking at old photographs or talking about your own feelings. When memories are buried or denied, children don't get the chance to master their feelings about what has happened, and later problems may emerge.

Art activities are helpful in this stage, too. Say something like "Let's draw some pictures about what happened to Grandma. We can draw what she looked like and things that we miss about her. Maybe we can put them in a scrapbook?"

The most typical symptom preschoolers have in this stage is to suddenly demonstrate behaviors from earlier times. Your child may no longer sleep through the night, or he may have difficulty falling asleep. He may wet the bed or have accidents during the day. He may want to use the bottle again and even begin to use baby talk. These are common behaviors immediately after a trauma, but if they persist for more than a few weeks, assume that they are symptomatic of continued emotional confusion and that professional advice should be sought.

SCHOOL-AGE CHILDREN

KEY TO PREVENTION: KEEP CHILDREN INFORMED AND ACTIVELY INVOLVED IN RECOVERY TASKS

School-age children between six and twelve years old may be the group most vulnerable to the long-term effects of a trauma. It will be years before they have the full power of cognitive understanding to help them put the trauma into perspective. Like younger children, they are still prone to misconceptions and fantasies, which can make them view their circumstances as much worse than they are in reality. Unlike adolescents, they are still largely dependent on their families for emotional support, and cannot yet turn to peers or adults who may be removed from the emotional impact of the trauma.

Often neighbors and teachers comment on how quietly and calmly children are behaving after a trauma. However, the inhibition of children's normal activity is a standard indicator of their degree of stress. Teachers must be alert to social withdrawal as a possible sign that the stress is continuing.

Other children may be hyper-alert and hyper-vigilant after a trauma. Following an earthquake in Armenia, elementary-school students jumped out of first-floor windows whenever a large truck rolled by and shook the ground.

As with younger children, there are many things you can do to help school-age children, and because of their increased understanding, you may see more immediate results from your efforts. As always, be alert for symptomatic behavior that may indicate the need for professional help. Even though long-term psychotherapy is not always feasible, an ongoing relationship with a counselor can guide you toward the different ways you can help your child as he grows.

AN OUNCE OF PREVENTION

Stage One: Trauma Preparedness

Help Your Children Know What to Do in an Emergency

Children should memorize their address and phone number, as well as the name and number of a close relative or neighbor. They should also know where to meet in case of an emergency. Some children may not be old enough to memorize all the important information, but they can carry a small index card listing emergency information.

Discuss Factual Information About What Can Cause Traumas

School-age children will have many opportunities to hear and learn about traumas. Talk about earthquakes, hurricanes, tornadoes, violent crimes, as well as about less dramatic events like severe illness.

Watch the news reports and read the paper together. Some parents try to protect their children from upsetting news, but this is a mistake. If you protect your children from minor stress, how will they learn to handle a major stress?

The Federal Emergency Management Agency sponsors an excellent Web site for teaching children about dangers and how to be prepared for them, called FEMA for Kids (www.fema.com/kids). This site offers a variety of interesting ways for children to learn about the importance of preparedness, from coloring books to stories to kid-oriented news articles.

Teach Problem-Solving Skills

Problem-solving skills are an important part of developing the emotional intelligence of all children, but they are critical when it comes to coping with a trauma. The five steps of solving a problem include: describing the problem, identifying possible solutions, comparing the different alternative solutions, deciding on the best one, and implementing the best potential solution. Encourage your child to apply those skills to everyday dilemmas. The more practice children have in problem-solving, the more automatic this skill will become. In the event of a trauma, they will be much more confident that they can handle both small and large decisions.

Teach Communication and Assertiveness Skills

These are two additional aspects of emotional intelligence that can help prepare your child to handle the intense emotions that are part of a traumatic event. When children learn to communicate their feelings and needs effectively, they are certainly less likely to allow themselves to be ignored in their everyday lives. But these skills should also be practiced as part of emergency preparedness. If you are listening to the news and hear about a fire, ask your child what she would do if she were in a fire and her parents weren't around. You may want to write down the various steps she would take and encourage her to think about additional ones. These steps should certainly include the following:

- Immediately find a safe place.

- Tell an adult what has happened.

- Call for emergency help.

- Tell an adult if you're in pain.

- Tell an adult if you're frightened.

- Tell an adult what you need.

Stage Two: Responding to the Trauma

Talk About What Happened

Encourage your child to describe everything that happened. Ask him what he saw, heard, smelled, felt, and thought. It is important for children to acknowledge the frightening parts of a disaster, even though they may be reluctant to do so.

It may help children to talk if you make it into a kind of game. If possible, get all family members involved. Say something like "It's important to talk about what happened so we can get out all of our feelings. Let's think about all the things we can remember. I'll start by saying, 'I remember when I first felt the ground shake and I knew it was an earthquake.' Now you say something that you remember, and then I'll go again." Children are much more willing to talk when they can do it in the context of an activity. However, even if they don't want to talk, they can benefit from hearing what you or other family members are saying.

Give Your Child Information

Tell children exactly what has happened and what will happen. The more you stimulate a child's thinking processes, the less likely her emotions will become overwhelming. Calmly and firmly explain the situation. As best you can, tell her what you know about what happened and explain what will probably happen next. For example, say, "Your brother was hurt in a car accident. We're going to the hospital right now, but you'll have to wait in another room while I visit with him. Daddy will meet us there, and we'll take turns staying with you and being with David. We'll tell you exactly how David is doing, even though you can't visit with him."

The way children see and understand their parents' responses is very important. Children are always aware of their parents' worries on some level, but they are particularly sensitive during a crisis. Parents should admit their concerns to their children, and also let them see that they are able to cope with the situation.

Include Children in Recovery Activities

School-age children are activity-oriented. They also feel important when they are helping adults. Give your children appropriate tasks that can aid you in the recovery process. Can they help you clean up an area? Can they help you sort through some papers? Assign them a finite task that can be accomplished in a relatively short period of time. It will give them a sense of control.

Find Out How Your School Will Handle the Trauma

Schools play an important part in helping children cope with a trauma. Let's say, for example, that a child's father has died of a sudden heart attack. The mother should talk to her child's teacher and the school psychologist about the best way to address this in his class. They will suggest ways to balance the child's need for privacy with his need for peer support.

Stage Three: Emotional Healing

Allow Time to Heal

Give each member of your family time to heal at his or her own pace. Don't try to "put things in the past" too quickly. Give and ask for support from family members, friends, and the community. Have family meetings to discuss feelings about the event as well as to handle the ordinary business (and annoyances) of family life. This will increase the sense of family togetherness that a child needs while the healing process is continuing.

Laugh

Humor is an important part of the healing process. Don't be afraid to joke and be silly with your child. Watch funny movies together. Have fun. Do not, however, use humor to avoid painful feelings.

Balance Tolerance with Ongoing Expectations

Certainly you need to be compassionate about the effects of the trauma on your child. You need to give her as much love and understanding as you can. But you must also enforce age-appropriate rules. Keep bedtimes consistent. Require the same schoolwork and chores. This is the best way to give your child the message that life can and should continue in as many normal ways as possible.

Provide Opportunities for Creative Expression

Like younger children, older children will benefit from various art experiences that will allow them to express how they feel. Offer them a variety of art supplies, including crayons, markers, paint, and clay.

Also encourage your child to write stories. At first let him write about whatever he wants. Then you can ask if he wants to write a story about what happened. Offer assurances that he doesn't have to share his stories if he doesn't want to. Some thoughts and feelings are private, and you should let him know that you respect his wishes.

Some children like to express themselves by play-acting. If you can, provide your child with a set of family dolls, puppets, or dress-up paraphernalia. Play along if you want to, but let her lead the play. Be noncritical and nonjudgmental. Let her tell the story through her play however she likes. You might make up your own story as well. Try creating one about how people realistically face their problems and find solutions for them.

Stage Four: Post-Trauma Awareness

Watch for Behaviors That Reveal an Ongoing Reaction

Following a trauma, some children may exhibit many signs of disturbance. But if after a month or so, if there is no diminishing of these disturbances, it might be that the child is developing a form of Post-Traumatic Stress Disorder. Symptoms can include:

- recurring nightmares about the trauma

- recurring thoughts about the trauma

- extreme withdrawal, sadness, and a reluctance to do normal activities

- continued fearfulness when hearing about anything about the trauma

- reluctance to go to school or to be with friends

- extreme alertness, as if waiting for something bad to happen again

Children may sometimes relive the trauma through repetitive play. If someone died for example, they may persist in making up dramas with their dolls or action figures about someone's dying and going to heaven. One eight-year-old who saw his father have a heart attack at home and watched him taken away in an ambulance, insisted on playing with a toy ambulance every day after school. This kind of play can be normal and healing for a time following the trauma, but after a few weeks, more natural types of play with other themes should replace it. Any type of preoccupation with a traumatic event can be a sign that a child needs some additional professional help in this stage.

Recognize Your Child's Vulnerability to Other Problems

Post-Traumatic Stress Disorder may mimic other disorders like depression or ADHD. It may precipitate physical symptoms, such as stomachaches or headaches. If your child has been through a trauma in the last three to six months, you should be particularly sensitive to the complaints or problems pointed out by his teachers. Seek professional help immediately if your child shows any signs of ongoing distress.

TEENAGERS

KEY TO PREVENTION: ENCOURAGING COPING SKILLS

An adolescent will respond to a trauma similarly to the way an adult will. Her immediate symptoms could include confusion, emotional numbing, sleep disturbances, and physical complaints. Post-trauma symptoms can include flashbacks, withdrawal and social isolation, school avoidance, and depression. The adolescent may feel extreme guilt over her failure to prevent injury or loss of life, and she may harbor revenge fantasies that interfere with recovery from the trauma.

Teenagers who are already good at coping with stress will likely be more resilient to a trauma. These teens will find solace from their friends, will seek out help when they need it, and will be able to develop some insight into their particular circumstances. They will see that their emotional conflicts are a reaction to the trauma, and that any symptoms will diminish after a period of time. They will soon develop a rationale that can explain the trauma. They might have a deep religious faith and put the trauma in that context, or they may go to the opposite extreme and take a fatalistic approach. In either event, they will try to find some meaningful context to understand what has happened.

Not surprisingly, teens who are already having adjustment problems, or do not do well with stress, will be more at risk. They will be prone to extreme emotional reactions, such as anger or sorrow, and they may even swing between these emotional states. If they are already experiencing any of the other problems discussed in this book—alcohol abuse, eating disorders, extreme shyness, underachievement—these will likely be amplified.

The probability of teens' experiencing some sort of trauma gets higher as they get older. Their parents will certainly be aging and likelier to have a serious illness. Because they are usually going to a much larger school with a more varied student body, the probability that something will happen to someone they know is much greater than it was in childhood. More of their friends or acquaintances will be participating in high-risk behaviors, such as drinking and driving, so it is probable that more tragedies will occur.

AN OUNCE OF PREVENTION

Stage One: Trauma Preparedness

Teenagers have a greater intellectual capacity than do younger children to help them be prepared for a traumatic event, yet few parents have had a discussion about this subject with their sons and daughters. Here are some practical things you should do as soon as possible. Assume that some sort of trauma will happen, and make sure that your teen is ready, particularly if he or she is already considered at risk for emotional and behavioral problems.

Find Out About Your School's Crisis Plan

As I mentioned earlier in this chapter, your family should have a Family Disaster Plan, and so should your school. With what has been happening in the schools lately, every school system should have contingency plans for a wide variety of problems. Ask the principal if there is a written copy of this plan. Perhaps it could be shared with all parents or published in a local paper. Talk about this plan with your teenager. Let her see that adults are aware of potential problems, and solicit her advice on what she could personally do as well.

Make Sure That Your Teenager Is Informed

Two of the common problems teenagers may encounter are aggressive classmates and classmates who are suicidal. Make sure that teens can recognize early warning signs of serious problems.

For example, teens who are prone to violence

- lose their temper frequently

- make threats or are involved in fights
- participate in vandalism or property damage
- regularly use drugs or alcohol
- talk about plans to hurt others
- carry weapons
- have been the victim of bullying
- feel constantly disrespected
- fail to acknowledge the rights of others
- are in deep conflict with parents

Potential suicide victims

- have made previous suicide attempts
- regularly use alcohol or drugs
- express thoughts of suicide, death, or dying
- show a sudden increase in moodiness, withdrawal, or isolation
- experience major changes in eating or sleeping habits
- express feelings of hopelessness, guilt, or worthlessness
- show a lack of interest in school and their usual activities
- get in trouble with authority figures
- expect everything in their life to be perfect
- give away important possessions
- hint about not being around in the future
- have close friends who committed suicide

Depending on your circumstances, your teen may be exposed to other types of traumas, like natural disaster. Teens should know the warning signs of these potential problems as well.

Teach Teens Stress Management

At several points in this book I've mentioned the importance of teaching children relaxation skills as a form of stress management. I've suggested many ways to help children calm themselves, such as using imagery, music, deep breathing, and progressive muscle relaxation. For teenagers, I often recommend an effective form of relaxation training called biofeedback. There are many forms of biofeedback that are used for a variety of medical purposes, but the simplest form measures the body's tension by minute changes in the sweat glands and pore size in the skin. This is called the "galvanic skin response," or GSR. The most inexpensive and durable equipment I have found is produced by a company called Thought Technology and sold on the Internet at www.mindgrowth.com. The teen simply puts his fingers on a palm-size plastic unit, and a tone is emitted. As he relaxes, the tone gets lower; as he becomes tense, it gets louder and higher-pitched. Because of this feedback, the teen will immediately know when he's achieved a state of relaxation, which significantly reduces the effects of stress.

Learning to relax, however, is just one part of stress management. Teens should also be taught how to maintain a healthy lifestyle (exercise, good food, and enough sleep), how to recognize early signs of stress, and how to manage their time and priorities.

Stage Two: Responding to the Trauma

Let Teens Know That It Is Normal to Feel Confused

Teenagers have many different emotional reactions to a trauma. Often these are so strong and confusing that teens feel that their life has suddenly taken a different direction. One teenager whose best friend died in an automobile accident told his counselor, "Nothing means anything to me anymore. Nothing looks the same to me. How do you just eat breakfast, and go to school, and come home, and see your friends, and pretend like everything is the same? It isn't. My life will never be the same."

It may take weeks or months, but teenagers do eventually return to a sense of normalcy.

Don't Criticize Regressive Behavior

It is common for adolescents to exhibit the behaviors of younger children as a reaction to a trauma. They may take out old toys or spend time watching cartoons. This is a perfectly normal reaction. It is an attempt to re-create memories of a calmer and safer time. You should be tolerant if your teen is not himself for a few weeks, even if he tries to pretend that the trauma never happened or has hardly affected him. You can help him understand that a trauma will elicit many different kinds of emotional reactions. In the long run it is always best for teens to be honest about their feelings and allow themselves to acknowledge their sense of loss and uncertainty.

Help Teens Understand Their Desire to Strike Back

Many times teens, particularly boys, become obsessed with a desire for retribution after a traumatic event. They have been brought up on stories and movies about fighting back when loved ones are hurt or victimized, and may feel that revenge will help make things "right." Teens rarely carry out these revenge fantasies, but they are still detrimental to emotional healing. Try to help your teen understand that this type of anger is a natural response, but that it's futile to respond with more violence. Hateful language or actions accomplish nothing good. Encourage your teen to get involved in actively helping others.

Stage Three: Emotional Healing

Encourage Teens to Discuss Their Feelings

Eventually your teen should talk to someone about his feelings. It may be his friends, other family members, a crisis counselor, or a peer counselor. Classroom discussions with a sensitive teacher may be enough. Help your teen find at least one place where the trauma can be discussed. Even if he doesn't want to talk, just listening to others can have a therapeutic benefit.

Encourage Teens to Read About Similar Traumas

An important part of this stage is for teens to get some perspective on the trauma. They need to understand that they are not alone in experiencing a tragedy of this nature, and to find out about the different ways other people have recovered. Your school or public librarian will be helpful in guiding you toward appropriate materials.

Help Teens Recognize and Change "Cognitive Distortions"

One of the most effective forms of psychotherapy used to help teen and adult victims of a trauma is called Cognitive Behavioral Therapy (CBT). In CBT the therapist helps the patient examine and reevaluate beliefs that are interfering with healing. Many trauma victims develop irrational beliefs, or "cognitive distortions," about the trauma. A teen may feel that something she could have done would have prevented her friend's suicide. Another teen might irrationally believe that she'll be involved in another car accident in the near future. Still other teens harbor a general belief that something very bad will happen again although they can't say what or why.

Without being critical of your teen, point out that cognitive distortions are common after a trauma, but that they interfere with the healing process. Have him write down all the thoughts and beliefs that seem to bother him. Then go over each one and see if it's logical or illogical. Only logical beliefs can be backed up by factual statements or evidence. Have your teen change his cognitive distortions into logical statements as I've done below:

Distortion: I could have done something to prevent my friend's suicide.

Logical Belief: People who commit suicide have deep emotional problems. If they're really intent on harming themselves, no one can stop them.

Distortion: I will be involved in another car accident, which could be even worse.

Logical Belief: Careless driving causes car accidents. If you drive safely in a safe car, your odds of having an accident are very small, and they have nothing to do with what happened before.

Distortion: Something bad is going to happen again to my family or me, although I don't know what.

Logical Belief: This is a common thought of trauma victims. But thoughts don't make things true.

Stage Four: Post-Trauma Awareness

Help Teens Understand the Nature of Post-Traumatic Stress Disorder

The estimated incidence of PTSD in children and teens varies widely, according to the nature of the trauma. For example, estimates range from 2 percent after a natural disaster (tornado), to 28 percent after an episode of terrorism (mass shooting), to 29 percent after a plane crash. It's more common for an adolescent to have just a few of the symptoms of PTSD than to develop the full-blown disorder.

The disorder may arise weeks or months after the traumatic event. PTSD may resolve itself without treatment, but some form of therapy by a mental-health professional is often required in order for healing to occur. Six to twelve sessions may be enough for a teen to overcome his symptoms, with follow-up sessions occurring at regularly prescribed intervals (e.g., once a month for three months after the therapy is over).

Since early treatment is always more effective, parents, teachers, and teens themselves should be aware of the different symptoms of PTSD:

- recurrent and intrusive thoughts about the trauma

- recurrent dreams about the event

- feeling as if the trauma were still occurring (having the same physical reactions or having "flashbacks")

- extreme reactivity to all kinds of stress

- avoidance of anything associated with the trauma (people, places, or objects that trigger memories)

- inability to recall certain aspects of the event

- emotional numbing

- a sense of a foreshortened future

- increased sensitivity and difficulty concentrating

- intense unexplained moods or mood swings

If any of these signs are present, professional consultation should be sought. If a teen resists going for counseling, she should be told that she's already suffered from the original trauma, and there is no need to suffer any longer. You can learn more about PTSD at the National Institute of Mental Health site (www.nimh.nih.gov; click on "For the Public").

HELP ADOLESCENTS REMAIN OPTIMISTIC

Sometimes survivors of a trauma don't develop specific symptoms, but they do develop a negative and pessimistic view of life. Teens should be helped to see that negative attitude is a type of cognitive distortion, and it can be just as detrimental to their development as can more recognizable symptoms. Pessimistic people are more prone to depression and underachievement than are people with a realistic and optimistic view of the world. As a parent, you may want to read Martin Seligman's books *The Optimistic Child* or *Learned Optimism* to find ways to help your teen, or yourself, become more optimistic.

Computers Can Help

I've already mentioned a number of Web sites that can guide parents and children through the different stages of trauma prevention. These include:

- The Dougy Centers to help grieving children (www.dougy.org)

- The Ronald McDonald House, which helps parents stay physically close to their hospitalized children (www.rmhc.org)

- The Starbright Foundation for chronically ill children and teens (www.starbright.org)

- The FEMA Web site for kids, to teach trauma preparedness (www.fema.com/kids/)

- The American Psychological Association site on teen violence (http://helping.apa.org/warningsigns/index.html

- The Yellow Ribbon site for suicide prevention in teens (www.yellowribbon.org).

• • •

It is unfortunate that most parents don't take time to think about how their children might be affected by a trauma. All children will experience significant losses or emotionally wrenching events in their lives, and many suffer needlessly after the event because they haven't been prepared to handle this kind of extreme stress. Preventive efforts can be made at four specific times: before a trauma occurs, as an immediate response to a trauma, in the period of emotional healing, and in the months and years that follow. Prevention techniques will, of course, vary with different ages, but at every age you can be assured that you are giving your child the tools to deal successfully with life's inevitable hardships.

Afterword

The Habit of Prevention

I've made dozens of suggestions in this book that can potentially change the course of your child's development, but will you implement them? As every psychologist knows, information is not always enough to change the way people act. Consider for a moment all the times you have pledged to eat more sensibly or exercise more often, and how difficult it has been to keep your resolutions.

Preventing emotional and behavioral problems requires more than just knowledge; it requires making prevention a parenting habit. Just as you make sure that your child is buckled up as soon as he gets into a car, or that she washes her hands before dinner, preventing mental health problems must become automatic. Prevention strategies that are only done occasionally, or are started and then neglected, rarely have any effect.

There are just three steps to making a permanent change in behavior, and these apply to parenting as well.

First, you must have the motivation to change. This is not usually a problem for most parents. Parents want the best for their children, and they will typically make extraordinary efforts and sacrifices if they know that their labors will help their children in any way.

Second, you must make a connection between the desired

behavior and some time-related event. When it comes to ensuring physical health and safety, you see to it that certain things happen at certain times. Your son brushes his teeth before bedtime. You probably take your daughter for a physical examination around the time of her birthday, or remind her to wear a bicycle helmet when you take her bike out for the season. You must do the same thing with prevention strategies, by associating them with some recurring event. Once you have determined what preventive actions you want to take, decide if they should be daily, weekly, or monthly, and then connect them in your mind with a predictable time or event. For example:

> Mrs. Arnold was concerned about her son's increasingly rude behavior. She reviewed the household "rules of respect" with him every night before dinner, and then during dinner she shared stories that reflected how much she valued good manners and consideration for others.

> Nine-year-old Hope was very shy and had a hard time making friends. Every Thursday night her parents made their weekend plans, scheduling at least one time period when Hope would do an activity with a neighbor or classmate. As soon as the time was set, Hope was encouraged to make the call immediately and plan the play date.

> Billy had ADHD, and there were five behaviors he was trying to improve. His teacher kept a weekly checklist of his progress, and so did his parents. On the first Monday of every month, Billy's parents and teacher had a standing phone appointment to go over what was working and what wasn't.

Reinforcement is the third and final step you must take to make prevention strategies into habits. Without meaningful reinforcement, even the best of intentions soon fade. Reinforcement works best when it is immediate, but the beneficial results of your preventive strategies may be months or even years away. For this reason, you must find ways to reinforce your own efforts, and researchers point out that the best way to change any habit is through social reinforcement. Talk frequently about what you are doing to help your child. Tell your spouse, your child's teacher, your own parents. Don't be afraid to brag a little bit. There's nothing more admirable than a dedicated parent, and you deserve all the praise that you will likely get.

If you follow these simple steps, within a few months preventing emotional and behavioral problems will become a habit. You will no longer have to think about it, because it will be incorporated into your parenting style. Of course, even the most dedicated parents can't prevent every problem. There are factors affecting the development of your child that are beyond your control. But you will soon find that your efforts to enhance the emotional well-being of your child will bring a new dimension to your parenting. Every moment you take to raise a happy, healthy, and successful child brings its own reward.

Appendix

Software and Internet Resources

Throughout this book I've recommended many different ways that the computer can be used to assist parents, teachers, and mental-health professionals in developing prevention programs. The following list includes software and Internet sites already mentioned, as well as some additional resources.

The most useful site I've found for finding and buying software is the PEP Registry for Educational Software Publishers, which provides ratings for children's software, a list of publishers, and a variety of places to purchase software. You can find them at www.microweb.com/pepsite/.

1: STOP EMOTIONAL PROBLEMS BEFORE THEY START

Software

Active Parenting Today

This CD-ROM teaches the basic principles of becoming an "authoritative" parent, clearly the most effective parenting style for prevention. (Active Parenting Publishers, at www.activeparenting.com)

Internet Sites

Family Cares (www.familycares.org)

This site is dedicated to helping families raise compassionate children.

Habitat for Humanity (www.habitat.org)

One of the effective and practical volunteer programs, this organization is dedicated to building decent, affordable homes. It emphasizes family and community involvement.

2: PREVENTING BEHAVIORAL PROBLEMS

Software

The Lie

A fun interactive story that teaches children how lying gets you into more and more trouble.
    (Knowledge Adventure, at www.knowledgeadventure.com)

The Berenstain Bears: Little Bears Make Big Helpers

These popular characters teach children the importance of doing chores and helping their parents.
    (Sounds Source Interactive, at www.soundsourceinteractive.com)

SMART-team CD-ROM

This program helps teens learn what makes them angry and how to express their feelings without resorting to violence.
    (Attainment Co., at www.attainmentcompany.com)

Straight Talk: A Substance Abuse Prevention Program

This CD-ROM covers substance abuse and violence prevention issues.
    (Attainment Co., at www.attainmentcompany.com)

Internet Sites

There are many sites that give parents advice on problem behavior. Some of the most popular are ParentSoup.com, Family.com, and Parents.com.

3: PREVENTING EATING PROBLEMS AND DISORDERS

Internet Sites

Something-fishy.com

This site has several chat rooms on mental-health issues, including one on eating disorders.

Concernedcounseling.com

Around-the-clock support for people with eating disorders and their families, sponsored by a residential treatment center for eating disorders.

4: PREVENTING UNDERACHIEVEMENT

Software

Jumpstart School Programs

This series of programs gives children fun ways to learn basic information from preschool through sixth grade.
    (Knowledge Adventure, at www.knowledgeadventure.com)

Thinkin' Things

Fun program that helps children learn logical thinking and problem-solving skills.
    (Edmark, at www.edmark.com)

Internet Sites

Kidsway (www.kidsway.com)

An organization devoted to helping children and teens learn entre-preneurial skills.

National Mentoring Partnership (www.mentoring.org)

Comprehensive site to learn how to find a mentor.

5: PREVENTING FEARS AND SHYNESS

Software

Pajama Sam and Who's Afraid of the Dark?

This fun program provides an interactive story of how a boy con-quers his fear of the dark. Designed for three- to seven-year olds.
    (Humongous Entertainment, at www.humongous.com)

Internet Sites

American Academy of Child and Adolescent Psychiatry (www.aacap.org)

Good site to learn about fears and anxiety disorders, as well as other mental-health problems.

6: PREVENTING PROBLEMS IN SEXUALITY, PERSONAL RELATIONSHIPS, AND GENDER IDENTITY

Software

Let's See About Me

This enjoyable and "hip" program is intended to help girls explore their identities. Also links to a Web site.
    (Simon & Schuster Interactive, at www.simonsays.com)

When No Means No

This program is aimed at teens and talks about the problem of date rape and how to avoid finding yourself in high-risk circumstances.
(Cambridge Educational Products, at www.cambridgeol.com)

7: LIMITING THE EFFECTS OF ATTENTION DEFICIT HYPERACTIVITY DISORDERS (ADHD)

Software

CyberPatrol

A popular filtering program to help parents keep their children away from inappropriate sites.
(The Learning Company, at www.cyberpatrol.com)

Improving Classroom Behavior

Techniques for teachers to use in preventing classroom behavior problems. Includes video demonstrations of how the techniques work.
(Savvy Knowledge Co., at www.savvyknowledge.com)

Internet Sites

Children and Adults with Attention Deficit Disorder (www.chadd.org)

The site of the self-help group for those concerned about ADHD.

8: PREVENTING THE LONG-TERM EFFECTS OF DIVORCE

Internet Sites

Kidshare.com

A site that helps parents work out custody and schedule problems.

DivorceCentral.com

This site gives parents a great deal of practical information about divorce, as well as links to other sites.

9: PREVENTING THE LONG-TERM EFFECTS OF A TRAUMA

Internet Sites

Dougy Centers (www.dougy.org)

This site directs parents to the Dougy Centers for grieving children and also gives information to help in the grieving process.

The Ronald McDonald Charities (www.rmhc.com)

This site helps parents find out how to stay at a Ronald McDonald House near the hospital of their chronically ill child, at little or no expense.

The Starbright Foundation (www.starbright.org)

This organization provides various services for chronically ill children and teens, including bedside computer hookups so that kids can talk and play with other sick children.

The FEMA (Federal Emergency Management Agency) Web site FEMA for Kids (www.fema.com/kids)

This site helps children learn to be prepared for various natural disasters.

The American Psychological Association Site on Teen Violence (www.helping.apa.org/warningsigns/index.html)

This site teaches teens about the various warning signs of teen violence and how to respond to them.

The Yellow Ribbon Suicide Prevention Program for Teens
(www.yellowribbon.org)

This site helps teens learn to recognize when someone is at risk for suicide and what to do about it.

References

1. Acredolo, Linda, and Goodwyn., Susan. *Baby Signs*. Chicago: Contemporary Books, 1996.
2. Alleman, Gayle P. *Save Our Child from the Fat Epidemic*. Rocklin, Calif.: Prima Publishing, 1999.
3. American Psychiatric Association. *Diagnostic and Statistical Manual of Mental Disorders, Fourth Edition*. Washington, D.C.: American Psychiatric Association, 1994.
4. Azrin, Nathan, and Besalel, Victoria. *How to Use Positive Practice, Self-Correction, and Overcorrection*. New York: McGraw-Hill, Inc., 1999.
5. Beal, Carole. *Boys and Girls: The Development of Gender Roles*. New York: McGraw-Hill, Inc., 1993.
6. Bernard, Michael. *You Can Do It!* New York: Warner Books, 1997.
7. Bigham, Vicki Smith, and Bigham, George. *The Prentice-Hall Directory of Online Education Resources*. Paramus, N.J.: Prentice-Hall, 1998.
8. Brown, Laurene K., and Brown, Marc. *The Dinosaurs Divorce*. Boston: Little, Brown & Co., 1986.
9. Bruer, John T. *The Myth of the First Three Years*. New York: The Free Press, 1999.
10. Covington, Martin. *Making the Grade*. New York: Cambridge University Press, 1992.

11. Crist, James. *ADHD: A Teenager's Guide*. Plainview, N.Y.: Childswork/Childsplay, 1996.
12. Damon, William. *Greater Expectations*. New York: Simon & Schuster, 1995.
13. ———. *The Moral Child*. New York: The Free Press, 1998.
14. Dinneen, Margo Holen. *If They Can Do It, We Can Too!* Minneapolis, Minn.: Deaconess Press, 1992.
15. Dworetzsky, John. *Introduction to Child Development, Sixth Edition*. St. Paul, Minn.: West Publishing Co., 1996.
16. Fallon, Ruth. *Kissed the Girls and Made Them Cry*. Planview, N.Y.: Childswork/Childsplay, 1998.
17. ———. *13 Steps to Better Grades*. Plainview, N.Y.: Childswork/Childsplay, 1998.
18. Garber, Stephen W.; Garber, Marianne Daniels; and Spizman, Robyn F. *Monsters Under the Bed and Other Childhood Fears*. New York: Villard Books, 1993.
19. Gardner, Richard. *The Parents Book About Divorce*. New York: Bantam Books, 1991.
20. Goleman, Daniel. *Emotional Intelligence*. New York: Bantam Books, 1995.
21. Gray, John. *Men Are from Mars, Women Are from Venus*. New York: HarperCollins, 1992.
22. Greene, Ross. *The Explosive Child*. New York: HarperCollins, 1998.
23. Haggerty, R. J.; Sherrod, L. R.; Garmezy, N.; and Rutter, M. *Stress, Risk, and Resilience in Children and Adolescescence*. New York: Cambridge University Press, 1994.
24. Harris, Judith Rich. *The Nurture Assumption*. New York: The Free Press, 1998.
25. Harvey, Neil. *Kids Who Start Ahead, Stay Ahead*. Garden City Park, N.Y.: Avery Publishing, 1994.
26. Hechtman, Lily. *Do They Grow Out of It?* Washington, D.C.: American Psychiatric Press, 1996.
27. Hirschmann, Jane, and Zaphiropoulos, Lela. *Preventing Childhood Eating Problems*. New York: Gurze Books, 1993.
28. Hooper, Judith, and Teresi, Dick. *The 3-Pound Universe*. New York: Tarcher/Putnam, 1992.
29. Ivey, Mark, and Bond, Ralph. *The PC Dads Guide to Becoming a Computer-Smart Parent*. New York: Dell Publishing, 1999.
30. James, Beverly. *Treating Traumatized Children*. New York: The Free Press, 1989.

31. Kalter, Neil. *Growing Up with Divorce*. New York: Fawcett Columbine, 1990.

32. Koplewicz, Harold S. *It's Nobody's Fault*. New York: Random House, 1996.

33. Marone, Nicky. *How to Father a Successful Daughter*. New York: Fawcett Crest Books, 1988.

34. Mindell, Jodi. *Sleeping Through the Night*. New York: HarperPerennial, 1997.

35. Money, John. *Principles of Developmental Sexology*. New York: The Continuum Publishing Co., 1997.

36. Nowicki, Stephen, and Duke, Marshall. *Helping the Child Who Doesn't Fit In*. Atlanta, Ga.: Peach Tree Publishers, 1992.

37. Orenstein, Julian. *365 Ways to Calm Your Crying Baby*. Holbrook, Mass.: Adams Media Corporation, 1998.

38. Orlick, Terry. *Cooperative Sports and Games Book*. New York: Pantheon Books, 1978.

39. Restak, Richard. *The Brain Has a Mind of Its Own*. New York: Crown Publishing, 1991

40. Rimm, Sylvia. *See Jane Win*. New York: Crown Publishers, 1999.

41. ———. *Why Bright Kids Get Poor Grades*. New York: Crown Trade Paperbacks, 1995.

42. Russel, Peter. *The Brain Book*. New York: Penguin Books, 1979.

43. Sammons, William. *The Self-Calmed Baby*. New York: St. Martin's Paperbacks, 1991.

44. Schaefer, Dan, and Lyons, Christine. *How Do We Tell the Children?* New York: New Market Press, 1993.

45. Schaefer, Charles, and Foy Digeronimo, Theresa. *How to Talk to Teens About Really Important Things*. San Francisco: Jossey-Bass, 1998.

46. Schaub, Janette. *Your Kid Has ADHD: Now What?* Minneapolis, Minn.: Beaver Press, 1998.

47. Seligman, M.; Reivich, K.; Jaycox, L.; and Gilham, J. *The Optimistic Child*. New York: HarperPerennial, 1996.

48. Shapiro, Lawrence E. *How to Raise a Child with a High EQ*. New York: HarperCollins, 1997.

49. Shure, Myrna. *How to Raise a Thinking Child*. New York: Henry Holt and Co., 1994.

50. ———. *I Can Problem Solve*. Champaign, Ill.: Research Press, 1993.

51. Teeter, Phyllis Anne. *Interventions for ADHD*. New York: The Guilford Press, 1998.

52. Wade, Nichols, Ed. *The Science Times Book of the Brain*. New York: The Lyons Press, 1998.
53. Walker, Phillip. *Baby Massage*. New York: St. Martin's Press, 1996.
54. Whitehead, Barbara Dafoe. *The Divorce Culture*. New York: Knopf, 1997.
55. Wilkoff, William. *Coping with the Picky Eater*. New York: Fireside Press, 1998.
56. Wolff, Rick. *Sports Parenting*. New York: Pocket Books, 1998.
57. Zimbardo, Phillip. *The Shy Child*. New York: Dolphin Books, 1982.

Index